Fifty cricket stars describe **My Greatest Game**

Edited by

Bob Holmes

and Vic Marks

MAINSTREAM
PUBLISHING

Other titles by the same author:
MY GREATEST GAME – FOOTBALL
MY GREATEST GAME – RUGBY

The moral right of the authors has been asserted

First published in Great Britain in 1994 by
Mainstream Publishing Company (Edinburgh) Ltd
7 Albany Street
Edinburgh EH1 3UG

ISBN 1 85158 633 4

A catalogue record for this book is available from the British Library

Typeset by Litho Link Ltd, Welshpool, Powys
Printed in Great Britain by Mackays of Chatham, Kent

Contents

Preface

If today's match reports are tomorrow's recycling, what point is there – you may wonder – in re-hashing accounts 10, 20, 40 and even 60 years later? One glance at the fixture list ought to be enough.

Like its rugby union counterpart, *My Greatest Game (Cricket)* is a collection of essays describing many of the sport's finest hours through the eyes of the men who made them. Many are famous occasions, even landmarks; there are epic team triumphs and those of a more individual nature. Whichever category they fall into, it is hoped that the stories excite interest and stir memories of unforgettable deeds in summers past.

Of course, they are not *straight* reports. The bones of the match are there but they've been fleshed out by liberal use of videos, newspapers and hindsight. One or two of the players may be surprised that the results of our snatched conversations/correspondence have been sprinkled across such a broad canvas. I just hope you feel that the portrayal is a fair reflection of what went on.

The essence of this series is that it is as much an attempt to look at the player through the game as the game through the player. And if its football predecessors are anything to go by, a source of major fascination is the choice itself. Here is the customary mix of obvious and obscure, vital and valedictory and, in a couple of cases, an inability to decide at all. I trust Keith Miller and Allan Border feel the author has done them justice?

No one was more spoiled for choice than Sir Donald Bradman yet his opting for Leeds in 1948 will be well understood. More batting mastery comes from Greg Chappell, Viv and Barry Richards, Ian Botham, Graeme Pollock and Neil Harvey. Sheer pace is provided by Frank Tyson, John Snow, Dennis Lillee and Jeff Thomson, spin by Ramadhin and Chandra. The glovemen are represented by Rod Marsh, Allan Knott and Jack Russell. As for the games, the majority are Tests (including both ties) but one-dayers are not forgotten – Pakistan's World Cup victory in 1992 being recalled by Wasim Akram. There are one or two surprises: Javed's incredible hitting in Sharjah while Harold Larwood prefers to talk about his *batting*! In the greater scheme of things, Clive Rice opts for South Africa's emotional return from the wilderness.

Although the emphasis is on Englishmen and Australians, the volume is truly international with every major Test-playing nation represented. And I would truly like to welcome aboard Vic Marks whose contacts with the modern English game have been invaluable. There are, of course, gaps but there always will be. And the careers of Lara, Warne and Tendulkar are still adding to the game's smörgåsbord of memorabilia. From the 50 morsels within these pages, it is hoped the cricket fan will not go hungry.

Jon Agnew

12, 13 August 1992

Born April 4 1960, Jon Agnew made his debut for Leicestershire in 1978, taking over 600 wickets for them until his retirement in 1990. He played three Tests for England, but withdrew from first-class cricket prematurely, foregoing a benefit, to work briefly for the Today *newspaper before becoming the BBC's cricket correspondent in 1991. Unjustly, his attempts to describe Botham's hit wicket dismissal against the West Indies in 1991 alongside Brian Johnston will probably linger in the memory of cricket enthusiasts longer than his prowess as a fast bowler.*

Jon Agnew had a fine career as a professional cricketer. As a lanky fast bowler he was a prolific wicket-taker, who mastered the art of swing and, as he is always keen to remind us, bowling uphill and into the wind in harness with one of Leicestershire's overseas pacemen. He had participated in Leicestershire's 1985 Benson and Hedges triumph over Essex. In 1988 he was one of Wisden's Five Cricketers of the Year, having taken 100 wickets the previous summer. He represented England three times in Test matches, all at home, and toured India as a replacement for Paul Allott. He was well known in Leicester and highly respected on the county circuit. However, soon after retirement in 1990, he was a household name nationwide. For after a brief foray into the world of tabloid journalism, Agnew was appointed the BBC's cricket correspondent. He has made the transition from player to commentator with apparent effortlessness and now his relaxed tones are instantly recognised by all cricket lovers.

Agnew chose the last game he played for Leicestershire. It was the NatWest semi-final against Essex in 1992 when he was lured out of retirement by his former club, which had been struck by an untimely injury crisis. Agnew explains how he briefly deserted the microphone: 'Jack Birkenshaw (Leicestershire's cricket manager) phoned me up two weeks before the semi-final in a mild panic, looking for bowlers for a Championship match at Edgbaston since David Millns and Vince Wells were both injured. He had already asked Les Taylor – who also retired in 1990 – to play, an offer politely declined by Les. I also turned him down, but he asked me to "stay fit" – an interesting use of the word "stay", since I had not bowled a ball since January when I had trundled a few overs in a charity match, arranged by Richard Hadlee in Auckland.

'A week before the game, Nigel Briers (the Leicestershire captain) phoned just before I was setting off to cover the Oval Test against

Pakistan. Again I was asked if I would play in the semi-final. I told him "you can't be serious", but he urged me to have a bit of practice at the Oval. I didn't and the more I mulled over the invitation, the more inclined I was to say "no". By Monday I'd just about made up my mind. I rang up Martin Johnson (once the cricket correspondent of the *Leicester Mercury* and now the *Independent*) and he said, "Ask yourself whether you can cope with complete disaster". It would be pretty tricky pontificating on the radio about the woefully inadequate bowling I was watching when I'd just been clouted all around Grace Road myself.

'Still, I turned up at Grace Road on the Tuesday, the eve of the match, and joined in the net practice and for fifteen minutes I bowled rather well. Briers took me to one side and repeated that he wanted me to play. Whatever happened, even if I dropped two catches and conceded 100 runs, he assured me that he would be happy with that decision. I said that I'd only bowled for fifteen minutes in the nets since January. He said "Whatever you do, don't bowl any more today". They were so desperate for me to play that in the end I could hardly refuse.

'In fact, I enjoyed the day of the match enormously. It began with an interview on the *Today* programme, after which I briefly became a cricketer again. On arrival at Grace Road it was raining, which meant a delayed start. When it began to clear the Leicestershire players went out to train and do their fielding practice. Birkenshaw instructed me not to bother with any of that so I sat in luxurious solitude in the dressing-room. In the press box at Grace Road and at the other semi-final venue at Edgbaston a sweepstake was underway among the journalists, guessing my final bowling analysis. The most optimistic was 0-40; Alan Lee of *The Times* plumped for the high 70s.

'We won the toss in damp conditions and put Essex in. Gooch and Stephenson went early and I didn't touch the ball until the eighth over when I surprised myself by sending an inch-perfect throw to the keeper, a good omen. When I came on to bowl, the two batsmen, Paul Prichard and Jonathon Lewis, were in a wary frame of mind; Essex's situation was unhealthy and they probably didn't want the ignominy of getting out to a creaking part-timer. My first ball was a wide half volley, which Lewis smashed square of the wicket; Winston Benjamin at cover point stuck his left arm out and pulled off a brilliant stop to prevent any runs. Thereafter I bowled well, though at no great pace, using my old Sunday League run. The pitch offered a little help and the ball swung a little. After six overs I'd only conceded four runs and I soon had Lewis caught behind (the *Wisden* reporter entering into the frivolity of the occasion, records that "his (Agnew's) return led to the entry 'c Nixon b Agnew' in the scorebook for the benefit of students of American history"). After eight overs Briers came up to me to see whether I wanted a rest. I told him that I had to keep going now or I would seize up so he let me bowl my overs straight through.'

Agnew's control did not waver; he did not concede any boundaries and finished with the highly respectable figures of 1-31 from 12 overs. Leicester restricted Essex to 226 in their 60 overs, a target they achieved the following day with several alarms, but without Agnew being required to bat. Just as well for he was 'hideously stiff'. After one glass of champagne Agnew slipped quietly away. He had enjoyed his day – 'It was the first time in my career that I'd really done myself justice in a big game; in three Tests and several semi-finals and the final of 1985 at Lord's I hadn't excelled; I had always bowled best in Championship cricket.' While he was flattered by his old club's determination to get him to play, he acknowledged that 'I didn't really feel part of the team; if anything the match confirmed that I had done the right thing in retiring'. So Leicestershire moved on to Lord's in September and a frenetic postscript. At 10.10 a.m. Agnew was in the commentary box preparing to broadcast the final to the nation when he received a frantic wave from Nigel Briers. In the dressing-room Briers asked him where his kit was (Wells was ill and Millns had complained of twinges in the nets). 'Back in Leicester,' replied Agnew, which was where it stayed. Briers also considered persuading Peter Willey, who was also working for the BBC to turn out, a tricky task.

In the end Millns played and Leicestershire succumbed to Northamptonshire in a forgettable final. Agnew wisely recognised that only one fairy-tale ending is permitted for mortal cricketers.

Result: Leicestershire won by five wickets

Essex

*G.A. Gooch c Benson b Benjamin	8
J.P. Stephenson c Benson b Mullally	0
J.J.B. Lewis c Nixon b Agnew	21
P.J. Prichard b Potter	87
N. Hussain b Parsons	40
D.R. Pringle c Potter b Parsons	3
N.V. Knight c Nixon b Benjamin	8
†M.A. Garnham b Benjamin	8
T.D. Topley not out	19
M.C. Ilott not out	10
Extras (LB 9, W 10, NB 3)	22
1/1 2/17 3/50 4/162 5/174 6/184 7/188 8/208	226

P.M. Such did not bat.

Bowling: Benjamin 12-1-40-3; Mullally 12-0-41-1; Parsons 12-3-29-2; Agnew 12-2-31-1; Potter 9-0-50-0; Benson 3-0-26-0

Leicestershire

T.J. Boon c Prichard b Topley 31
*N.E. Briers c Hussain b Ilott 88
J.J. Whitaker c Stephenson b Ilott 46
W.K.M. Benjamin c Stephenson b Pringle 1
P.E. Robinson c Gooch b Topley 15
J.D.R. Benson not out 25
L. Potter not out 7
     Extras (LB 7, W 5, NB 4) 16
     1/52 2/138 3/145 4/176 5/213   229
†P.A. Nixon, G.J. Parsons, J.P. Agnew, A.D. Mullally did not bat.

Bowling: Ilott 12-2-36-2; Topley 12-1-58-1; Stephenson 11.5-1-56-0; Pringle 12-2-35-1; Such 12-0-37-0

Wasim Akram

World Cup final, Melbourne, 25 March 1992

Born in Lahore on 3 June 1966, Wasim Akram is the living proof that cricketers grow up quickly in Pakistan. Two years after skippering his school, he took seven wickets against the touring New Zealanders on his first-class debut. At 18, he took 10 in his second Test; by 21, he was a gnarled veteran of 15 Tests. Having completed his apprenticeship at the late Colin Milburn's Burnopfield in County Durham and been signed by Lancashire, he was being hailed as the best left-arm paceman since Alan Davidson. At 6' 3" and with a natural in-swinger, he is a blur of fluid motion and pent-up energy. On his day he can be unplayable but can still infuriate with the bat. One of Imran Khan's early 'tigers', Wasim is a mood cricketer who has yet to fully realise his enormous potential, especially with the bat. But he remains one of the game's great match-winners and, with Waqar Younis, forms the most lethal new ball pairing in the world. In England in 1992, Wasim took 82 first-class wickets at 16. 21 to become a Wisden 'Cricketer of the Year'. He had already been 'Man of the Match' in the World Cup final.

When 87,182 Melburnians began filing into their beloved mausoleum of sport, the MCG, to watch 'the Pakis' and 'the Poms' contest the fifth World Cup final, the main talking point was still the rain rule. No expletive seemed adequate in condemning a regulation that had changed South Africa's semi-final requirement from a gettable 22 off 13 balls to an impossible 22 off one ball after the briefest of showers. Mercifully for the Australian players, it helped switch the criticism of their own failure to reach the semis on to the 'boofheads' behind the laws. It had been an exciting tournament and deserved better, but now no one quite knew what to expect – on or off the field.

Some may argue that is 'situation normal' for the mercurial Pakistanis who had already displayed their best and worst sides in this competition. Rolled over for 74 by England in a group match in Adelaide, only rain (and the accompanying rule) had allowed them to escape with a point – the same as England. But while England had begun impressively, they were now running out of steam, having lost to Zimbabwe and New Zealand. As Pakistan were getting their act together, England were getting injured and grumpy. Botham and Gooch walked out of the pre-final dinner in protest at some mild rubbishing of the royals, an act which would hardly have lessened Imran's growing feeling that things were going Pakistan's way. Or the neutral Aussies from leaning toward

11

Pakistan. As for Wasim: 'I had had a lousy tournament but felt good going into the final. I had hardly taken a wicket or scored a run, but was pretty confident we would win.' Indeed, as Imran put it: 'England had more experience, we had more talent.' And no one had more talent than Wasim. He was due a good one.

Pakistan had recovered from the loss of Waqar, who returned home with a stress fracture in his back, and the injury to Javed to time their run for the tape to perfection. In Inzamam-ul-Haq and Mushtaq Ahmed, they had discovered brave young players for a crisis and, in Imran and Javed, had two of the wisest old heads in the game. Both had played in all four previous World Cups. Imran won a vital toss and batted. But two early wickets by Pringle and then a period when Imran and Javed seemed becalmed, encouraged satellite television viewers in England that their early rise would be rewarded. Indeed, as Pakistan's two veterans pushed and prodded, it was *their* judgment that was being questioned, a mere 70 runs off 25 overs being a pretty meagre halfway total. The two appeared to be playing into England's containing hands although Gooch spilled a skier off Imran. 'It was too slow,' says Wasim, 'even though we had planned to take our time and wait for the final overs. I must admit, I was concerned at that stage.'

But slowly, imperceptibly at first, the tempo changed and runs began to flow. Javed found the gaps and the niggardly Pringle, whose eight-over spell (two for 13) might have been a match-winner, had to be saved for the end. In contrast, Lewis's first four overs went for 42 and Botham, too, was belted. And when Javed finally perished from a reverse sweep of Illingworth for 58, England's joy was short-lived. In came Inzamam, whose swashbuckling 60 not out had won the man of the match award in the semi-final with New Zealand, and immediately the run-rate soared. Scoring 28 off his first 15 balls, the tall youngster altered the complexion of the match and Wasim, padded-up and next man in, was heartened. 'Suddenly we were in control,' says the Lancashire all-rounder. And when Imran holed out for 72, Wasim came in with the situation made for him.

'Although we had batted a little too slowly,' he says, 'the important thing was we had wickets in hand.' Like a relay runner who could hardly wait to receive the baton, he knew he had ground to make up. And from the way he swung that redwood trunk that passed for his bat, he felt he could do it. Driving with immense power, he smashed England's bowlers to the four corners of the great ground which, for once, did not look so huge. With Inzamam, who made 42, he put on a whirlwind 52, hitting a pulverising 33 off just 18 balls. By the time he was run out suicidally off the last ball of the innings, Pakistan had reached 249, a scorching 170 coming off the final 20 overs. It was devastating stuff and looked like a winning total. England, however, had some experienced campaigners in Gooch, Botham and Lamb. In Stewart, Hick and Fairbrother, they also had men who knew all about chasing targets. But they did not have Robin Smith, whose class they decided they could do without for the 'bits and pieces' player, Reeve. England still regrets what Gooch called 'the toughest decision I've ever had to make'.

To make 250 under lights was, as the Australians say, 'a big ask' and Wasim was supremely confident at the interval. 'Imran asked me how I felt at tea and I told him I felt light. And when I feel light, I always perform,' he explains. But in spite of removing Botham to a dubious caught behind, Wasim performed below par in his opening spell. Although swinging the ball sharply both ways, he was wayward and England were able to keep the scoreboard ticking. Perhaps he should have had Stewart but umpire Aldridge annoyed the Pakistanis as much by ruling not out as he had Botham by raising his finger. Stewart did not last long, though, and at 21 for two, England were in deep trouble. Hick and Gooch began to right the ship but Imran's bold decision to bring on Mushtaq early was rewarded when the leg-spinner removed both batsmen midway through his spell. Gooch top-edged a sweep but Hick might have been reading Urdu, so bewildered was he by the googly.

Lamb and Fairbrother brought England back into it again with a stand of 72 but just when the final seemed intriguingly poised at 141 for four, back came Wasim. 'I had told Imran that I wanted to come back. We discussed it and I said that I was ready. We needed something as the game was getting away from us a bit.' The 'something' was two successive balls that would have bowled Bradman. The first, to Lamb, swung into him before jagging away to hit off-stump. It was nigh on unplayable and it turned the match. In walked Lewis, a hero in an earlier run-chase but now facing an altogether more daunting task. In came Wasim, round the wicket. Would it be another leg-cutter? He let fly. Lewis's forward push was beaten as the ball came back into him off to hit the stumps off an inside-edge. Two in two balls. Game over.

Led by the plucky Fairbrother, England did not give up the chase, the last four batsmen all reaching double figures, but the task was beyond the mere improviser – it needed batting of the highest class for this was bowling of the highest class. The margin was 22 runs but, as Gooch acknowledged, 'it was pretty conclusive.' Wasim had swung it first with the bat, now with the ball and there was no contender in sight for man of the match. 'It was real joy,' he said. 'Winning the World Cup is wonderful, of course, but, at one stage, I did not think we would get to the semi-finals. Yes, this is my greatest game – no doubt about it.' That's Wasim, a big-time player who had swung bat, ball and match on the biggest stage of all.
Result: Pakistan won by 22 runs

Pakistan

A. Sohail c Stewart b Pringle 4
R. Raja lbw b Pringle 8
*I. Khan c Illingworth b Botham 72
J. Miandad c Botham b Illingworth 58
Inzamam-ul-Haq b Pringle 42
W. Akram run out Stewart 33
S. Malik not out 0
    Extras (LB 19, W 6, NB 7) 32
    1/20 2/24 3/163 4/197 5/249 6/249   249
I. Ahmed, M. Khan, A. Javed did not bat

Bowling: Pringle 10-2-22-3; Lewis 10-2-52-0; Botham 7-0-42-1; DeFreitas 10-1-42-0; Illingworth 10-0-50-1; Reeve 3-0-22-0.

England

*G.A. Gooch c Aqib b Mushtaq 29
I.T. Botham c Khan b Akram 0
A.J. Stewart c Khan b Aqib 7
G.A. Hick lbw b Mushtaq 17
N.H. Fairbrother c Khan b Aqib 62
A.J. Lamb b Akram 31
C.C. Lewis b Akram 0
D.A. Reeve c Rameez b Mushtaq 15
D.R. Pringle not out 18
P.A.J. DeFreitas run out (Malik-Moin) 10
R.K. Illingworth c Rameez b Imran 14
    Extras (LB 5, W 13, NB 6) 24
    1/6 2/21 3/59 4/69 5/141 7/180 8/183 9/208   227

Bowling: Akram 10-0-49-3; Aqib 10-2-27-2; Mushtaq 10-1-41-3; Ijaz 3-0-13-0; Imran 6. 2-0-43-1; Sohail 10-0-49-0.

Paul Allott

Headingley, 12, 13, 14, 16 July 1984

Paul Allott was born in Altrincham, Cheshire, on 14 September 1956. A graduate of Durham University, he made his debut for Lancashire in 1978 and his Test debut in 1981. In all, he represented England in 13 Test matches and 13 one-day internationals. He was released by Lancashire at the end of the 1992 season, but has since returned to Old Trafford in the guise of the club's bowling coach. In between teaching Wasim Akram how to bowl he is now a regular contributor to BBC radio sport as well as finding time to write for national newspapers. In both roles he has successfully curbed some of the language he employed when bowling in the middle.

1984 was not a memorable year for English cricket. England had never before been beaten in all five Tests of a home series. The narrowest margin of defeat against Clive Lloyd's West Indians was eight wickets. Not many Englishmen could find any solace from such a drubbing. David Gower with the harshest initiation to the England captaincy imaginable averaged 19 in five Tests. Two untried openers, Andy Lloyd and Paul Terry, made their Test debuts only to be ruled out of the series, having received crushing blows from the West Indian pacemen; Lloyd was struck on the helmet by Malcom Marshall seven overs into his Test career and missed the rest of the series; in his second Test Terry broke his arm. Of the English batsmen only Allan Lamb with three centuries in the series could cope with Marshall, Garner and Holding. For Ian Botham, that coveted century against the West Indians remained elusive. Bob Willis was carted around our Test arenas and soon retired from both international and county cricket. A melancholy summer.

However, I found one Englishman who could look back on that series with justifiable pride – that most English of seam bowlers – Paul Allott. Allott was – and is – a no-nonsense Lancastrian with a no-nonsense approach to bowling. His goal was simple; to pound the ball into the pitch on a good length at off stump. He rarely swung the ball but he did hit the seam regularly at a lively, though seldom terrifying pace.

Often his tongue could be more intimidating. It is a curiosity that the most vociferous of bowlers are usually just short of extreme pace; maybe they feel the need to atone for that missing yard. The likes of Robin Jackman and Paul Allott seldom scorned an opportunity to give the batsmen the benefit of their opinion of the latest passage of play and they were not always totally objective. By contrast Michael Holding or Malcolm Marshall never opened their mouths. If you were on the same side or met them off the field both Jackman and Allott were – and are – the most delightfully entertaining companions.

Allott mulled over several options for his chosen match. His Test debut at Old Trafford against the Australians in 1981 was memorable. It was played on his home ground, he scored a few runs (66 in all), took four wickets and England won, but it has already been taken up elsewhere in these pages. He accepted this rather more graciously than any rejected lbw decision. He considered the 1987 season when Lancashire were chasing the Championship and won six games out of six only to finish second: 'I remember a low scoring game at Edgbaston, when I scored runs, which, like all bowlers, I enjoyed immensely. No one knew what would happen when I went out to bat except that if I survived for two overs you could guarantee that I would play all the shots in the coaching books and one or two that weren't.' Allott, a mean and niggardly bowler, who moaned but never whinged, was an expansive, free-spirited batsman.

He finally selected the Headingley Test of 1984. This was Allott's recall after two years out of the Test side, an occasion that can be as traumatic as a Test debut. After five Tests in 1981 and 1982 he had learnt how fleeting a Test career can be during his two-year absence. Nonetheless he recalls that 'I was determined to enjoy the occasion. I knew that I was bowling better than at any stage of my career even if our opponents were the West Indies.'

Gower won the toss and batted. Thanks to a Lamb century England reached 236-5 against an attack that was soon deprived of Marshall, who sustained a double fracture of the left thumb when fielding in the gully. But on the second morning the English innings subsided in familiar fashion to 270 all out.

To Allott's surprise he was invited to take the new ball. 'There was a strong breeze blowing towards the football stand at Headingley. Willis obviously wasn't going to bowl uphill into the wind – he hadn't done that since 1981 – and Botham made it plain that he wasn't going to either, so Gower turned to me.'

Despite the elements Allott was comfortably England's most dangerous bowler. 'I bowled Haynes through the gate with one that nipped back and then had Richards, who was somewhere near his prime, caught at mid wicket in my first spell.' When he returned, Dujon was lbw and Baptiste and Harper followed in swift succession. At stumps the West Indies were 239-7 and indebted to the unflappable Larry Gomes. Allott had returned to Test cricket with 5-42.

The next morning a ferocious assault by Michael Holding on Bob Willis in an innings of 59, which included five sixes, gave the West Indies the lead. Allott clung on to a monumental skier to dismiss him, a wise move for a Lancastrian playing for England at Headingley. When Garner was run out for a duck everyone assumed that the innings would close, even though Gomes was on 96. But out came Marshall with his left hand in plaster; his appearance allowed Gomes to reach three figures and presented Allott with a peculiar problem.

'I hadn't bowled to a man in plaster before. Botham, in the slips, shouted that I should bounce him. I thought there was no need since he was bound to be bowled by a straight ball. I pitched the ball on a full length and he scythed it over the slips for four. Botham still wanted a bouncer. Again I pitched up and he swung and missed; the next ball he swung again and edged it straight to Botham.' This wicket gave Allott figures of 6-61, his best in Test cricket. For the foreseeable future at least, he would now be a regular in the England side.

Allott did not make another significant contribution to this match, though to everyone's consternation Malcolm Marshall did. Defying doctor's orders he entered the field with his plastered hand and bowled England out, taking 7-53 as the home side crumpled for 159 and lost the match by eight wickets.

Allott remained in the England team for the rest of the series, picking up 14 wickets at an average of 20. He was chosen as the senior pace bowler for the tour to India, but was thwarted by injury. He came back to play four Tests against the 1985 Australians but he would never bowl as well for England as he did in a losing cause at Headingley in 1984.

Result: West Indies won by eight wickets

England

G. Fowler lbw b Garner	10	c&b Marshall	50
B.C. Broad c Lloyd b Harper	32	c Baptiste b Marshall	2
V.P. Terry c Harper b Holding	8	lbw b Garner	1
*D.I. Gower lbw b Garner	2	C Dujon b Harper	43
A.J. Lamb b Harper	100	lbw b Marshall	3
I.T. Botham c Dujon b Baptiste	45	c Dujon b Garner	14
†P.R. Downton c Lloyd b Harper	17	c Dujon b Marshall	27
D.R. Pringle c Haynes b Holding	19	lbw b Marshall	2
P.J.W. Allott b Holding	3	lbw b Marshall	4
N.G.B. Cook b Holding	1	c Lloyd b Marshall	0
R.G.D. Willis not out	4	not out	5
Extras: (B 4, LB 7, NB 8)	29	(LB 6, NB 2)	8

1/13 2/43 3/53 4/87 270
5/172 6/236 7/237 8/244 9/254

1/10 2/13 3/104 4/106 159
5/107 6/135 7/138 8/140
9/146

Bowling: *First Innings* – Garner 30-11-73-2; Marshall 6-4-6-0; Holding 29.2-8-70-4; Baptiste 13-1-45-1; Harper 19-6-47-3. *Second Innings* – Garner 16-7-32-2; Marshall 26-9-53-7; Holding 7-1-31-0; Harper 16-8-30-1.

West Indies

C.G. Greenidge c Botham b Willis	10	c Terry b Cook	49
D.L. Haynes b Allot	18	c Fowler b Cook	43
H.A. Gomes not out	104	not out	2
I.V.A. Richards c Pringle b Allott	15	not out	22
*C.H. Lloyd c Gower b Cook	48		
†P.J.L. Dujon lbw b Allott	26		
E.A.E. Baptiste c Broad b Allott	0		
R.A. Harper c Downton b Allott	0		
M.A. Holding c Allott b Willis	59		
J. Garner run out	0		
M.D. Marshall c Botham b Allott	4		
Extras (LB 3, NB 15)	18	(LB 2, NB13)	15
1/16 2/43 3/78 4/148	302	1/106 2/108	131
5/201 6/206 7/206 8/288 9/290			

Bowling: *First Innings* – Willis 18-1-123-2; Allott 26.5-7-61-6; Botham 7-0-45-0; Pringle 13-3-26-0; Cook 9-1-29-1. *Second Innings* – Willis 8-1-40-0; Allott 7-2-24-0; Pringle 13-3-26-0; Cook 9-2-27-2.

Mike Atherton

The Oval, 19-23 August 1993

Born 23 March 1968, Mike Atherton was educated at Manchester Grammar School and Downing College, Cambridge, where he read history and captained the University side. He made his debut for Lancashire in 1987 and was appointed the club's vice-captain in 1992. A well-organised, phlegmatic batsman and once a promising leg-spinner, an unfortunate combination of a back injury and a rapid loss of confidence has restricted his bowling. He made his Test debut at the age of 21 against Australia in 1989 and soon formed one of England's most fruitful opening pairs with Graham Gooch, for whom Atherton has obvious admiration. He was appointed England captain after the resignation of Gooch in 1993.

I suppose it was inevitable that Mike Atherton would become England's captain. His Cambridge colleagues spotted this when he was only 19 so they scrawled the initials F.E.C. (Future England Captain) on his cricket coffin, although his earthier Lancashire team-mates deciphered the acronym rather differently; that the 'E' stood for 'Educated' is all that can be revealed here. He had all the right credentials; captain of school sides since the age of eleven, captain of England Under 19 and Cambridge University, vice-captain of England A and in 1991, vice-captain to Graham Gooch. He obviously had a brain, scored enough runs, did not quarrel with umpires or invite barmaids to his room and was not known to be an adherent of optional nets.

And yet in January 1993 while touring India no one thought of him as a F.E.C. There he admitted that 'for years I've been fed up with the label, but I'm starting to miss it now'. Atherton had just been omitted from the Test team and could not even be consoled by the fact that the side were playing so well that no place was available. England were playing dreadfully and he still could not get into the team. Yet within seven months he was in charge.

In fact, England's dire performances in India and Sri Lanka and against Border's 1993 tourists conspired to elevate him from an outsider to the leading candidate for the job. When Gooch resigned after the Headingley Test of 1993, it was clear that a change of emphasis was required. The other candidate, Alec Stewart, was a strict adherent of the Gooch philosophy of leadership – 'work hard and then work some more'. After a run of eight defeats in nine Tests, this was patently not working so Ted Dexter, in one of his last decisions as Chairman of Selectors, turned to his fellow Cantab. Not that Atherton is the archetypal Oxbridge amateur; he drinks ale in northern pubs, speaks with a quiet Mancunian twang and fervently supports Manchester United, where his father was briefly on the books. He has an unsentimental view of the game and prides himself on his 'professionalism'. He is no glamorous dilettante. That he overcame the burden of expectation is a testimony not only to his ambition but also his dogged level-headedness.

It did not take him long to choose the match of his life. He flirted briefly with a Benson and Hedges match at the Oval in May 1993, in which Surrey required 25 with nine wickets remaining and yet still contrived to lose to Lancashire by six runs – 'it was undoubtedly the biggest turnaround in a game that I have ever seen'. But this stunning victory was surpassed by the Oval Test against Australia in August.

It was Atherton's second match in charge of the England team. The first at Edgbaston had been lost by eight wickets on a pitch unusually helpful to spinners, which was therefore ideal for the tourists, Shane Warne and Tim May sharing 13 wickets in the game. Atherton admits he was unusually nervous as he went out to open the batting on the first morning. 'As captain, your priorities change a little; I was conscious that if I failed, the immediate conclusion might be that I was affected by the burdens of captaincy.' He scored top in England's first innings with 72 and all were agreed that he handled his bowlers shrewdly in the field, but this was scant consolation in another English defeat.

Before the Oval Test Atherton was reminded vividly of the pitfalls that come with responsibility. Atherton stayed as a house guest of Robin Smith in Southampton during a county game. 'At the end of my stay,' he recalls, 'I had to tell my host that he was dropped from the England team – if only he'd cook the black pudding correctly in the morning!' There were other significant changes since the pace attack was revamped with recalls for Devon Malcolm, Angus Fraser and Steve Watkin.

Atherton won the toss, batted and played his part in 'the most entertaining first day's play that I can remember in a Test match'. Gooch and Atherton rattled up 88 for the first wicket in even time and even though none of the English batsmen consolidated their starts, this tempo was maintained throughout the day, which ended with England 353-7.

The following morning this was extended to 380, sufficient to give the bowlers some confidence; more importantly this was the one pitch in the 1993 series to encourage fast bowlers, since it was generous in pace and bounce. Malcolm, hurtling in from the Vauxhall End, undoubtedly appreciated it. Occasionally wild, but always fast, he dismissed Slater and Boon cheaply and disconcerted the others. For the first time in a long summer, the Australians looked vulnerable. Fraser, at last restored to full fitness, dealt with a middle order, that leant heavily on the irrepressible Ian Healy, and England, for the first time in the series, had conjured a first innings lead of 77.

England's second innings began even more frenetically than the first. 29 runs were taken from the first three overs and when Gooch off drove Reiffel to the boundary the crowd rose to acknowledge the highest English runscorer in Test cricket. However, in this innings Atherton was outpacing Gooch, contributing 42 in a quickfire stand of 77. Maybe the captaincy was affecting Atherton's batting, after all. Shorn of the need to justify his selection, he played with unfamiliar fluency – 'it was not a conscious decision; it just happened through a combination of a good pitch, some wayward bowling and the need to give ourselves plenty of time to bowl out the Australians a second time'.

Australia were set a target of 392, but heavy rain on the fourth evening put this beyond their reach. On the last morning Steve Watkin, assisted by one dubious umpiring decision and Boon's reluctance to play a shot to his first delivery, rocked the Australians. Mark Waugh was in princely form, but he was caught, hooking a ball to the square leg boundary, where Ramprakash had been meticulously placed by Atherton moments before. This was the second time an unusual field placement had resulted in a wicket; was this beginner's luck or the intuition that selectors had been seeking when they appointed their new captain?

The pace bowlers were juggled skilfully with the spin of Such and Hick and when Warne was lbw to Fraser with an hour's play remaining, England had won their first Test in eleven attempts and Atherton's appointment to lead the side to the Caribbean the following winter had become a formality.

Celebrations of the triumph were necessarily brief; the bulk of the side had to return to their counties though Atherton admits that the following day, 'I awoke with a particularly heavy head, having celebrated with some of my old Cambridge team-mates, to whom a cricket victory was equally rare.' After all, this was the first time in 13 Tests that Atherton had been on the winning side against Australia.

Result: England won by 161 runs

England

G.A. Gooch c Border b S Waugh	56	c Healy b Warne	79
*M.A. Atherton lbw b S Waugh	50	c Warne b Reiffel	42
G.A. Hick c Warne b May	80	c Boon b May	36
M.P. Maynard b Warne	20	c Reiffel b Hughes	9
N. Hussain c Taylor b Warne	30	c M Waugh b Hughes	0
†A.J. Stewart c Healy b Hughes	76	c M Waugh b Reiffel	35
M.R. Ramprakash c Healy b Hughes	6	c Slater b Hughes	64
A.R.C. Fraser b Reiffel	28	c Healy b Reiffel	13
S.L. Watkin c S Waugh b Reiffel	13	lbw b Warne	4
P.M. Such c M Waugh b Hughes	4	lbw b Warne	10
D.E. Malcolm not out	0	not out	0
Extras (LB 7, W 1, NB 9)	17	(B 5, LB 12, W1, NB 3)	21
1/88 2/143 3/177 4/231	380	1/77 2/157 3/180	313
5/253 6/272 7/339 8/363 9/374		4/180, 5/186 6/254 7/276	
		8/283 9/313	

Bowling: *First Innings* – Hughes 30-7-121-3; Reiffel 28.5-4-88-2; S. Waugh 12-2-45-2; Warne 20-5-70-2; M. Waugh 1-0-17-0; May 10-3-32-1. *Second Innings* – 31.2-9-110-3; Reiffel 24-8-55-3; Warne 40-15-78-3; May 24-6-3-1.

Australia

	1st Innings		2nd Innings	
M.A. Taylor c Hussain b Malcolm	70	b Watkin	8
M.J. Slater c Gooch b Malcolm	4	c Stewart b Watkin	12
D.C. Boon c Gooch b Malcolm	13	lbw b Watkin	0
M.E. Waugh c Stewart b Fraser	10	c Ramprakash b Malcolm	49
*A.R. Border c Stewart b Fraser	48	c Stewart b Malcolm	17
S.R. Waugh b Fraser	20	lbw b Malcolm	26
†I.A. Healy not out	83	c Maynard b Watkin	5
M.G. Hughes c Ramprakash b Watkin	7	c Watkin b Fraser	12
P.R. Reiffel c Maynard b Watkin	0	c&b Fraser	42
S.K. Warne c Stewart b Fraser	16	lbw b Fraser	37
T.B.A. May c Stewart b Fraser	15	not out	4
Extras (B 5, LB 6, W 2, NB 4)	17	(B 2, LB 6, W 2, NB 7)	17

1/9 2/30 3/53 4/132   303
5/164 6/181 7/196 8/196 9/248

1/23 2/23 3/30 4/92   229
5/95 6/106 7/142 8/143 9/217

Bowling: *First Innings* – Malcolm 26-5-86-3; Watkin 28-4-87-2; Fraser 26.4-4-87-5; Such 14-4-32-0; Hick 14-4-32-0. *Second Innings* – Malcolm 20-3-84-3; Watkin 25-9-65-4; Fraser 19.1-5-44-3; Such 9-4-17-0; Hick 8-3-11-0.

Trevor Bailey

The Oval, 16-20 August 1953

Born on 3 December 1923 at Westcliff-on-Sea, not only did Trevor Bailey play cricket for Essex, where he was both club captain and county secretary, but he was also a fine footballer in his youth winning an FA Amateur Cup winner's medal with Walthamstow. He played 61 Tests for England between 1949 and 1959. He is now a highly respected broadcaster, whose observations are more entertaining than his batting in the first televised match in Australia in 1958. At Brisbane he reached his 50 in three minutes under six hours, which is still the slowest half-century on record.

It is easy to forget how good Trevor Bailey was. Bailey still has a prominent voice in English cricket; those clipped, authoritative tones are frequently heard analysing Test matches on the radio, but – unlike some pundits – his observations rarely include any glowing references to his own career.

There is a foolproof way of measuring the worth of an all-rounder; it is clinical and objective, the sort of method that Bailey himself would applaud. Simply examine the batting and bowling averages of the player concerned. If the batting average is higher, then we have an all-rounder of exceptional ability.

Bailey is one of only four post-war English Test all-rounders to meet this measurement. In international cricket, Ian Botham averages 33 and 28 respectively, Tony Greig 40 and 32. Ted Dexter is surprisingly well-placed (47 with the bat and an average of 34 with those deceptive swingers that accounted for 66 Test batsmen). In 61 Tests Bailey averaged 29.7 with the bat and 29.2 with the ball. In domestic cricket, he achieved the coveted double eight times, the same number as W. G. and Frank Woolley. There is no question that he finds himself in rarified company.

Bailey was an amateur, seemingly of the classic mould, educated at Dulwich College and Cambridge University. But he played like a professional and was much valued by the arch professional, Len Hutton, in the successful England sides of the fifties. He began as a tearaway fast bowler, but soon he recognised the virtues of accuracy and clever variations. This is his own estimate of his pace in relation to his colleagues in the day before the dreaded radar gun: 'On the tour of Australia in 1954-5 the difference in pace between Statham and myself was about the same as between Statham and Tyson.'

He readily agrees that 'I was nothing if not a pragmatic cricketer', an assessment which tallies with his reputation as a Test batsman — the 'barnacle', with that trademark forward defensive stroke, the use of which could be justified in almost every circumstance. 'Batting at number 6, I reasoned that if I stayed in, the tail was good enough to add on average another 100 runs. Two from Evans, Laker, Lock and Trueman, who could all bat a bit, would probably get 20 or 30.'

Bailey chose the Oval Test of 1953. His own contribution may not have been spectacular, but the occasion certainly was. If he had concentrated on personal achievements he might have plumped for one of several county games for Essex; perhaps the game at Romford in 1957 when he scored 130 once out and took 14-81 against Hampshire, or a match at Headingley in 1960 (106 once out and 12-101). At international level, the Kingston Test of 1954 when he took 7-34 on a benign wicket was an obvious candidate. 'But,' he explains, 'for tension and elation the Oval Test was the match.' England had to win the match against Lindsay Hassett's Australians to regain the Ashes for the first time in 19 years and the public interest was unprecedented.

'Pressure,' says Bailey, 'is not a term that means much to me; the bigger the crowd and the occasion, the more I enjoyed it.'

Bailey had displayed his 'pragmatism' earlier in the series by helping to secure unlikely draws at Lord's in a memorable partnership with Willie Watson and at Headingley, where he bowled several overs outside the leg stump to stem an Australian run chase. Bailey was no Corinthian; he was prepared, at his captain's behest, to slow the over rate and adopt negative tactics to avoid defeat; no doubt Gubby Allen would have disapproved. Indeed one reason why Bailey never assumed the England captaincy, for which his tactical acumen — and his amateur status — were clearly suited, was that he published an account of the 1954 West Indian tour in defiance of the establishment, confirmation that the wariness of the masters at Lord's towards 'free speech' among players is not a new phenomenon.

At the Oval, Hassett won the toss but Australia were unable to compile a formidable score thanks to the excellence of Alec Bedser, who had already taken 36 wickets in the series, and Fred Trueman. Yet their total of 275 was only just surpassed by England. Hutton scored 82, but it was left to Bailey with 64 and that tail to conjure a modest lead of 31.

Bailey, of course, was immovable as Neville Cardus described in his account for the *Guardian*: 'Bailey batted according to his Test match habit — blade to the ball, which he met in the middle of it, statuesque in the manner of some monumental stonemason, emulating Michelangelo . . . He is not only an anchor for England; he barnacles the good ship to the floor of the ocean.' Perhaps the same role as Botham, but most certainly a different method.

In Australia's second innings Hutton swiftly tossed the ball to his spinners, Laker and Lock, on their own patch and they soon undermined the tourists. 'By now,' wrote Hutton in his memoirs, 'there was real turn, but fortunately not too fast and, equally fortunately Australia's attack was not as well balanced as England's' — they had omitted Richie Benaud. England needed 132 for victory and even though Hutton was run out cheaply, the victory was achieved by the peerless popular duo, Compton and Edrich, who, along with their captain, had shared the torment of being constantly trounced by Australian sides since the end of the war.

The nation rejoiced and Peter Wilson, father of the BBC racing correspondent, Julian, reached for superlatives in the *Daily Mirror*, seldom used by his son even in the sensational '90s. 'By the beard of W.G., we've done it! After 19 years of frustration, war, humiliation and near misses we've got those old Ashes back where they belong – in England, where we have taught the best part of the world how to play cricket . . . and what it means . . . This was the match that counted.' Forty years on Trevor Bailey – after due consideration – agrees.

Result: England won by eight wickets

Australia

*A.I. Hassett c Evans b Bedser	53	lbw b Laker	10
A.R. Morris lbw b Bedser	16	lbw b Lock	26
K.R. Miller lbw b Bailey	1	c Trueman b Laker	0
R.N. Harvey c Hutton b Trueman	36	b Lock	1
G.B. Hole c Evans b Trueman	37	lbw b Laker	17
J. de Courcy c Evans b Trueman	5	run out	4
R. Archer c&b Bedser	10	c Edrich b Lock	49
A.K. Davidson c Edrich b Laker	22	b Lock	21
R.R. Lindwall c Evans b Trueman	62	c Compton b Laker	12
†G.R. Langley c Edrich b Lock	18	c Trueman b Lock	2
W.A. Johnston not out	9	not out	6
Extras (B 4, NB 2)	6	(B 11, LB 3)	24
1/38 2/41 3/107 4/107	275	1/23 2/59 3/60 4/61	162
5/118 6/160 7/160 8/207 9/245		5/61 6/85 7/135 8/140 9/144	

Bowling: *First Innings* – Bedser 29-3-88-3; Trueman 24.3-3-86-4; Bailey 14-3-42-1; Lock 9-2-19-1; Laker 3-0-34-1. *Second Innings* – Bedser 11-2-24-0; Trueman 2-1-4-0; Lock 21-9-45-5; Laker 16.5-2-75-4.

England

*Hutton b Johnston	82	run out	17
W.J. Edrich lbw b Lindwall	21	not out	55
P.B.H. May c Archer b Johnston	39	c Davidson b Miller	37
Compton c Langley b Lindwall	16	not out	22
Graveney c Miller b Lindwall	4		
T.E. Bailey b Archer	64		
Evans run out	28		
Laker c Langley b Miller	1		
Lock c Davidson b Lindwall	4		
Trueman b Johnston	10		
Bedser not out	22		
Extras (B 9, LB 5, W 1)	15	(LB 1)	1
1/37 2/137 3/154 4/167	306	1/24 2/88	132
5/170 6/210 7/225 8/237 9/262			

Bowling: *First Innings* – Lindwall 32-7-70-4; Miller 34-12-65-10; Johnston 45-16-94-3; Archer 10.3-2-25-1; Davidson 10-1-26-0; Hole 11-6-11-0. *Second Innings* – Lindwall 21-5-46-0; Miller 11-3-24-1; Johnston 29-14-52-0; Archer 1-1-0-0; Hassett 1-0-4-0; Morris 0.5-0-5-0.

Allan Border

WEST INDIES V AUSTRALIA

Trinidad, 16, 17, 18, 20, 21 March 1984

Born in Sydney on 27 July 1955, Allan Robert Border sends shudders down Australian spines when he says that, as a schoolboy, he preferred baseball to cricket – so immense has his contribution to the national game been. Brought up in Mosman, he extended his apprenticeship to England where he played for the same Gloucestershire village (Downend) as W. G. Grace. Having made his New South Wales debut in 1976/77, he was soon wearing the baggy green cap and has never been out of it. Just 5'8" tall, he epitomised the Aussie battler and was at his best when the going was tough – as it was for much of his early years when the Australian game was riven by the World Series dispute. In 1984, he moved to Queensland and enjoyed two seasons (1986 and 1988) with Essex. Although neither a great stylist nor a natural leader, Border became a man for all seasons, all occasions. Carrying a side weakened by defections, he mastered the Indian spinners and was unwavering in the face of successive Caribbean cyclones. The captaincy was thrust upon him when Kim Hughes tearfully resigned in 1984 but he has emerged as a genuine giant of the game, winning the World Cup in 1987 and three Ashes series. A heroic run-getter, superb fielder and useful slow left-arm bowler, his career statistics alone demand a sizable volume. In 1993, he surpassed 'Sunny' Gavaskar to become the highest run-scorer in Test history and a year later topped 11,000. Known as 'Herby' in England, 'A.B.' at home and occasionally 'Captain Grumpy', he may have sometimes lacked imagination as a skipper but if VCs were awarded for batting, he would be among the first in line.

Burdened by responsibilities and, perhaps, by sheer weight of runs, Allan Border found it difficult to single out one particular game for this book. Such is the magnitude of his achievements that only Sir Donald Bradman could have found the task more onerous. There are the endless Anzac rearguard actions, runs by the container-load, big hundreds and a couple of double hundreds, catches and even the marvellous triumph with the ball in Sydney when he took 11 wickets to rout the West Indies in 1989. But when assessing Border's contribution to the game, it is impossible to ignore either his cussedness or his courage: not for him a sparkling 70, although he could demolish the best of attacks, but an epic against the odds, carved in blood, swathed in bandages, a cricketing Gallipoli. Defying gravity is the quintessential Border, a Digger to his bootstraps. But one innings, no matter how monumental, can scarcely do him justice so when, on a previous occasion, he enthused over both digs in the same

27

match, there was no need to look elsewhere. It was in Trinidad in 1984 that he declared: 'Critics have said it was my finest hour in cricket; I prefer to regard it as my finest ten hours.'

Australia's tour to the Caribbean in 1984 was always going to be tough. After returning to the fold following the Packer interlude, the rebellious legends of the previous decade, Marsh, Lillee and Greg Chappell, bowed out. Yallop, the side's leading run-scorer in the previous series, had to stay behind with a knee injury and skipper Hughes hardly boosted morale when he acknowledged: 'The West Indies are the strongest, most disciplined and professional side I have seen.' Helped by rain, Australia drew the first Test but Hughes again made it hard for his team when he angered the Trinidadians by putting up the shutters in a match against the islanders.

Not even Clive Lloyd's absence from the second Test was of much encouragement to the visitors when they saw Joel Garner raging in at them. Overlooked for a recent tour of India, the 'Big Bird' had a point to prove and Australia were soon 16 for three. Border joined Hughes who fell just before the break when Australia had reached 55 for four. Garner had taken all four. Mercifully for the visitors, rain fell for the rest of the day but the respite was only temporary: Hookes perished at 85 and in stalked debut boy Dean Jones. The cocky Victorian was of the right stuff but Border, overcome by sickness, struggled throughout their 100-run partnership. Jones fell for a brave 48 and Border's concentration was not helped by further rain interruptions. Although ill at ease, he still had the stomach for the fight and reached 92 not out at the end of the second day. Australia were 248 for eight. The next morning he had clawed his way to 98 when Hogg went and Alderman, a renowned rabbit, came in. The recalled Garner, a foot taller than his adversary, was in no mood for sentiment and pinned Border down for 27 minutes before Alderman was removed. Australia were finally all out for 255 with Border left on 98 not out. But such was the awesome nature of his five-hour resistance, many observers are proud to say 'I was there'.

In drier conditions and against less hostile bowling, West Indies reached 218 for four by the close but the real onslaught was still to come. On the fourth day, Logie and Dujon hammered 158 for the sixth wicket. Dujon going on to 130, his second Test century, before acting skipper Viv Richards called a halt at 468 for eight after tea. The daunting task of survival depended on the elements and Allan Border, but it looked beyond them when Phillips was run out with only one on the board. Worse was to follow as Wessels and Ritchie went before the close. It was at this point that Border recalls saying to himself: 'I had made up my mind that if I was going to join the procession back to the pavilion it was going to be after a fight.'

When he came in, Australia were 114 for four and five hours were left in the match. Nightwatchman Hogan soon went but there was a glimmer of hope – Garner went down with food poisoning and Daniel had a stomach virus. Border, ever self-critical, took note when he said: 'I have analysed many of my innings and that first innings was the best. The state of the match was disastrous, the pitch wasn't good for batting, the opposition bowling was a hell of a standard and I reckon my technique was as good as I have ever produced.' With two men out of the attack, the second dig was obviously a doddle.

Richards used himself and Gomes for much of the final day, the pair wheeling away for 52 overs and claiming Hookes (caught off Gomes) and Jones (bowled by Richards). By mid afternoon, Australia were still trailing by 51 and not even staunch resistance from Lawson and Hogg seemed likely to delay the inevitable West Indies victory. That looked even more certain when Alderman, whose Test average was 'five-ish', joined Border just after tea and Australia led by just 25 runs. Hughes admits: 'I had a gut feeling that luck might just turn for us and that Terry might be able to hang on long enough for Allan to make his century.' Draw? That was pure *Boys' Own*.

But Alderman, to the amazement of his own dressing room, offered a straight bat to everything and the minutes ticked away. Border continued to accumulate and approached three figures. Alderman approached double figures. A second new ball was taken but still the pair could not be shifted. Writing in *Beyond Ten Thousand*, Border remembers a previous occasion when Garner made him feel 'out of my depth'; Richards was 'enjoying my discomfort. I gritted my teeth and thought, "I'll show you, you mug." Nothing derogatory, Viv ... just the time-worn Aussie expression that says "One day I'm coming to get you".' With Alderman as a partner, it did not look like the day but Border insists: 'I told him, "All you have to do is keep out the ball that might hit the stumps and leave the rest to me".' He remembers the crowd chanting 'Border, Border, Border' as if it were in Australia and at the end, he says he felt steam-ironed. 'But the 105 minutes and 61 runs I shared with "Clem" Alderman will remain with me forever.'

Richards reverted to spin but to no avail. Finally, he tossed the ball to Logie and Border drove the four to reach his century. Richards then shook Border's hand and called off the hunt. 'We've always rated Allan highly,' said Richards, 'and he was unlucky not to make a hundred in the first innings.' Hughes said: 'It was one of the most inspirational things I've ever seen in cricket.' Indeed. It was pure Allan Border.
Result: Match drawn

Australia

K.C. Wessels c Gomes b Garner 4	lbw b Garner 4
†W.B. Phillips c Dujon b Garner 4	run out 0
G.M. Ritchie b Garner 1	b Small 26
*K.J. Hughes c Dujon b Garner 24	lbw b Marshall 33
A.R. Border not out 98	(6) not out 100
D.W. Hookes b Garner 23	(7) c Richardson b Gomes 21
D.M. Jones c and b Richards 48	(8) b Richards 5
G.F. Lawson c and b Daniel 14	(9) b Marshall 20
T.G. Hogan c Greenidge b Daniel 0	(5) c Logie b Daniel 38
R.M. Hogg c Marshall b Daniel 11	c Garner b Richards 9
T.M. Alderman c Richardson b Garner 1	not out 21
Extras (B 6, LB 4, NB 17) 27	(B 6, LB 1, NB 14, W 1) 22
1/4 2/7 3/16 4/50 255	1/1 2/35 3/41 (9 wkts) 299
5/85 6/185 7/233 8/233 9/253	4/114 5/115 6/153 7/162
	8/196 9/238

Bowling: *First Innings* – Garner 28. 1-9-60-6; Marshall 19-4-73-0; Daniel 15-2-40-3; Small 10-3-24-0; Gomes 10-0-33-0; Richards 10-4-15-1. *Second Innings* – Marshall 22-3-73-2; Garner 15-4-35-1; Small 14-2-51-1; Daniel 9-3-11-1; Richards 25-5-65-2; Gomes 27-5-53-1; Logie 0. 1-0-4-0.

West Indies

C.G. Greenidge c Phillips b Hogg 24
D.L. Haynes run out 53
R.B. Richardson c Wessels b Alderman . 23
I.V.A. Richards* c Phillips b Alderman . 76
H.A. Gomes b Lawson 3
A.L. Logie lbw b Hogan 97
P.J.L. Dujon† b Hogan 130
M.D. Marshall lbw b Lawson 10
J. Garner not out 24
W.W. Daniel not out 6
M. A. Small
        Extras (B 7, LB 12, NB 1, W 2) 22
1/35 2/93 3/124 4/129   (8 wkts dec.) 468
5/229 6/387 7/430 8/462

Bowling: Lawson 32-3-132-2; Hogg 31-2-103-1; Alderman 35-9-91-1; Hogan 28-3-123-2.

Umpires: D. M. Archer and C. E. Cumberbatch

Ian Botham

Brisbane, 14, 15, 16, 18, 19 November 1986

Born 25 November 1955, Ian Botham, a useful right-arm pace bowler and middle-order batsman – is that sufficient? – made his debut for Somerset in 1974, before moving on to Worcestershire in 1987 and Durham in 1992. The most charismatic cricketer of his generation, he thrust cricket on to the front pages, usually for the right reasons but not always. In between playing 102 Tests for England, he raised over one million pounds for Leukaemia Research, admitted to smoking marijuana and played football for Scunthorpe United. He became the first player in Test history to score 3000 runs and take 300 Test wickets. He retired in 1993, but remains public property as a team captain in 'A Question of Sport' and a regular performer in pantomime. His most recent role was 'Silly Mid-Off', the captain's mate in 'Dick Whittington'. Described by Mike Brearley as 'the greatest match-winner the game has ever known'.

One learnt to expect the unexpected from Ian Botham. Surely he was bound to choose one of those matches in 1981 without any hesitation? At Headingley, Edgbaston and Old Trafford his performances defied belief yet he ignored them. However, it is possible to understand why. His astonishing achievements in that series tossed him into a 'Catch 22' situation. By performing so miraculously he added fuel to the argument that he was unable to play to his potential when saddled with the England captaincy; that he was at his most lethal when he had leeway to be a little irresponsible. If he had been captain at Headingley he would have felt duty bound to play properly rather than indulging in what seemed to be a forlorn slog (Botham, remember, had already booked out of his hotel) and Australia would have won the Test match.

To this day Botham remains reluctant to accept this theory, but very few of his contemporaries would agree with his protestations. Moreover, the heroics of 1981 haunted him for the rest of his career. Thereafter every time he entered the arena he was expected to produce the extraordinary. It is remarkable how often he achieved it.

Even so, the Brisbane Test of 1986 was not an obvious choice. What about the centenary Test in Bombay in 1980 when he scored a century and took 13 wickets? He is not one of those cricketers blessed with a detailed recall of matches past; perhaps it all took place too long ago. His choice reflects his happiest overseas tour. 'My wife, Kath, and the family joined me for much of the tour. We had a suite in most of the hotels, which was often used as an additional team room. Mike Gatting as captain led a relaxed regime (so relaxed that Gatting overslept before one match). It was Micky Stewart's first tour as manager, but he was on trial then and he was very much Gatt's subordinate. It was not like the rigid regime operated by Stewart and Gooch later on. Also, we were written off by the press of both sides before the series began, yet we ended up winning everything, the Tests and two one-day competitions. There's nothing better than stuffing the Aussies in Australia and making fools of a few pressmen in the process. '

In the autumn of 1986 Botham's career was in a state of flux. He had just left Somerset, appalled by their decision to sack Viv Richards and Joel Garner and was about to join Worcestershire. He declared that this was to be his last overseas tour (he was to change his mind later; after consultations with Micky Stewart, he made himself available for the Caribbean tour of 1990 and was furious to be omitted; and in 1992 – once his pantomime commitments were fulfilled – he joined the tour of New Zealand prior to the World Cup in Australia). His plan was to spend his winters playing for Queensland (in fact this scheme disintegrated after one stormy Australian season) so there was every incentive to excel in Brisbane.

Everyone outside of the England party expected Australia to win, so lack-lustre had England's performances been in the preliminary matches. Yet Australia's pace trio; Bruce Reid, Merv Hughes and Chris Matthews had only played nine Tests between them, a fact conveniently forgotten as England blundered around the states early in the tour, losing to Queensland and narrowly avoiding defeat against Western Australia.

At the Gabba, Border won the toss, fielded but endured a frustrating day. Although Chris Broad was soon caught behind off Reid, his bowlers were off target, with debutant Chris Matthews showing signs of Test match nerves. The Australians' only other success on a rain-shortened day was the wicket of Gatting, but not until he had scored 61. By the close England were 189-2, with Bill Athey a dogged 76 not out.

The following morning began disastrously. Allan Lamb was lbw to Hughes' first ball and Athey was caught behind off Chris Matthews without adding to his overnight score. England's two new batsmen were mightily experienced, but devoid of form. Gower had just collected a pair in Perth while Botham's batting had been sketchy, though he had assured any doubters 'I'll be fine once the Tests start.'

Botham was the more secure of this illustrious pair. Gower was dropped on 0 by the luckless Chris Matthews who was surprised to be stationed in the slips and gradually regained his form in a 127-run partnership. As usual when the new ball was taken, Botham regarded this as the signal to open his shoulders. Three of the first four balls from Hughes were crashed to the boundary; he tried another booming drive to the fifth but missed, prompting Gower to stroll casually down the wicket and confide, 'I think I should tell you exactly what Gatt is saying in the dressing room at this very moment, but perhaps I won't.' Botham blocked the sixth with a dutiful straight bat and thereafter settled for selective rather indiscriminate hitting.

Gower departed for 51, caught at mid-wicket from a fierce pull and Jack

Richards and John Emburey soon followed, but Phil DeFreitas allied to laudable Australian sportsmanship gave Botham time to reach his century. On three DeFreitas edged the ball to second slip, where Border dived forward. Umpire Mel Johnson immediately raised his finger. Border was uncertain whether the ball had carried and Botham enquired, 'How can you give him out when Border says he isn't sure whether the catch was clean?' The umpires consulted; Johnson's partner, Tony Crafter said that he was unsighted whereupon Greg Ritchie, who had been fielding at cover point said that he thought the ball had bounced.

DeFreitas, who had been 'mothered' early in the tour by Botham, went on to score 40 on his Test debut and gave his mentor plenty of time to reach his century. When Botham was caught at long leg, hooking for 138, the highest Test score by an Englishman at the Gabba, England were in an unassailable position. Australia were forced to follow on and finally lost the match by seven wickets and were tormented by this 'hopeless' side for the rest of the summer.

This was Botham's only significant contribution with the bat in the Test series, but he remained a contented contributor in an excellent team performance throughout an arduous season. At Melbourne he was compelled to bowl at a gentle medium pace following a rib injury and he conjured five wickets in the match that retained the Ashes. In the one-day finals against Australia he was declared man of the series.

By the end of the tour he had earnt his captain's gratitude. Reflecting on the tour Gatting commented, 'I don't think I could have asked much more of him either on or off the field. He attended every fielding and net session he was asked to and produced more than a few words at team meetings that got the rest of the lads in the mood. He was never short of advice on the field either.' Unusual plaudits for Botham and he must have cherished them as much as anything written post 1981. However, this assessment was not shared by his next captain in Australia, Allan Border at Queensland.

Result: England won by seven wickets

England

B.C. Broad c Zoerhrer b Reid	8	not out	35
C.W.J. Athey c Zoerhrer b Matthews	76	c Waugh b Hughes	1
*M.W. Gatting b Hughes	61	c Matthews G b Hughes	12
A.J. Lamb lbw b Hughes	40	not out	15
D.J. Gower c Ritchie b Matthews C	51		
I.T. Botham c Hughes b Waugh	138		
†C.J. Richards b Matthews C	0		
J.E. Emburey c Waugh b Hughes	8		
P.A.J. DeFreitas c Matthews C b Waugh	40		
P.H. Edmonds not out	9		
G.R. Dilley c Boon b Waugh	0		
Extras (B 3, LB 19, NB 3)	25	(B 2, NB 3)	5
1/15 2/116 3/198 4/198	456	1/6 2/25 3/40	77
5/136 6/324 7/351 8/443 9/451			

Bowling: *First Innings* – Reid 31-4-86-1; Hughes 36-7-134-3; Matthews C. 35-10-95-3; Waugh 21-3-76-3; Matthews G. 11-2-43-0. *Second Innings* – Reid 6-1-20-1; Hughes 5.3-0-28-2; Matthews C. 4-0-11-0; Matthews G. 7-1-16-0.

Australia

G.R. Marsh c Richards b Dilley	56	b DeFreitas	110
D.C. Boon c Broad b DeFreitas	10	lbw b Botham	14
†T.J. Zoerhrer lbw b Dilley	38	not out	16
D.M. Jones lbw b DeFreitas	8	st Richards b Emburey	18
*A.R. Border c DeFreitas b Edmonds	7	c Lamb b Emburey	23
G.M. Ritchie c Edmonds b Dilley	41	lbw b DeFreitas	45
G.R. J. Matthews not out	56	c&b Dilley	13
S.R. Waugh c Richards b Dilley	0	b Emburey	28
C.D. Matthews c Gatting b Botham	11	lbw b Emburey	0
M.G. Hughes b Botham	0	b DeFreitas	0
B.A. Reid c Richards b Dilley	3	c Broad b Emburey	2
Extras (B 2, LB 8, W 2, NB 6)	18	(B 5, LB 6, NB 2)	13
1/27 2/97 3/114 4/126	248	1/24 2/44 3/92	282
5/159 6/198 7/204 8/239 9/239		4/205 5/224 6/262 7/266	
		8/266 9/272	

Bowling: *First Innings* – DeFreitas 16-5-32-2; Dilley 25.4-7-68-5; Emburey 34-11-66-0; Edmonds 12-6-12-1; Botham 16-1-58-2. *Second Innings* – DeFreitas 17-2-63-2; Dilley 19-6-47-1; Emburey 42.5-15-80-5; Edmonds 24-8-46-0; Botham 2-0-2-0.

Mike Brearley

MIDDLESEX V SURREY

8, 9 August 1977

Born in Harrow on 28 April 1942, Mike Brearley followed his father into the Middlesex team. Horace Brearley played twice in 1949 so that father and son could claim to have ushered in and out the career of Fred Titmus. At Cambridge University he gained a first in Classics and a 2:1 in Moral Sciences as well as captaining the University side for two seasons. He made his debut for England in 1976 – aged 34 – and went on to play 39 Tests. He retired from first-class cricket in 1982. He now runs a psychotherapy practice in London, as well as contributing to a leading Sunday newspaper.

Mike Brearley's Test career is well documented. Statistically he is England's most successful captain ever. In 31 games in charge he led the side to victory 18 times and lost just four matches. Equally well established is his annoyingly modest record as a Test batsman – 1,442 runs at an average of 22.88.

These figures are so striking that it is easy too overlook the impact that Brearley had on English domestic cricket. He was a prolific student cricketer at Cambridge scoring 4,068 runs, which is a record. In 1964 he was selected for the MCC's tour of South Africa; he scored a few runs, but saw enough to join the campaign to cancel the 1970 South African tour to England. In 1965/6 he captained the England Under 25 side to Pakistan, scoring 312 not out in Peshawar, but by then he had already decided upon an academic career, which meant that he made only sporadic appearances for his county. However, in 1971 he was enticed back to first-class cricket on a full-time basis by the invitation to lead the Middlesex side. Thereafter he had a prolific county record as a batsman, equal to those who played Test cricket with him, and during his 12 years at the helm Middlesex won the Championship four times and the Gillette Cup twice.

Brearley inherited a heirarchical dressing room at Middlesex, where the senior professionals, Fred Titmus, Peter Parfitt and J.T. Murray ruled the roost. Delicately, Brearley sought to change such a rigid system. As the Middlesex players made their way through the Long Room to their dressing room, denims and scarves began to replace the club blazers. More importantly, although he was without question in charge, he actively encouraged a more open atmosphere, in which anyone in the team could make a contribution or suggestion.

One illustration of the changing atmosphere from Brearley: 'I once harangued the side for about ten minutes at Cheltenham, along the lines that we seemed to be assuming that we only had to turn up on the ground to win; and I focussed on the recently developed vogue of playing, endlessly, mindless card games. These games went on while the side was batting; players would play with their pads on and curse when a wicket fell in the middle of a hand. The climax of my speech was that there were to be no more card games during hours of play over the next few days. When I stopped there was absolute silence for about ten seconds. Suddenly the tension broke as a voice from the back was heard to say "Who's got the cards then?" Such a remark would have been unthinkable during Titmus's captaincy.'

Brearley's readiness to listen to the ideas of his teammates was spectacularly rewarded in his chosen game. It was a Championship match at Lord's against Surrey in 1977. This was the year in which Brearley took over the England captaincy from Tony Greig, who had alarmed the establishment by signing for Mr Kerry Packer. It was an invigorating summer for Brearley. By the first week in August England were 2-0 up in the Ashes series and Middlesex were pressing for their second consecutive Championship title.

The first day's play (Saturday) was completely washed out. On the Monday only five overs were possible, during which Surrey scored eight runs for the loss of Alan Butcher's wicket. Because these overs had been bowled before tea time, it was impossible for the match to become a one innings contest even though eleven and a half hours had been lost. Middlesex's Championship challenge appeared to be receding.

Brearley recalls: 'When the covers were removed on the Tuesday morning the pitch was still damp and green, ideal conditions for seam bowling. As the wickets started to fall, Mike Selvey reckoned that we could bowl them out twice in the day and win the match. Then I think it was Clive Radley, who suggested that we should consider forfeiting our first innings to force Surrey to bat again on the still damp pitch.

'When Surrey lost their sixth wicket (for 31) I ran off the field. None of us knew whether forfeiting was permitted by the laws of cricket, so I consulted with Donald Carr, Secretary of the Test and County Cricket Board. He sucked on his pipe as he was wont to do in tense situations and eventually replied that a side could not forfeit its first innings, only its second. No one knew why and this law was subsequently changed, thanks to our attempt. So, having bowled Surrey out for 49, we had to bat for one ball, which meant a waste of 11 minutes.'

Surrey fared little better the second time around, even though Middlesex dropped five catches throughout the day. Monty Lynch, playing his first county match at Lord's, had the dubious distinction of recording a pair before lunch. None of the Surrey batsmen appeared to have the technique or the stomach to cope with the Middlesex seamers. In the match Wayne Daniel, with his muscular pace took 8-39, Mike Selvey with his unerring medium-paced seamers captured 6-60, while Mike Gatting, ever optimistic but surely not lethal, finished with extraordinary match figures of four wickets and three runs. To compound Surrey's misery, Geoff Arnold, their most potent bowler in these conditions, was struck on the foot by a Daniel yorker and was unable to bowl when Middlesex set about their target of 139 in 27 minutes plus 20 overs.

They romped home against demoralised opponents by nine wickets with 11 balls to spare. Brearley himself was unbeaten on 66, but remembers little of the innings except that 'I played pretty well'. Surrey, whom Middlesex have always taken special pleasure in beating, sped home across the Thames without tarrying at HQ. Middlesex took 16 points from the match. At the end of that season as well as winning the Gillette Cup, they shared the Championship with Kent. But for that elusive combination of luck, ingenuity and self confidence at Lord's on that Tuesday (plus some mighty fine bowlers) – qualities that made Brearley a special captain – Middlesex would have been compelled to settle for second place.

This was not the last time that Brearley oversaw a miraculous victory. After that remarkable sequence of Tests against Australia in 1981 a correspondent to the *Guardian* wrote 'On Friday I watched J. M. Brearley directing his fieldsmen very carefully. He then looked up at the sun and made a gesture which suggested that it should move a little squarer. Who is this man? '

Result: Middlesex won by nine wickets

Surrey

A.R. Butcher c Gould b Daniel	1	b Daniel 10
G.P. Howarth c Edmonds b Selvey	9	c Gould b Selvey 8
M.A. Lynch c Gould b Daniel	0	b Selvey 0
Younis Ahmed c Featherstone b Daniel	4	c Gould b Daniel 14
D.M. Smith lbw b Selvey	0	c Radley b Emburey 10
Intikhab Alam b Daniel	15	c Barlow b Daniel 2
*R.D. Jackman b Daniel	0	c Brearley b Selvey 1
I.R. Payne lbw b Selvey	6	c Smith b Daniel 5
G.G. Arnold not out	8	not out 19
†C.J. Richards c Edmonds b Gatting	1	c Emburey b Gatting 6
P.I. Pocock b Gatting	3	c Edmonds b Gatting 0
Extras (w1, nb1)	2	(b3, lb8, w1, nb2) 14
1/7 2/8 3/12 4/12	49	1/14 2/14 3/31 4/46 89
5/26 6/31 7/32 8/38 9/45		5/48 6/53 7/58 8/59 9/83

Bowling: *First Innings* – Daniel 9-5-16-5; Selvey 11-2-29-3; Gatting 2.5-2-2-2. *Second Innings* – Daniel 15-8-23-4; Selvey 19-6-31-3; Gatting 1.3-1-1-2; Emburey 9-4-17-1; Edmonds 6-4-3-0.

Middlesex

J.E. Emburey not out	0		
†I. J. Gould not out	0		
M.J. Smith (did not bat)		st Richards b Pocock	51
*J.M. Brearley (did not bat)		not out	66
C.T. Radley (did not bat)		not out	21
Extras:	0	(b3,nb1)	4
Total: (no wkt, dec)	0	(1 wkt)	142

M.W. Gatting, G.D. Barlow, N.G. Featherstone, P.H. Edmonds, M.W.W. Selvey and W.W. Daniel did not bat.

Bowling: *First Innings* – Jackman 0.1-1-0-0-0. *Second Innings* – Jackman 12.1-0-61-0; Payne 2-0-19-0; Butcher 2-0-11-0; Intikhab 3-0-20-0; Pocock 6-0-27-1.

Sir Donald Bradman

Born in Cootamundra, New South Wales, on 27 August 1908, Donald George Bradman was the son of a carpenter and grandson of an English farmhand who migrated from Suffolk in 1852. Growing up in Bowral, he spent countless hours throwing a golf ball at a corrugated-iron rainwater tank and hitting the rebound with a cricket stump! Having perfected his hand-eye co-ordination, he made his first 100 for Bowral at the age of 12. Double and triple centuries followed but he played tennis almost as well and in the summer of 1923/24 he did not pick up a bat. The following season, he returned to the crease to face Bill O'Reilly in a local bush derby – and made 234 not out; in 1927/28 he scored 118 on his first-class debut at the Adelaide Oval and the legend was born. In 1928/29, he became the youngest player to score a Test century (against England), hit 340 (the highest total at Sydney) in the Sheffield Shield and saved Australia from a series whitewash with another 100 in the final Test. He was not yet 21. In 1929/30, he made 452 not out for New South Wales yet, when he sailed for England in 1930, there were still doubts about his technique. Maurice Tate told him he would have to play straighter on the soft English wickets. He did – making four hundreds, five double-hundreds, and one triple, including 309 in a day at the Headingley Test. At home, he feasted on the attacks of West Indies and South Africa before England's infamous Bodyline strategy (devised specifically to counter Bradman) reduced him to a mere mortal in 1932/33. But still he topped the batting averages at 56.67. A lingering appendicitis induced another fallow period on his second tour of England but he managed his 'traditional 300' at Leeds before his illness was diagnosed. In 1935, he moved to Adelaide but maintained his prolific output as he did when appointed captain of Australia. Only the War halted him but he came back for a final, undefeated tour of England in 1948, when a second ball duck in his final innings deprived him of a Test average of 100. In all, he made 117 first-class centuries, scoring better than one in every three visits to the crease. He was knighted in 1949.

Every sport has its saloon bar wrangles about who was the greatest. Opinions differ from genre to generation and neither stop-watches nor computers can sway impressions moulded in the formative clay of youth. Who can say between such as Ali or Marciano, Lewis or Owens, di Stefano or Pele? No such disputes occur in cricket, however, when it comes to choosing the best batsman. Donald George Bradman is so far ahead of the rest that the only discussion surrounds who comes second – and the legendary likes of Hammond, Hobbs, Hutton, Pollock, Chappell, Gavaskar, Headley, Sobers and both Richardses are reduced to the ranks of the also-batted. As Bill Bowes once said, 'Bradman is not head and shoulders above the rest, he is better from the ankles up.'

Statistically, Bradman was 40 runs an innings better than most of the above and 40 is a respectable Test average. So what, practice apart, was the secret of his remorseless infallibility? Barely 5'7", he had small hands but strong wrists and was as nimble as he was nerveless. His stance was motionless and he moved into the stroke late, like a tiger waiting and then pouncing. His footwork was near-perfect as was his range of strokes, yet he never betrayed the human trait of being a stylist. Perfect balance, timing and temperament were other factors in his relentless stockpiling of runs which he did as if on piecework. However, even he had his critics. Let us leave them to Sir Neville Cardus: 'People say,' he wrote, 'that he hasn't the charm of McCabe, or the mercury of McCartney, or the dignity of Hammond'; the objection is a little unintelligent, as though a lion were criticised for lacking the delicacy of the gazelle, the worrying tenacity of the terrier or the disdainful elegance of a swan or camel.

Asking Sir Donald to choose the game of his life was akin to demanding to know Shakespeare's favourite verse. For lesser mortals, it usually comes down to one of several peaks, a highest score, a match-saving hundred or even a swift 70 to win a game. But for Bradman, whose run-scoring was of Himalayan proportions, the double-centuries were almost routine, while even the triples too numerous to mention. And when he was out for a mere 100, sighs of disappointment were often heard. A London paper's billboard once screamed: 'Bradman fails'. He had made 80. So the man, himself, says: 'If I were forced to name my most memorable match, it would probably be the fourth Test at Leeds in 1948. I was then 39, on my last tour of England and on the final day England declared leaving us 345 minutes to get 404 runs.'

It had never been done and even for Bradman's all-conquering 'Invincibles', it was thought impossible. But not by Yardley who batted on for five minutes on the last morning before setting the target. By doing so, England's captain had the choice of the roller and opted for 'heavy'; Bradman just had a steamroller – his own. An ageing yet inexperienced side, the Australians had made triumphant progress around ration-book Britain. Welcomed as heroes by a war-torn nation – Bradman even delivered food parcels – the likes of Lindwall and Miller, Morris and Barnes, Toshack and Tallon, not to mention Bradman, made the Brits feel the war really was over. Vast crowds flocked to glimpse the charismatic visitors who were treated like pop stars and the Australian captain was lent a secretary to handle his 600 letters a day. But on the field, it was the blitz all over again as the men in green caps won the first two Tests – and every other game – by a country mile. The rain-affected third Test at Manchester was drawn with England in a promising position, so all eyes were on Bradman's beloved Headingley for the decisive fourth Test in late July. Purposeful early batting took England to 496, their highest total of the summer, and had it not been for Neil Harvey, in for the injured Sid Barnes, making a magnificent 112 on his debut, Australia would have trailed by more than 38 on first innings.

Bradman made just 33 and worse was to come for the tourists as

Hutton and Washbrook fashioned their second century opening stand of the match. Although both fell at 129, England gathered the quick runs Yardley needed to give his bowlers a chance of bowling Australia out – and keeping England in the series – in the fourth innings. The home side had outplayed Bradman's men for four days. Attendance records were broken and long queues formed outside the packed ground in the early morning. Thousands were turned away. As Morris and Hassett set about the 'impossible' task, the early editions of the evening papers concluded: 'the best they can hope for is a draw.' Bradman refused to countenance such an outcome.

With only Laker as a front line spinner, England's options were limited and it wasn't long before Compton's occasional spin was employed. But he soon had Hassett caught and bowled and might have had Bradman shortly afterwards. The great man was given perhaps the greatest ovation Headingley has heard when he came in at 57 for one. But he should have been out twice in Compton's seventh over, edging to slip on both occasions. The part-timer was also unlucky when Evans missed a stumping chance from Morris. Then Bradman was dropped by Yardley off Cranston and England's morale dropped with it. Compton was wayward, Laker tired and Morris and Bradman helped themselves. The skipper made just 35 in half an hour before lunch – it was to be a mere appetiser for the afternoon feast.

Allowing the elegant left-hander to lead the onslaught, Bradman eagerly clasped Morris's hand when the opener reached his century, getting to his own 50 in just an hour. Rattling along at two runs a minute, the pair carved up a demoralised attack, Bradman arriving at his own hundred at ten past four, just two hours and 25 minutes after coming in. With rasping drives, murderous pulls and rapier-like cuts, he had once again demonstrated that *Wisden* was right when it wrote: 'At the crease, he is the master; the bowler is the servant.' At tea, Australia needed 116 to win in 105 minutes and few were betting against them. After the break, Bradman and Morris carried on remorselessly before Morris finally perished, caught by Pollard off Yardley for a magnificent 182. The pair had put on 301. There was time for Miller to fall to Cranston but when Harvey belted the winning run, Australia were home by seven wickets with 13 minutes to spare. Bradman was 173 not out. 'It was the first time in history,' he says, 'that any side had won a Test with 400 in the fourth innings. Winning the Test won us the Ashes and the attendance was 158,000, then an all-time record for any match in England. It was memorable for me as a finale to my career as captain. What else can I say?'
Result: Australia won by seven wickets

England

L. Hutton b Lindwall	81	c Bradman b Johnson	57
C. Washbrook c Lindwall b Johnston	143	c Harvey b Johnston	65
W.J. Edrich c Morris b Johnson	111	lbw b Lindwall	54
A.V. Bedser c and b Johnson	79	(9) c Hassett b Miller	17
D.C.S. Compton c Saggers b Lindwall	23	(4) c Miller b Johnston	66
J.F. Crapp b Toshack	5	(5) b Lindwall	18
N.W.D. Yardley* b Miller	25	(6) c Harvey b Johnston	7
K. Cranston b Loxton	10	(7) c Saggers b Johnston	0
T.G. Evans+ c Hassett b Loxton	3	(8) not out	47
J.C. Laker c Saggers b Loxton	4	not out	15
R. Pollard not out	0		
Extras (B 2, LB 8, NB1, W 1)	12	(B 4, LB 12, NB 3)	19
1/168 2/268 3/423 4/426 5/447	496	1/129 (8 wkts dec.)	365
6/473 7/486 8/490 9/496		2/129 3/232 4/260 5/277	
		6/278 7/293 8/330	

Bowling: *First Innings* – Lindwall 38-10-79-2; Miller 17.1-2-43-1; Johnston 38-12-86-1; Toshack 35-6-112-1; Loxton 26-4-55-3; Johnson 33-9-89-2; Morris 5-0-20-0. *Second Innings* – Lindwall 26-6-84-2; Miller 21-5-53-1; Johnston 29-5-95-4; Loxton 10-2-29-0; Johnson 21-2-85-1.

Australia

A.R. Morris c Cranston b Bedser	6	c Pollard b Yardley	182
A.L. Hassett b Crapp b Pollard	13	c and b Compton	17
D.G. Bradman* b Pollard	33	not out	173
K.R. Miller c Edrich b Yardley	58	lbw b Cranston	12
R.N. Harvey b Laker	112	not out	4
S.J.E. Loxton b Yardley	93		
I.W. Johnson c Cranston b Laker	10		
R.R. Lindwall b Crapp b Bedser	77		
R.A. Saggers+ st Evans b Laker	5		
W.A. Johnston c Edrich b Bedser	13		
E.R.H. Toshack not out	12		
Extras (B 9, LB 14, NB 3)	26	(B 6, LB 9, NB 1)	16
1/13 2/65 3/68 4/189 5/294	458	1/57 2/358 (3 wkts)	404
6/329 7/344 8/355 9/403		3/396	

Bowling: *First Innings* – Bedser 31.2-4-92-3; Pollard 38-6-104-2; Cranston 14-1-51-0; Edrich 3-0-19-0; Laker 30-8-113-3; Yardley 17-6-38-2; Compton 3-0-15-0. *Second Innings* – Bedser 21-2-56-0; Pollard 22-6-55-0; Cranston 7.1-0-28-1; Laker 32-11-93-0; Yardley 13-1-44-1; Compton 15-3-82-1; Hutton 4-1-30-0.

Umpires: H. G. Baldwin and F. Chester

Bhagwat Chandrasekhar

The Oval, 19, 20, 21, 23, 24 August 1971

Born in Bangalore on 17 May 1945, Bhagwat Subrahmanya Chandrasekhar was stricken by polio at the age of five but turned the handicap to his advantage. With an indomitable spirit and a withered right arm, he became one of the great leg-break bowlers of all time – just when the art, itself, was withering away. At 17, he played for Mysore in the Ranji Trophy and a year later took four for 67 in 40 overs on his Test debut against England. Regarded as either a phenomenon or a freak, he would hold the ball in both hands like a bowls player, then trundle in some ten paces before sending down a potpourri of leggies, googlies and top spinners at around 'Underwood' pace. Although he bowled with his emaciated right arm, he threw with his left. As a batsman, it didn't matter which way he faced: 'Chandra' was not merely a rabbit at the crease, he was permanently caught in the headlights. But with the ball this slim, bearded south Indian was a master, totalling 242 wickets at 29. 74 in 58 Tests. Although his finest hour was at the Oval in 1971, his match figures of 12 for 104 in Melbourne bowled India to a first Test win on Australian soil in 1978.

'Who would have imagined,' asked former Indian batsman Rusi Modi, 'that a victim of poliomyelitis would one day paralyse the best batsmen in the game?' But in his early career, 'Chandra', as he was universally known, had other worries. 'My nagging ankle problem caused me to be sent back from the tour of Australia in 1968,' he says. 'I would even say that I was driven into oblivion. Back home my mental and physical agony were aggravated by a road accident! I missed the home series against New Zealand and Australia but, much to my delight, my mind and limbs became better co-ordinated than ever before. The next domestic season I took a lot of wickets – enough, I felt sure, to go to the West Indies in 1971. But I was not there.

'What else should I do to get back into the national side? I wondered. Months passed without much cricket in Bangalore, the Indian team came back with a sensational win from the West Indies and thoughts turned to the tour of England that began in June. I did not have even a ghost of a chance of being there but the chairman of the selection committee, the late Vijay Merchant, took "a calculated risk" by including me. Naturally, I was delighted. But then the term "calculated risk" began to irk me. Yet I had no choice but to gulp it and grin. As the tour progressed, I developed an uncertainty about my future as a cricketer. I had done nothing to live up to the tag "calculated risk" and was just another bowler. But the team manager Colonel Adhikari kept telling me that my day would come before the end of the tour. No one could have served me a stronger dose of tonic at that juncture.

'The first two Tests failed to produce a result. Before the third and final Test at the Oval, there was a game against Nottinghamshire and the soothing words of Colonel Adhikari strengthened my will. 11 wickets in that match meant I was playing at the Oval. England began on a grand note blasting 355 runs on the opening day but they were all out.' It is worth noting that Chandra had to be content with two for 76 off 24 overs, but had the satisfaction of bowling Illingworth, the skipper, with a top spinner, and having D'Oliveira caught in the deep, driving. Sages said the wicket would turn later and England, thanks largely to John Jameson hitting a robust 82, Alan Knott a typically ebullient 90 and Richard Hutton hammering 81 after tea, were reasonably satisfied. The second day was washed out and on the third, the cricket was as grey as the weather, India doggedly batting through it for 234 for seven. No batsman took command; Engineer top-scoring with 59, but a final total of 284 kept the visitors very much in the match. And the wicket was turning as any Illingworth-watcher was well aware. The home skipper was renowned for under-bowling himself but on this occasion he churned down 34.3 overs for a final haul of five for 70. Chandra was heartened. And when England began their second innings with a lead of 71, it was Chandra who made the breakthrough – but not in the way he intended.

'Luckhurst drove me straight back,' he recalls, 'and I put my right hand to the hot cherry. It went on to hit the stumps at the non-striker's end with Jameson stranded outside the crease.' It was the second time in the match that the burly Warwickshire opener had been run out. 'Back home it was Ganesha Day. Ganesha being worshipped by Indians before beginning a commitment. It was a historic coincidence that we Indian cricketers began to build our international reputation on that day, a day when English wickets tumbled much to the cricket world's astonishment. Dilip Sardesai, for whom horse-racing is a favourite pastime, used to call me "Mill Reef" after the most favoured and admired horse of that period. He told me: "Come on, Mill Reef, it could be your day."'

In the last over before lunch, Chandra suggested that he could well be the horse to back with a perfect illustration of his varied repertoire. After yorking Edrich with a quicker one, his next ball was a googly. Fletcher pushed forward, edged and Solkar dived to take the catch. Chandra lunched on a hat-trick. With two balls remaining to complete the over, six fieldsmen crowded the bat. D'Oliveira blocked the first but edged the second ball to Sardesai at slip, but the turf lover downed a sharp chance. In Chandra's next over, D'Oliveira was dropped again, this time by Solkar at short leg. The South African-born all-rounder was a doughty fighter and with Luckhurst coping admirably at the other end, there was the feeling that India's misses could prove costly. The truth was that, although D'Oliveira delivered a couple of telling blows to disperse the field, he was not as comfortable as he looked and he eventually holed out to deep mid-on off Venkat who then had Knott caught at short leg. That was 55 for five and Chandra was just getting warmed up.

Three wickets in three overs for no runs put paid to any hope of an England recovery. Extracting snake-like venom from the pitch, he had Luckhurst caught off a top-spinner – 'a blinder by Venkat at slip' – Illingworth caught and bowled off a slower ball and then held an easy return catch to remove Snow. He recalls: 'I bowled at a stretch except for one over from Bedi. Ajit [Wadekar], my skipper, did well to effect that change as there was no success for me for two overs. I came back to mop up the tail and England went reeling to 101 all out. We had to make 173 to win.

'Thus winning a Test match in England appeared a certainty. We lost wickets, no doubt out of sheer tension, but we knew the game was ours. The victory chase featured some game efforts from Wakedar (45), Sardesai (40), Viswanath (33) and Engineer (28 not out), with Abid Ali confirming it with a firm cut to the fence. We were through by six wickets. India became a feared and respected cricket-playing nation and I, the "calculated risk", went on to play for my country for the next eight years. The Oval triumph shaped my career and gave a new image to our country. Amazingly, one of my most respected English friends, the great Ken Barrington, had predicted the miracle. In his column on the eve of England's second innings, he wrote that "Chandra is India's trump card and England could be in a nasty spot if he turns it on tomorrow." It turned out to be so.'

Indian cricket was renowned for its grace: on the final day it supplied the grit, too, as England, who had beaten Australia, West Indies, Pakistan and New Zealand, fought them every step of the way. When Wadekar was run out without addition to the overnight score of 76 for two, it looked as if the home side might yet sneak it. But they did not possess a bowler of Chandra's bite and, amid great jubilation from the Indian section of the crowd, history was made. The festival of Ganesha was celebrated in appropriate fashion and all that was needed was Kenneth Wolstenholme to say: 'there is an elephant on the pitch.' India's long wait was over – 'Mill Reef' had come home.

Result: India won by four wickets

England

J.A. Jameson, run out	82	run out	16
B.W. Luckhurst, c Gavaskar, b Solkar	1	c Venkataraghavan, b Chandrasekhar	33
J.H. Edrich, c Engineer, b Bedi	41	b Chandrasekhar	0
K.W.R. Fletcher, c Gavaskar, b Bedi	1	c Solkar, b Chandrasekhar	0
B.L. d'Oliveira, c Mankad, b Chandrasekhar	2	c sub, b Venkataraghavan	17
A.P.E. Knott, c & b Solkar	90	c Solkar, b Venkataraghavan	1
R. Illingworth, b Chandrasekhar	11	c & b Chandrasekhar	4
R.A. Hutton, b Venkataraghavan	81	not out	13
J.A. Snow, c Engineer, b Solkar	3	c & b Chandrasekhar	0
D.L. Underwood, c Wadekar, b Venkataraghavan	22	c Mankad, b Bedi	11
J.S.E. Price, not out	1	lbw, b Chandrasekhar	3
Extras (B 4, LB 15, W 1)	20	(LB 3)	3
Total	355		101

1/5 2/111 3/135 4/139 5/143 6/175
7/278 8/284 9/352

1/23 2/24 3/24 4/49 5/54
6/65 7/72 8/72 9/96

Bowling: *First Innings* – Abid 12-2-47-0, Solkar 15-4-28-3, Gavaskar 1-0-1-0, Bedi 36-5-120-2, Chandrasekhar 24-6-76-2, Venkataraghavan 21. 4-3-63-2 *Second Innings* – Abid Ali 3-1-5-0, Solkar 3-1-10-0, Venkataraghavan 20-4-44-2, Chandrasekhar 18. 1-3-38-6, Bedi 1-0-1-1

India

A.V. Mankad, b Price	10	c Hutton, b Underwood	11
S. Gavaskar, b Snow	6	lbw, b Snow	0
A.L. Wadekar, c Hutton, b Illingworth	48	run out	45
D.N. Sardesai, b Illingworth	54	c Knott, b Underwood	40
G.R. Vishwanath, b Illingworth	0	c Knott, b Luckhurst	33
E.D. Solkar, c Fletcher, b D'Oliveira	44	c & b Underwood	1
F.M. Engineer, c Illingworth, b Snow	59	not out	28
S. Abid Ali, b Illingworth	26	not out	4
S. Venkataraghavan, lbw, b Underwood	24		
B.S. Bedi, c D'Oliveira, b Illingworth	2		
B. S. Chandrasekhar, not out	0		
Extras (B 6, LB 4, NB 1)	11	(B 6, LB 5, NB 1)	12

1/17 2/21 3/114 4/118   284
5/125 6/222 7/230 8/278 9/284 10/284

1/2 2/37 3/76   (6 wkts) 174
4/125 5/134 6/170

Bowling: *First Innings* – Snow 24-5-68-2, Price 15-2-51-1, Hutton 12-2-30-0, D'Oliveira 7-5-5-1, Illingworth 34. 3-12-70-5, Underwood 25-6-49-1 *Second Innings* – Snow 11-7-14-1, Price 5-0-10-0, Underwood 38-14-72-3, Illingworth 36-15-40-0, D'Oliveira 9-3-17-0, Luckhurst 2-0-9-1

Greg Chappell

ENGLAND V AUSTRALIA

Lord's, 22, 23, 24, 26 June 1972

Born in Adelaide on 14 August 1948, Gregory Stephen Chappell was always going to be a cricketer. With Vic Richardson for a granddad, a first-grade player in his own Dad and big brother Ian as mentor and tormentor in backyard 'Tests', young Greg learned the game quickly. At 18, a century on his debut for South Australia underlined his potential and another, in his first Test, confirmed it. A classic right-hander, immaculate in technique and appearance, he is widely regarded as the best Australian batsman since Bradman, under whose admiring gaze his early brilliance flowered. His marvellous 131 at Lord's in 1972 announced his arrival as a new master. A superb slip and useful seamer, he had two seasons with Somerset, moved to Queensland in 1974/75 and took over the Australian captaincy from his brother a year later. After World Series Cricket, he returned to skipper his country to an Ashes win in 1982/83. His only blemishes were the seven ducks in 1981/82 and the infamous – and later regretted – last ball underarm he asked his younger brother Trevor to bowl against New Zealand. But he finished his Test career as he began it – with a century. In that farewell game at Sydney in 1984, he also broke Cowdrey's record 120 catches and Bradman's 6,996 runs, ending with 7,110 (av. 53.86). An appropriate way for a master to bow out.

Bob Massie didn't want to talk about it but Greg Chappell did. The unforgettable Lord's Test of 1972 might have gone down in history as 'Massie's match', which is reasonable enough when the hitherto-unknown paceman took 16 wickets on his Test debut. But not even that could totally overshadow Chappell's first-innings century, always regarded by the man, himself, as his best. It also was a bigger influence on the match and the series than was realised amid all the Massie mania. 'We'd been beaten in the first Test,' he recalls, 'and were two for seven when I went in. England had made 272 which wasn't that bad in conditions that were very much in favour of bowling.'

But let us give due credit to Massie, whom, two seasons earlier had been playing for Kilmarnock in the Scottish League. Yes, at cricket. Moving the ball prodigiously both in the air and off the pitch from around the wicket, he caused so much panic among the England batsmen that some suspected him of using lip-salve to aid his swing. If it had been that easy, he would surely have bought another tube when he lost his touch. As it was, the Western Australian was already celebrating a five-wicket haul when England struggled to 249 for seven at the end of the first day. He

47

soon polished off the tail but Aussie joy was shortlived when both openers (Stackpole and Francis) were removed with seven runs on the board. It was murky and ideal for swing bowling when Greg walked in to join his brother Ian.

'It was always going to be difficult,' remembers Greg. 'They had an experienced batting side yet had made hard work of it. We were pretty inexperienced, especially in those conditions.' England, thanks to their dogged lower-middle order, had fought back from 97 for five and now unleashed Snow on the visitors. Tearing in from the pavilion end, he was a tough proposition but, with their parents and younger brother Trevor watching, the Chappells stood firm. 'Ian tried to meet fire with fire,' says Greg, 'while I just stayed there. The bowling was accurate rather than venomous but in those conditions, they would have expected to win.' Having declared that he'd had 'a gutful of bouncers', Ian was true to his word – and hooked them. The stroke brought him five fours and a thrilling six into the Mound stand before it brought his downfall, caught by a tumbling Smith on the long-leg fence.

Eighty-two for three and Walters came in to face his *bête-noire*, Snow. Predictably, he did not last long and, just as predictably, he was caught in the gully. Eighty-four for four and crisis time once again. Edwards joined Chappell who waited three hours before scoring his first boundary. Locked in concentration, Chappell was judicious in picking the balls to leave, the balls to punish. Marooned on 14 for an hour, he had been totally unperturbed and showed a bat that was ramrod straight. At the same time, watchful and imperious, he gradually took on the mantle of stroke-maker, driving powerfully between cover and mid-wicket. With Edwards offering valuable support, Chappell defied everything Illingworth could think of and was nearing his century when Edwards, swinging at the England captain, was well held by Smith in the deep. Gleeson was sent in as nightwatchman and Chappell duly completed his first century at Lord's just before close of play. At 201 for five, the game was tantalisingly poised – thanks to the admirably straight bat of the younger Chappell. He received a tremendous, standing ovation, the England players joining the 29,000 to salute what John Arlott called a 'faultless innings'.

'I had just decided to bat as long as I could, hoping the wicket would get easier as the match wore on,' he says. 'Illingworth complained that England had the worst of the conditions but it was movement off the pitch as much as in the air that did for them. We found it was searing around a bit and wanted to get as close as we could to their score, hoping that batting would get easier. My knock seemed to go on forever. Physically, I was as good as gold but mentally I was tiring.' Arlott added: 'Already at 23, he is a mature, responsible and informed cricketer.' The next morning Gleeson didn't last long but England's hopes of a first innings lead were dashed by the bold hitting of Marsh, the perfect foil to Chappell's measured mastery. He had reached 131 when he dragged a ball from D'Oliveira on to his stumps. 'I had wanted to force the pace the next morning,' he says, 'and it was the first mistake I'd made. I got another terrific reception – and it was my first 100 at Lord's. That added something to it.' He had hit 14 fours and had not given a chance.

Marsh made 50 and Australia totalled 308, a lead of 36, with Snow finishing with five for 57 off 32 overs. The match was still anybody's but not for much longer. After Lillee had taken the first two wickets, Massie took over once more and by tea, the home side were 25 for four. Worse was to follow as this time the redoubtable middle order of Greig, D'Oliveira, Knott and Illingworth had no more answers to Massie than Messrs Boycott, Edrich, Luckhurst and Smith. With Greg Chappell picking up two catches at slip, England slumped to 86 for nine, a lead of 50 with two days to play. Massie had taken seven, giving him 15 in the match.

There was no miracle – and no respite from Massie – on Monday and Australia duly levelled the series, knocking off the runs (81) for the loss of Francis and Ian Chappell. Fittingly Greg was at the crease (seven not out) when Stackpole made the winning hit. It will forever be Massie's match – as it should be with 16 for 137. But Greg Chappell would have won an Oscar for one of the finest supporting roles of all time. 'It was my most complete innings,' he says. At the time Ian declared: 'I doubt whether he'll play a much better innings than that one.'

Result: Australia won by eight wickets

England

G. Boycott b Massie	11	b Lillee	6
J.H. Edrich lbw b Lillee	10	c Marsh b Massie	6
B.W. Luckhurst b Lillee	1	c Marsh b Lillee	4
M.J.K. Smith b Massie	34	c Edwards b Massie	30
B.L. D'Oliveira lbw b Massie	32	c G.S. Chappell b Massie	3
A.W. Greig c Marsh b Massie	54	c I.M. Chappell b Massie	3
†A.P.E. Knott c Colley b Massie	43	c G.S. Chappell b Massie	12
*R. Illingworth lbw b Massie	30	c Stackpole b Massie	12
J.A. Snow b Massie	37	c Marsh b Massie	0
N. Gifford c Marsh b Massie	3	not out	16
J.S.E. Price not out	4	c G.S. Chappell b Massie	19
Extras (LB 7, NB 2)	13	(NB 4, W 1)	5
1/22 2/23 3/28 4/84	272	1/12 2/16 3/18 4/25	116
5/97 6/193 7/200 8/260 9/265		5/31 6/52 7/74 8/74 9/81	

Bowling: *First Innings* Lillee 28-3-90-2; Massie 32. 5-7-84-8; Colley 16-2-42-0; G. S. Chappell 6-1-18-0; Gleeson 9-1-25-0. *Second Innings* – Lillee 21-6-50-2; Massie 27.2-9-53-8; Colley 7-1-8-0.

Australia

K.R. Stackpole c Gifford b Price	5	not out	57
B.C. Francis b Snow	0	c Knott b Price	9
*I.M. Chappell c Smith b Snow	56	c Luckhurst b D'Oliveira	6
G.S. Chappell b D'Oliveira	131	not out	7
K.D. Walters c Illingworth b Snow	1		
R. Edwards c Smith b Illingworth	28		
J.W. Gleeson c Knott b Greig	1		
†R.W. Marsh c Greig b Snow	50		
D.J. Colley c Greig b Price	25		
R.A.L. Massie c Knott b Snow	0		
D.K. Lillee not out	2		
Extras (LB 7, NB 2)	9	(LB 2)	2
1/1 2/7 3/82 4/84 5/190	308	1/20 2/51	(2 wkts) 81
6/212 7/250 8/290 9/290			

Bowling: *First Innings* – Snow 32-13-57-5; Price 26. 1-5-87-2; Greig 29-6-74-1; d'Oliveira 17-5-48-1; Gifford 11-4-20-0; Illingworth 11-4-20-0. *Second Innings* – Snow 8-2-15-0; Price 7-0-28-1; Greig 3-0-17-0; D'Oliveira 8-3-14-1; Luckhurst 0. 5-0-5-0.

Umpires: D. J. Constant and A. E. Fagg

Martin Crowe

Christchurch, 13, 14, 15 March 1987

Born in Henderson, Auckland, on 22 September 1962, Martin David Crowe is one of the handful of great New Zealand batsmen. The son of D.W., who played for Wellington and Canterbury, and younger brother of Jeff, a predecessor as his country's skipper, Martin's childhood was a cricket tutorial. At 17, he played for Auckland, made his Test debut at 19 and by 25 was regarded as one of the top five batsmen in the world. He honed his technique on the Lord's ground staff and in the Bradford leagues, proved a worthy replacement for Viv Richards at Somerset (in 1984 and 1987) and played a key role in his country's emergence as a force on the international scene. By giving the great Richard Hadlee something to bowl at, Crowe starred in victories over England, Australia and West Indies, his immaculate technique and complete range of strokes earning him the accolade of master batsman. Personable and articulate, he has been plagued more by illness, injuries and the scurrilous elements of the Kiwi press than by any bowler, but became a national hero by guiding New Zealand into the World Cup semi-final in 1992. His brilliant batting and innovative captaincy made him the 'Man of the Tournament'. In 1987, he joined la crème de la crème by amassing over 4,000 runs in a calendar year. The other members of this exclusive club? Bradman, Hammond, Sutcliffe and Hutton . . .

With just seven victories in their first 102 Tests, New Zealand suddenly began to get it together in the 1970s. Historic wins over Australia, India and England gained new respect for the Shaky Isles, who were determined to maintain this belated momentum. With the incomparable Richard Hadlee as the spearhead, they knew they could dismiss any side but inconsistency, especially in the batting, continued to dog them. Still, thanks to the emergence of a world-class middle order strokeplayer, the 1980s became even more memorable, the most celebrated triumph being the win in Brisbane in 1985 (Hadlee's match).

But throughout this decade, discerning teams would judge themselves by how they did against the all-conquering West Indies, whose battery of fast-bowlers regarded reputations as fair-ground customers do coconuts. Crowe had already proved his mettle with a magnificent 188 off Marshall, Garner and Holding in Georgetown and began the 1986/87 home series by scoring two centuries in three innings. Proud of their unbeaten home record in the 1980s, New Zealand were mortified to lose the second Test of three in Auckland. And even 1-0 down with skipper Coney having a

51

bitter spat with Hadlee, few would have backed them to level against the likes of Richards, Greenidge and Haynes, Marshall, Garner, Gray and Walsh. When the first day was washed out, the task, according to the *New Zealand Herald*, became 'impossible'.

'We won the toss, which was a start,' says Crowe, 'and put them in. It was the best – perhaps, only – chance we had. We really wanted to preserve that record.' There was no better man to exploit the green top than Hadlee, but he admitted to being 'totally unprepared mentally after the conflict with Coney.' Still, being the professional he was, he tore into the West Indian batsmen. He bowled Haynes in the second over and then Chatfield bowled Greenidge. Six for two. Gomes and Richardson took it to 44 but Chatfield had probably already delivered the ball that won the match, the West Indies being scarcely able to believe that Greenidge, the double-century-making hero of Auckland, had been removed in such a way. Crowe actually dropped Gomes at slip off Chatfield but his brother Jeff made amends off the same bowler, who then had Richards caught behind. Martin Crowe then held Richardson off Hadlee before Dujon and Marshall also fell. It was 67 for seven! 'They somehow scrambled to 100,' says Crowe and, in spite of Hadlee refusing to speak to Coney, he took six wickets [for 50], and Coney held three brilliant catches! But Chatfield, although his reward was just four for 30, had been the more effective. If anything could have promoted harmony in the New Zealand dressing room, it was surely dismissing the Windies for 100 but, says Crowe, 'Hadlee still refused to speak to Coney.'

Like a wounded tiger, the West Indies were expected to strike back immediately and they did not disappoint, Wright and Horne being removed with just 23 on the board. But this brought together the Crowe brothers and, recalls Martin, 'we put on our best partnership in Tests (156).' It turned out to be the critical stand of the match as another wicket would have had New Zealand struggling to top the West Indies' first innings total. But recalling their backyard battles as kids, when the virtues of playing straight were drummed into them by Dad, the Crowes saw their side into the lead on the first day. And few New Zealanders could believe the score at stumps – 17 in front and eight wickets in hand.

It was not vintage Martin Crowe and both brothers were fortunate to survive chances. But this was gritty, Test cricket, the West Indies were slowing the over rate to a crawl and Richards was beginning to glower. The fielding was becoming ragged and no balls made a healthy contribution to the Kiwi total (28 in all). The younger Crowe had begun to play shots toward the end of an unforgettable day but the pair were just happy to be there – and ecstatic to be resuming the next morning. That same *New Zealand Herald* dared to mention victory. Martin, after what he describes as 'an aggressive 83', was eventually bowled by Marshall, and Patel and Jeff soon followed. Three wickets fell for the addition of two runs but 181 for five was still fantasyland. Coney, Bracewell and Hadlee ensured the Crowes' work was not wasted, taking the total to 332 for nine declared. 'It was a good lead but important that we made inroads right away,' says Crowe, 'which we did.'

Haynes and Greenidge both went at 37 but the visitors were making a fight of it, Richards even threatening to take control. Of the first nine balls Hadlee bowled to him, he thrashed five to the fence. Murderously. He had raced to 38 before Snedden induced an edge to Smith. With Martin Crowe having dismissed Gomes with a rare bouncer, West Indies were just not able to get a big enough partnership going until New Zealand started to tire. But then Hadlee broke through just before tea, Martin Crowe took his third catch and the innings was over at 264. Just 33 runs were wanted.

'The West Indies fast bowlers came out, guns blazing, in an amazing spell,' recalls Crowe. 'We were three for two and 30 for five. But John Bracewell and I scraped the final runs in singles to give New Zealand a famous victory inside three days. And Hadlee still refused to talk to Coney!' Crowe had run like a 100 metres champion to scamper that last single and had grabbed a stump as a souvenir. Who can blame him? As the *Herald* was justified in claiming: 'The win was the stuff of legend and deserves a special place in the pantheon. Forget the dross at the end,' it urged readers, 'forget the ghastly memories of the 26 [when New Zealand collapsed at Eden Park] 33 years ago, but remember instead one of the great performances by New Zealand cricket. It was also fitting that Martin Crowe, with 1,676 runs from his incredible summer, was there at the end.' The impossible had actually happened.

Result: New Zealand won by five wickets

West Indies

C.G. Greenidge b Chatfield	2	c Smith b Hadlee	16
D.L. Haynes b Hadlee	0	c Horne b Chatfield	19
R.B. Richardson, c M. Crowe b Hadlee	37	c M. Crowe b Hadlee	19
H.A. Gomes c J. Crowe b Chatfield	8	c Coney b M. Crowe	33
I.V. Richards c Smith b Chatfield	1	c Smith b Snedden	38
A.L. Logie c Coney b Hadlee	6	c J. Crowe b Snedden	19
P.J. Dujon c Coney b Hadlee	6	c M. Crowe b Snedden	39
M.D. Marshall c Snedden b Chatfield	2	b Hadlee	45
J. Garner c Coney b Hadlee	0	c Wright b Snedden	11
A.H. Gray not out	10	c M. Crowe b Snedden	3
C.A. Walsh b Hadlee	14	not out	8
Extras (6 LB, 8 NB)	14	(2 B, 4 LB, 8 NB)	14

1/2 2/6 3/44 4/56   100   1/37 2/37 3/80 4/129   264
5/56 6/64 7/67 8/70 9/75 10/100   5/133 6/160 7/237 8/241
                                     9/255 10/264

Bowling: *First Innings* – Hadlee 12.3-2-50-6; Chatfield 18-8-30-4; Snedden 6-1-14-0. *Second Innings* – Hadlee 23-2-101-3; Chatfield 16-3-42-1; Bracewell 7-0-34-0; Snedden 18.3-2-68-5; M. Crowe 6-0-13-1.

New Zealand

P.A. Horne c Richards b Garner	9	c Gray b Walsh 0
J.G. Wright c Richards b Walsh	6	c Richards b Gray 2
J.J. Crowe c Dujon b Gray	55	c Gray b Walsh 2
M.D. Crowe b Marshall	83	not out 9
D.M. Patel c Dujon b Gray	0	c Richardson b Walsh 9
J.V. Coney run out	36	c Gray b Garner 2
J.G. Bracewell c Haynes b Garner	66	not out 2
R.J. Hadlee not out	25	
L.D. Smith c Dujon b Garner	7	
M.C. Snedden c Logie b Garner	7	
E.J. Chatfield not out	1	
Extras (2 B, 6 LB, 1 W, 28 NB)	37	(7 NB) 7
1/12 2/23 3/179 4/180 (9 wkts decl)	332	1/1 2/3 3/13 4/27 (5 wkts) 33
5/181 6/270 7/294 8/307 9/330		

Bowling: *First Innings* – Marshall 27-2-75-1; Garner 19-2-79-4; Walsh 24.5-3-78-1; Gray 17-4-47-2; Richards 9-3-29-0; Gomes 4-1-10-0. *Second Innings* – Walsh 5.1-0-16-3; Gray 4-1-14-1; Garner 1-0-3-1.

Umpires: George Morris and Steve Woodward

Alan Davidson

Melbourne, 31 December 1958 – 5 January 1959

Born in Lisarow, near Gosford in New South Wales, on 14 June 1929, Alan Keith Davidson belonged to a family that lived for cricket. Demons at local level, they first had Alan bowling chinamen but he achieved greater success when he turned to speed. After three games for his state, he was chosen for an Australian 2nd XI tour to New Zealand where he took 10 for 29 and scored 157 not out in the same match. It was only the fifth time such a feat had been achieved at first-class level. Other performances such as his six for 13 against South Australia at Sydney in 1952 and some celebrated big hits made his name, but his international reputation took longer to establish: just 16 wickets in his first 12 Tests, 170 coming in his last 32! He is now regarded as the finest left-arm opening bowler Australia has produced. A big man, barrel-chested and broad of shoulder and beam, he developed a withering late inswinger to complement his natural drift away from the right-hander. He could also be very quick. With the bat, he seldom did himself justice although he made runs when they were needed, most notably in the tied Test in Brisbane and at Manchester in 1961. Retiring at his peak in 1963, this popular and enthusiastic all-rounder notched 1,328 runs (av: 24.59) and 186 wickets (at 20.59) in his 44 Tests.

The tearaway in Alan Davidson was tamed early in his career – by a leg injury that caused him to reduce his run-up to 15 paces; the tiger in him never was. Even on that relatively short approach, Davo's muscular frame was an intimidating sight to batsmen who had to endure that slow walk back to his mark, trouser legs bulging with those boab tree thighs. With the tension deliberately built and his strength finally gathered, he would turn and begin those measured strides of mounting purpose. And then he would drive into that wheeling action and thunder down another searing delivery. As a batsman, he was just the man captains loved to have in the lower middle order, offering the broad blade as readily as the long handle. Although he never made a Test 100, his two best international knocks were worthy of a dozen other three-figure innings. And he was capable of the genuine blacksmith's strike – the best remembered being a six off Colin Cowdrey on to the roof of the old Brewongle Stand at the S.C.G. and another off David Allen that landed on the wall between Old Trafford and the nearby railway yards. Davo's career was studded with startling feats and if his incredible double against Wairarapa at Masterton and his world record of 11 wickets and 124 runs (in two innings) in the tied Test with West Indies are probably the highlights, his 'proudest moment' was one over against England at Melbourne on New Year's Eve, 1958. 'It really ripped the guts out of them,' he remembers, 'and was the decisive Test in us regaining the Ashes.'

When Peter May's England sailed for Perth on the *Iberia* in the autumn of 1958, the Ashes were not thought to be in serious danger. With May, Cowdrey and Graveney the heart of the batting, Laker and Lock as the spinners and Trueman, Statham, Tyson and Loader as fearsome a fast bowling quartet ever to leave the 'Old Dart', the team had an 'invincible' look to it – as Davidson wrote in his autobiography, *Fifteen Paces*. As for Australia, they had yet to rebuild after the retirements of Keith Miller and Lindsay Hassett, while Ian Craig was stricken with hepatitis. Richie Benaud was a controversial choice as captain ahead of Neil Harvey and Colin McDonald, which led one Melbourne scribe to claim: 'Down go Australia's chances'. But England, too, had their troubles; Wardle being omitted after criticising Yorkshire in the *Daily Mail*, Watson injuring a knee on the voyage and Subba Row breaking a wrist on the eve of the first Test. Ted Dexter and John Mortimore were flown out as replacements.

'No one gave us a chance,' remembers Davidson, 'and the critics didn't approve of Benaud. The main objections seemed to be that he was not skipper of his state (N.S.W.) and we had not been successful with bowler-captains.' But Benaud was a revelation with his aggression and tactical astuteness, not to mention his openness with the media. And in Davidson, Australia had a great all-rounder who had finally 'arrived' after a lengthy spell in the shadows of Lindwall and Miller. Once handed the new ball, Davo took more than a shine to it, his six for 34 against South Africa in Johannesburg (1958) being the turning-point of his career. Even so, England were hot favourites when the Ashes series began at Brisbane almost 12 months later. 'It was supposed to be one of the really great England sides,' says Davidson, 'and it was the first series to be televised.' Unfortunately, some players seemed to find the cameras inhibiting – Trevor Bailey's glacial 68 in 458 minutes doing little for the ratings and still not being enough to save England from defeat by eight wickets.

'My own contribution was five wickets and 66 runs but I was ill and had to be carried from the field,' recalls Davidson. 'I'd picked up a bug in Africa but I was fit for the second Test which was always going to be the decisive one.' It was also the most controversial; Fleet Street being convinced that half of Australia's pacemen 'chucked'. The furore built up after the thrilling draw against South Australia whose opening bowlers Peter Trethewey and Alan Hitchcock were dubbed 'Trethrowey and Pitchcox'. Even an Australian wag shouted: 'Put Harvey on – he throws straighter.' In working up a lather over this, left-armer Ian Meckiff being the main suspect, the English camp overlooked Davidson who had made little impact on his two tours there. Australia, however, still had painful memories of how England, hammered in the first Test on their previous visit, had roared back to dominate the series. And as the public descended on M.C.G. in their customary droves, the question was not so much whether their own bowlers were chuckers but whether the Poms were chokers. Could they fight back again?

They had their answer in the second over. England were seven without loss as Davidson took his customary 15 paces. 'First to go,' recalls Davo, 'was left-hander Peter Richardson who flicked at an outswinger some way from his body and edged to Wally Grout's vigilant gloves.' Willie Watson, another left-hander, walked in first drop and survived the next two deliveries. For his third, Davidson sent him a swinging yorker which bowled him middle and off. There were howls of delight from a crowd still settling in their seats but there was more to come. In walked Tom Graveney, a player who could delight the most partisan spectators with his graceful strokeplay. The scene was set for just such a knock but, at seven for two, it was graft England needed most of all. Alas for them, they got neither as Graveney shouldered arms to a ball that was outside the off-stump. Tragically for him, it dipped in late and trapped him leg before. Seven for three, the crowd going wild and Davo . . . was simply deified.

In his autobiography, *Fifteen Paces*, he wrote: 'Here in the space of a handful of deliveries, the Ashes had been virtually plucked from England and were on their way back to Australia.' But there was still some way to go as May joined the redoubtable Bailey. They took the score to 92 before Meckiff removed Bailey only for Cowdrey to share a stand of 118 with May who made a magnificent 113. England battled to 259, Davidson coming back to finish the job and end with six for 64, his best against the old enemy. It was then Harvey's turn, a brilliant 167 ensuring the home side had an ultimately decisive lead of 49. Davidson was fourth top scorer with 24. England folded again in the second innings, but this time it was Meckiff who was the main destroyer.

In less than three hours, this much-vaunted battling line-up had subsided to their lowest total for half a century – a paltry 87 all out, leaving Australia the formality of making 42, a task they achieved for the loss of two wickets. Although Davo's role was mainly supportive in this shambles, he chipped in with three more wickets and what he describes as 'one of the great catches' to get rid of May. He caught three in each innings. But it was his bowling on the first day that most observers agree was the decisive spell that brought back the Ashes. As the chucking controversy raged on, Australia produced one of cricket's biggest upsets with a 4-0 rout. And in Davo, they discovered a giant of their own.
Result: Australia won by eight wickets

England

P.E. Richardson c Grout b Davidson 3	c Harvey b Meckiff	2
T.E. Bailey c Benaud b Meckiff 48	b Meckiff	14
W. Watson b Davidson 0	b Davidson	7
T.W. Graveney lbw b Davidson 0	c Davidson b Meckiff	3
*P.B.H. May b Meckiff 113	b Meckiff	17
M.C. Cowdrey c Grout b Davidson 44	c Grout b Meckiff	12
†T.G. Evans c Davidson b Meckiff 4	run out	11
G.A.R. Lock st Grout b Benaud 5	c and b Davidson	6
J.C. Laker not out 22	c Harvey b Davidson	3
J.B. Statham b Davidson 13	not out	8
P.J. Loader b Davidson 1	b Meckiff	0
Extras (B 1, LB 2, W 3) 6	(B 1, LB 1, NB 2)	4

1/7 2/7 3/7 4/92 5/210 259
6/218 7/218 8/233 9/253

1/3 2/14 3/21 4/27 87
5/44 6/57 7/71 8/75 9/80

Bowling: *First Innings* – Davidson 25.5-7-64-6; Meckiff 24-4-69-3; Mackay 9-2-16-0; Benaud 29-7-61-1; Kline 11-2-43-0. *Second Innings* – Davidson 15-2-41-3; Meckiff 15.2-3-38-6; Benaud 1-0-4-0.

Australia

C.C. McDonald c Graveney b Statham . 47	lbw b Statham	5
J.W. Burke b Statham 3	not out	18
R.N. Harvey b Loader 167	(4) not out	7
N.C. O'Neill c Evans b Statham 37		
K.D. Mackay c Evans b Statham 18		
R.B. Simpson lbw b Loader 0		
*R. Benaud lbw b Statham 0		
A.K. Davidson b Statham 24		
†A.T.W. Grout c May b Loader 8	(3) st Evans b Laker	12
I. Meckiff b Statham 0		
L.F. Kline not out 1		
Extras (LB 3) 3		

1/11 2/137 3/255 4/257 308
5/264 6/261 7/295 8/300 9/300

1/6 2/26 (2 wkts) 42

Bowling: *First Innings* – Statham 28-6-57-7; Loader 27.2-4-97-3; Bailey 16-0-50-0; Laker 12-1-47-0; Lock 17-2-54-0. *Second Innings* – Statham 5-1-11-1; Loader 5-1-13-0; Laker 4-1-7-1; Lock 3.1-1-11-0.

Umpires: M. J. McInnes and R. Wright

Kapil Dev

Madras, 18-22 September 1986

Born in Chandigarh, Punjab on 6 January 1959, Kapil Dev Ramlal Nikhanj might have played for Pakistan had his parents not emigrated from Rawalpindi. He might have been a spinner, too, but switched to seam as a schoolboy. He might also have descended from another planet. To a nation as renowned for its lack of top pacemen as for its plethora of wrist spinners and arty stroke-makers, any strapping six-footer who bowled quick and belted sixes was bound to earn film-star status. But Kapil's popularity has far exceeded that. Since taking six for 39 in his Ranji Trophy debut as a 16-year-old, he has swept through the sub-continent's cricket scene like the Ganges in flood. He's India's answer to Botham, Imran and Miller and it would take Kipling to do his biography justice. Known as the 'Haryana Hurricane', he became the youngest player to the Test double of 100 wickets and 1,000 runs, and to 200 and 2,000. As captain, he won the World Cup, unleashed countless blitzes with bat and ball until, finally and triumphantly, he broke the world record for Test wickets, passing Hadlee's 431, in 1994.

'Even in a vast land of 750 million people,' wrote Mike Coward in the *Sydney Morning Herald,* 'there was but one man who could have denied Australia the right to enforce the follow-on in the first Test with India at the Chidambaram Stadium.' Facing the visitors' monumental 574 for seven declared and with the cream of the batting already gone, it is doubtful if any other number 7 in the world could have steered his side around that particular hurdle from 206 for five. And it is absolutely certain that no one else could have done so in the manner of a maddened Maharajah.

In his pomp, Kapil was among the elite quartet of world-class all-rounders that comprised Botham, Imran, Hadlee and himself. And with the bat, he was probably the most dazzling to watch of the four, employing the traditional Indian rapier as well as his own individual bludgeon. Who could ever forget his blazing 175 not out to rescue his side from the ruins of 17 for five against Zimbabwe? Or the corruscating 89 off 55 balls at Lord's? 'But I am primarily a bowler,' he always insisted. Indeed. His world record brooks no argument there and if it took him longer (130 Tests) to reach the milestone than Hadlee (86), account must be taken of his mostly lone battle on soul-destroying pitches. And here we have the essential Kapil – a 'Hurricane' who never stopped blowing for his country. But back to the searing heat of Madras and a crisis midway through the first match in a five-Test series. Like the cornered pirate, he knew only one way to fight his way out of it – by attacking.

With the pitch already beginning to turn, the Australian spinners, Matthews and Bright, looked odds on to bowl Allan Border's team to an innings victory after Dean Jones's heroics had built the perfect platform. Defying 40 degree heat, dehydration, sickness and the deliberately cruel jibes of his skipper, the Victorian ground out an epic 210 to leave his country in an unassailable position and himself on a saline drip. After Boon's 122 had laid the foundations, Jones constructed a massive total but risked his health in doing so. After occupying the crease for nigh on two days in the humid dust bowl of a stadium, he could no longer run twos and threes, and was brought glucose drinks every couple of overs. Literally tottering between balls, vomiting and twice urinating in his trousers, he still managed to smack the Indian bowlers to the fence with frightening regularity. When he'd made 160, he told skipper Allan Border, who was at the other end in their 178-run partnership: 'Mate, I've had enough. I can't move my arms. I've just pissed in my pants and I'm in a mess.' Border's response was devastating: 'OK, we'll get somebody tough out here – a Queenslander.' Brisbane's Greg Ritchie was next man in but Jones was stung. He somehow carried on to make his double century and by the time he was bowled by Yadav for 210, he had faced 330 balls, smacked 27 fours and two sixes, and lost a stone in weight. Coach Bob Simpson said: 'No one has ever been asked for more on a cricket field.'

Having witnessed such a Homeric knock at first hand, Kapil was not going to surrender without a 'captain's innings' of his own and, in his own inimitably belligerent way, smote both spinners out of the attack and out of the ground. Showing equal disdain for Reid and McDermott, who were summoned to halt the rampage, Kapil treated the 37,000 crowd to an exhibition of one-day hitting. Without quite slogging, he tore the previously tight attack apart, racing from 50 to his 100 with just 16 scoring strokes, 11 boundaries, a two and four singles. His 119 came off just 138 balls and he 'died' as he had lived – by the sword, caught by Border off Matthews who ended with five for 103. The follow-on was avoided and the game had undergone a psychological shift. 'I had set out to avoid the follow-on,' he says. 'And just tried to do it in the best way I knew. Australia were dominating and I wanted to do something to get us back in the game. The fact that we avoided the follow-on meant that we were still in it – even though a long way behind.'

Shastri had also contributed stoutly with a defiant 62 and Srikkanth had made his customary blazing start with a half-century at a run-a-minute. Azharuddin, too, reached 50 in a total of 397. Border hid his disappointment at not being able to make India bat again, declaring that his hopes of victory were very much alive. And his batsmen appeared to agree, racing to 170 for five by stumps to give Australia an overall lead of 347 with a day left.

Border's spinners could hardly conceal their delight at how much the ball was turning (Maninder and Shastri sharing the wickets) but the timing of the declaration was a delicate task. On the one hand, he wanted to give his bowlers time and anything over 300 was always a tall order in the fourth innings. On the other hand, India had the batsmen to reach it, if anyone could. They had Gavaskar, Azharuddin, Srikkanth and, above all, Kapil. Courageously, Border declared at his overnight total.

'I think it was a brave declaration,' says Kapil. 'I always felt that we could get the runs (348 to win) and we certainly went for them. We started pretty well with Gavaskar and Srikkanth, and were quite well-placed at lunch (94 for one).' Border, who had banked on the pitch providing Matthews and Bright with considerable help, looked deep in thought for much of the morning. In the afternoon, he began to look worried. Helped by a half-century from Amarnath, Gavaskar looked to be guiding India to an improbable victory. Tea was taken with India 193 for two.

With the heat and humidity showing no sign of relenting, excitement in the crowd mounted and Australian frustration began to boil over. In a smouldering final session, there were even several altercations between batsmen and fielders, while umpire Dara Dotiwalla and Border appeared to be rehearsing for the Mike Gatting/Shakoor Rana show in Pakistan a year later. Even when Gavaskar went for 90, there was no respite for the Australians, Azharuddin and Pandit taking the score to 251 before Azharuddin was held on the fence off Bright. When Kapil fell for one in the next over, the Aussies were back in the game but Shastri was in aggressive mood and reduced the rate from 6.6 to less than five per over. When Pandit was the sixth man out at 331, only 17 runs were wanted. But India panicked; More, Sharma and Yadav all falling to Bright in the space of three overs. When Matthews prepared to bowl the final over – his 40th in succession – four runs were still required by India, one wicket by Australia.

'It was nothing like the Brisbane tie,' says Kapil, 'as we knew exactly what was needed. But the tension was quite something. Shastri forced a two and then a single to leave Maninder on strike. The scores were tied and there were three balls left. The crowd held its collective breath as Matthews came in. Maninder could not score but survived. Two balls to go. Matthews came in again with that springy run of his. Maninder went back but was rapped on the pads. A ferocious appeal came from the Australian fields and umpire Vikramraju raised his finger. 'The Australians were jubilant, we were sad,' says Kapil, 'as for most of that final day, we thought we would win. For most of the first four days, they thought they would win. It made for a fascinating match and an easy answer to your question.'

Result: A tie

Australia

D.C. Boon c Kapil Dev b Sharma ..	122	(2) lbw b Maninder Singh	49
G.R. Marsh cKapil Dev b Yadav	22	(1) b Shastri	11
D.M. Jones b Yadav	210	c Azharuddin b Maninder Singh	24
R.J. Bright c Shastri b Yadav	30		
*A.R. Border c Gavaskar b Shastri	106	(4) b Maninder Singh	27
G.M. Ritchie run out	13	(5) c Pandit b Shastri	28
G.R.J. Matthews c Pandit b Yadav ...	44	(6) not out	27
S.R. Waugh not out	12	(7) not out	2
†T.J. Zoehrer			
C.J. McDermott			
B.A. Reid			
Extras (B 1, LB 7, NB 6, W 1) ..	15	(LB 1, NB 1)	2
1/48 2/206 3/282 (7 wkts dec.)	574	1/31 2/81 (5 wkts dec.)	170
4/460 5/481 6/544 7/573		3/94 4/125 5/165	

Bowling: *First Innings* – Kapil Dev 18-5-52-0; Sharma 16-1-70-1; Maninder Singh 39-8-135-0; Yadav 49.5-9-142-4; Srikkanth 1-0-6-0. *Second Innings* – Sharma 6-0-19-0; Kapil Dev 1-0-5-0; Shastri 14-2-50-2; Maninder Singh 19-2-60-3; Yadav 9-0-35-0.

India

S.M. Gavaskar c and b Matthews	8	c Jones b Bright	90
K. Srikkanth c Ritchie b Matthews ...	53	c Waugh b Matthews	39
M. Amarnath run out	1	c Boon b Matthews	51
M. Azharuddin c and b Bright	50	c Ritchie b Bright	42
R.J. Shastri c Zoehrer b Matthews ...	62	(7) not out	48
C.S. Pandit c Waugh b Matthews	35	(5) b Matthews	39
*Kapil Dev c Border b Matthews ...	119	(6) c Bright b Matthews	1
†K.S. More c Zoehrer b Waugh	4	(9) lbw b Bright	0
C. Sharma c Zoehrer b Reid	30	c McDermott b Bright	23
N.S. Yadav c Border b Bright	19	b Bright	8
Maninder Singh not out	0	lbw b Matthews	0
Extras (B 1, LB 9, NB 6)	16	(B 1, LB 3, NB 2)	6
1/62 2/65 3/65 4/142	397	1/55 2/158 3/204	347
5/206 6/220 7/245 8/330 9/387		4/251 5/253 6/291 7/331	
		8/334 9/344	

Bowling: *First Innings* – McDermott 14-2-59-0; Reid 18-4-93-1; Matthews 28.2-3-103-5; Bright 23-3-88-2; Waugh 11-2-44-1. *Second Innings* – McDermott 5-0-27-0; Reid 10-2-48-0; Matthews 39.5-7-146-5; Bright 25-3-94-5; Border 3-0-12-0; Waugh 4-1-16-0.

Umpires: D. N. Dotiwalla and V. Vikramraju

John Emburey

Born in Peckham on 20 August 1952, John Emburey made his debut for Middlesex in 1973, where he was groomed to replace Fred Titmus. He played 62 Tests for England over a period of 15 years, taking 144 wickets and he's still going strong at the age of 42. These figures could have been even more impressive since Emburey was the only player to embark on both of the rebel tours of South Africa. This decision debarred him from around 50 Test matches and probably cost him the Middlesex captaincy, though he did lead England twice in 1988 against the West Indies. He possesses a textbook bowling action – side on, arm high, feet close to the stumps, a model for all youngsters. However, they should be blindfolded when he is batting; his own carefully developed method works but is inimitable.

John Emburey's choice was a surprising one – an English Test defeat on a triumphant tour. He selected the final Test of the 1986/7 tour of Australia at Sydney. It was England's only setback of the winter, but in this match Emburey's dogged allround skills were displayed to the full.

England had already retained the Ashes despite a rocky start to the tour, which had prompted one English scribe to observe that 'there's only three things wrong with this English side – they can't bat, can't bowl and can't field.' Yet they won the first Test at Brisbane, secured the Ashes in Melbourne and carried off two one-day tournaments for good measure. Goodness knows what our expert made of the Aussies by the end of a long Antipodean season.

Under the leadership of Mike Gatting England fielded a traditional side throughout the Test series – two opening bowlers, Botham as the all-rounder and two canny, accomplished spinners, Edmonds and Emburey. In a grand team effort Emburey, with 18, was the leading wicket-taker. Emburey was Gatting's vice-captain on that tour, though in many ways he qualified as the archetypal senior pro (curiously the Corinthian David Gower held this role in 1986/7). Emburey has the reputation of being a miserly bowler, who analyses the intricacies of his craft minutely; he would happily spend an evening discussing the vagaries of his arm ball while his colleagues were sampling the delights of Sydney's nightlife. His partner, Edmonds, who once mused 'I could never be a 100 per cent professional like John Emburey', might be wayward, temperamental and sometimes brilliant, Emburey by contrast offered rock-solid reliability. And yet he has had an extraordinary Test career.

It spanned 15 years, during which he twice condemned himself to exile by embarking – without regret – on rebel tours of South Africa. He captained England twice in the madcap summer of 1988 and had no complaints about being dropped – 'I was bowling poorly and the next match was at Headingley.' In Calcutta in 1993 he virtually talked himself out of a Test place, an error he does regret, and at the age of 40 he was recalled to play against Australia in 1993 – to no great effect – yet in the same season he was easily the country's leading all-rounder and a vital component of Middlesex's romp to the Championship. Hardly the career of a dogged senior pro.

In Sydney in January 1987 England were expected to win the Test for a variety of reasons. As usual the pitch was expected to turn and this should have suited England with their superior spin combination. Moreover, the Australians were showing signs of demoralization and disarray. Allan Border's captaincy was being constantly questioned and before the match there was an element of farce, which delighted English visitors. The Australian selectors, when they announced their side, included a debutant, named Taylor. The Australian press assumed this was the New South Wales opener, who was to establish himself spectacularly on the 1989 tour of England and they conducted all the usual interviews with the unfortunate Mark. For it transpired that the Australians had not chosen Mark, but Peter, a sandy-haired, thirty-year-old offspinner, who had played four Sheffield Shield matches for New South Wales and had taken eight first-class wickets in Australia in his life. The selectors were ridiculed – at least for a few days. Australia won the toss, batted and were entirely indebted to Dean Jones, who scored 184 out of the home side's 343. Emburey recalls 'we thought we had him caught down the legside off Gladstone (Small) for 5.' It was to be a match of numerous debatable umpiring decisions and constant appealing, yet is still a classic. Small and Edmonds were England's most successful bowlers in Australia's first innings; Emburey despite bowling 30 nagging overs remained wicketless.

In reply England slumped to 17-3 after a rare failure from Chris Broad. The innings was restored first by Gower with a mellifluous 72 and then Emburey with a slightly less elegant 69. Elegance is not the prime consideration of Emburey at the crease. To be blunt, he doesn't consider it at all. He has in his armoury an ugly collection of swats, shovels, sweeps and nurdles as well as the impassive block. Occasionally he unveils surprising power despite having no recognisable backlift, as he once revealed in South Africa when he hit six sixes in seven balls playing for Western Province. Not bad for a man who started his career as an automatic number 11; indeed, there were times when the quality of his batting secured his Test place.

At Sydney he was soon hampered by a groin strain acquired when scampering for a second run and Bill Athey was summoned as a runner. Nonetheless Emburey frustrated the Australian spinners by thrusting out his left leg and padding away anything off line – ungainly, painful but effective. With Jack Richards he ensured that Australia's first innings lead was restricted to 68. When Australia batted again, Border was soon fuming since Emburey, who had batted for three hours with a runner, was soon starting a spell that culminated in his best Test figures, 7-78

A high-flying Paul Allott demonstrating a classic fast-bowling action straight from the coaching manual.

A well-protected Mike Atherton manages to keep his eye on the ball and his balance after hooking down to long leg.

Bristling with defiance under the baggy green cap, Allan Border looks as if much more than his wicket is at stake.

Putting some beef behind it: Ian Botham wielding his sledgehammer bat to put cover point in mortal danger.

Don Bradman.

Rodney Hogg once claimed that Mike Brearley 'had a degree in people.' But besides having legendary leadership skills, the Middlesex and England captain was a fine opening batsman.

Trevor Bailey: the kind of classic all-rounder and man for a crisis that modern English captains would kill for.

At 19, Neil Harvey was the baby of Bradman's 1948 'Invincibles' but soon announced his arrival as another master. It was later said of him that he 'never grew old.'

Harold Larwood, the Notts Express, smiles beneath his county cap. Still, he won't talk about bodyline but he's included for his batting – an epic 98 at Sydney.

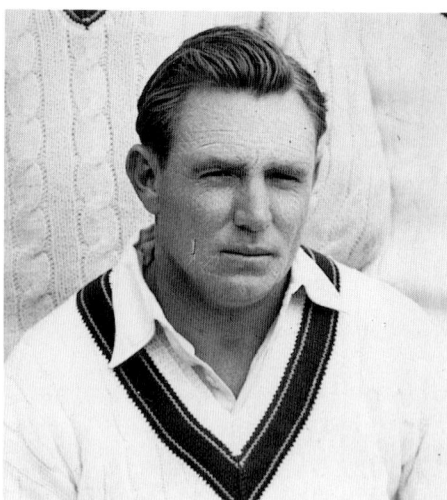

Ray Lindwall, who began as a batsman but was inspired by Larwood to bowl fast. With Keith Miller, he formed one of the legendary pace pairings of all time.

Kapil Dev, the world record wicket-taker in Tests, in full flight.

No one has made the difficult art of batting look so ridiculously easy as David Gower.

from 46 overs. 'Is this India or Australia?' Border mused not very philosophically. Emburey was unable to run, but he could bowl and the pitch was turning. Steadily he eked out the frontline batsmen and at 145-7 Australia were struggling. Now Steve Waugh survived a tricky stumping chance off Edmonds and with that man Taylor, who had already vindicated the selectors spectacularly by taking 6-78 in England's first innings, 98 vital runs were added.

England needed 320 in just over seven hours and captain Gatting, with the Ashes secure, did not rule out victory. The last day fluctuated magnificently. At one point just before lunch England were 91-1, but by the end of the first over after the interval they were 102-5, with Botham having succumbed to Taylor's first ball. Then Gatting, taking advantages of several wayward deliveries from Taylor and Peter Sleep, batted the rest of the afternoon session alongside Jack Richards so that an English victory was an enticing 133 runs away at the tea interval. At the start of the last 20 overs, 90 were required when the England captain, on 96, spooned an agonising return catch to Steve Waugh. As he passed Emburey (minus a runner this time) he halted briefly to say 'It's still on. Get yourself in and then have a word with Jack to reassess the situation.' But when Richards misread Sleep's googly the tactics were clear – survival.

Edmonds, however, failed to survive a single delivery but Small accompanied Emburey for eight overs until he was caught behind off Reid with 14 balls remaining. Emburey was on strike for the penultimate over from Sleep and he blunted the first five deliveries. As Sleep approached to bowl the last ball of the over Emburey recalls 'I was keen to try to pick up a single so that I would be on strike for the last over of the match.' This was sound thinking, but it may have cost him his wicket and England the match. Emburey tried to turn a leg spinner to the on side for a single. The ball kept devilishly low and he was bowled. Emburey with 91 runs in the match, 7 wickets all achieved with a debilitating injury, had to be satisfied with heroic and painful failure. The Australians, of course, were cock-a-hoop. This victory ended a run of 14 Tests without a victory, the longest in their history; it also enabled Border to keep the captaincy.
Result: Australia won by 55 runs

Australia

G.R. Marsh c Gatting b Small	24	c Emburey b Dilley	14
G.M. Ritchie lbw b Dilley	6	c Botham b Edmonds	13
D.M. Jones not out	184	c Richards b Emburey	30
*A.R. Border c Botham b Edmonds	34	b Edmonds	49
D. Wellham c Richards b Small	17	c Lamb b Emburey	1
S.R. Waugh c Richards b Small	0	c Athey b Emburey	73
P.R. Sleep c Richards b Small	9	c Lamb b Emburey	10
†T.J. Zoerhrer c Gatting b Small	12	lbw b Emburey	1
P.L. Taylor c Emburey b Edmonds	11	c Lamb b Emburey	42
M.G. Hughes c Botham b Edmonds	16	b Emburey	5
B.A. Reid b Dilley	4	not out	1
Extras (B 12, LB 4, W 2, NB 8)	26	(B 5, LB 7)	12
1/8 2/58 3/149 4/184	343	1/29 2/31 3/106	251
5/184 6/200 7/232 8/271 9/338		4/110 5/115 6/141 7/145	
		8/243 9/248	

Bowling: *First Innings* – Dilley 23.5-5-67-2; Small 33-11-75-5; Botham 23-10-42-0; Emburey 30-4-62-0; Edmonds 34-5-79-3; Gatting 1-0-2-0. *Second Innings* – Dilley 15-4-48-1; Small 8-2-17-0; Botham 3-0-17-0; Emburey 46-15-78-7; Edmonds 43-16-79-2; Gatting 2-2-0-0.

England

B.C. Broad lbw b Hughes	6	c&b Sleep	17
C.W.J. Athey c Zoerhrer b Hughes	5	b Sleep	31
*M.W. Gatting lbw b Reid	0	c&b Waugh	96
A.J. Lamb c Zoerhrer b Taylor	24	c Waugh b Taylor	3
D.I. Gower c Wellham b Taylor	72	c Marsh b Border	37
I.T. Botham c Marsh b Taylor	16	c Wellham b Taylor	0
†C.J. Richards c Wellham b Reid	46	b Sleep	38
J.E. Emburey b Taylor	69	b Sleep	22
P.H. Edmonds c Marsh b Taylor	3	lbw b Sleep	0
G.C. Small b Taylor	14	c Border b Reid	0
G.R. Dilley not out	4	not out	2
Extras (B 9, LB 3, W 2, NB 2)	16	(B 8, LB 6, W 1, NB 3)	18
1/16 2/17 3/17 4/89	275	1/24 2/91 3/91	264
5/119 6/142 7/213 8/219 9/270		4/102 5/102 6/233 7/257	
		8/257 9/262	

Bowling: *First Innings* – Hughes 16-3-58-2; Reid 25-7-74-2; Waugh 6-4-6-0; Taylor 26-6-78-6; Sleep 21-6-47-0. *Second Innings* – Hughes 12-3-32-0; Reid 19-8-32-1; Waugh 6-2-13-1; Taylor 29-10-76-2; Sleep 35-14-72-5; Border 13-6-25-1.

Graeme Fowler

Madras, 13, 14, 15, 17, 18 January 1985

Graeme Fowler was born 20 April 1957 at Accrington, the same birthplace as his mentor, David Lloyd. He made his debut for Lancashire in 1979 when he was sometimes used as a stopgap wicketkeeper, but soon won more plaudits as an attacking left-handed opening batsman. He was released by Lancashire in 1992 and moved to Durham where he was once a student. He played 21 Tests for England and has a highly respectable record – 1,307 runs at an average of 35. Indeed after 20 Tests, Fowler had scored more runs than most of England's leading batsmen over the same period; 100 more than Boycott and Edrich, 200 more than Gooch. However, his technique did not always suggest stability and he was soon discarded when the South African rebels returned. Whenever possible he relaxes by playing the drums.

England's tour of India in 1984/5 was an unforgettable experience for all those who took part. Twenty-four hours after landing in Delhi, most of the participants, whether pressman or player, assumed that it would be cancelled. As the players meandered down for their first breakfast the news filtered through that India's Prime Minister, Indira Gandhi, had been assassinated. Amid the ensuing chaos, reflected by smoke billowing into the sky from fires in the centre of Delhi, the continuation of a cricket tour seemed a trifling priority. Yet after prolonged negotiations with the Indian cricket authorities and the British High Commission, it was decided that the tour should proceed once the England party had spent a week in the 'safe haven' of Sri Lanka.

On the eve of the first Test in Bombay there was another tragedy. The British Deputy High Commissioner, Percy Norris, who had entertained the England party handsomely on the previous evening, was also assassinated. Again it was assumed that the tour would be abandoned; this was the course of action favoured by the majority of team members and journalists. Again it was decided that the tour must go on.

At the time this was an unpopular decision, but two months later no one regretted it. Despite the inconvenience of ever-present armed guards, England's tourists were charmed by the country and the hospitality of its inhabitants; moreover, the cricket was to be fascinating and from an English viewpoint, uplifting.

This was Graeme Fowler's third and final England tour. In 1982 his ascent to the Test side had been rapid, no doubt assisted by his prolific performances for Lancashire against Warwickshire, who were then led by England's current captain, Bob Willis. In July he scored 150 at Edgbaston; three weeks later the two sides met again at Southport in an incredible match which Fowler considered as his selection. After a record stand of 470 between Geoff Humpage and Alvin Kallicharan, Warwickshire declared at 533-4 in their first innings, yet still lost the match by 10 wickets. Fowler scored a century in each innings, both with the aid of a runner – that's the way to play cricket.

A month later he made his debut for England against Pakistan at Headingley. However, his achievements in India were more substantial. By now he was a more mature batsman after a frantic start to his Test career. He explains why, 'I'd only played two seasons for Lancashire when I went to Australia (in 1982/3) and I'd received very little coaching – except from David Lloyd. Suddenly after one game for England, simply everyone wanted to coach me – especially since I'd been labelled an unorthodox player. So in Australia I tried to play as I thought an England player should and I hardly scored a run. It was only after talking to Clive Lloyd that I began to see the light. He said that batting should be an extension of your personality and only then did I revert to the method I used in county cricket.' By the Indian tour Fowler was well established in the side. In Bombay England lost the first Test by eight wickets. Although captain David Gower refused to use the Norris assassination as an excuse it was obviously a factor in the defeat as was the leg spin bowling of Laxman Sivaramakrishnan, who took 12 wickets in the match. In the second Test at Delhi, England gained a dramatic victory when the Indian middle order self-destructed on the final afternoon. After a tedious draw in Calcutta, the fourth Test in Madras was obviously crucial especially since the final match was scheduled for Kanpur, where results are as rare as an empty Indian bus.

The first day's play was stunning. In less than five hours and 68 overs, India were bowled out for 272. Indian Test matches were reputed to be boring but this was champagne cricket from the Indian batsmen, magnificent to watch but highly irresponsible. Neil Foster, exploiting the bounce in the wicket, finished with six wickets and Gower and his team knew they had been presented with a great chance of victory if they could bat for two days. They probably could have batted for two weeks. Reflect on the scoreboard at various stages of the English innings for these figures do not occur very often: 178-0, 419-1 and 563-2. Fowler batted for nine and a half hours in partnership with Tim Robinson and Mike Gatting.

Fowler's initial concern was a patch of rough outside his off stump, which seemed an ideal aid to Siva's legspin. However, Siva was also all too conscious of the possibilities. Fowler sensed this, 'Siva was disappointed after every over if he hadn't beaten the bat and exploited the rough'. Fowler's patience outlasted that of the Indian leg spinner. Earlier in the series he had been dismissed by Siva trying to flick through mid-wicket, so at Madras he decided to deadbat all full-length deliveries and await short balls. Steadily these became more frequent.

On that second day the only wicket to fall was that of Tim Robinson, who edged the perfect leg spinner to the keeper. Fowler and Gatting, taking no risks but punishing anything off line unerringly, guided England into an impregnable position. On 97 Fowler pushed into the off-side and went for a quick single. Siva throwing from cover, hit the stumps and the ball sped to the boundary so he reached his hundred with a five. He says that 'without Gatt I wouldn't have gone on to 200; he maintained a barrage of encouragement after every over. My knees had gone septic and I was tiring, but Gatt kept me going.' In the last over of the day Gatting lent more concrete and selfless support. Fowler on 149, was now exhausted so Gatting, on strike, rejected an obvious single so that he could take responsibility for the final four deliveries.

The following day Fowler had two personal targets; the first was to surpass Gooch's 150 on that ground (Fowler had gained his England place partly because of Gooch's decision to go to South Africa and everyone was aware that Gooch was available for England again the following summer). The second was to overhaul the 214 scored by his mentor and friend, David Lloyd against India in 1974. The first goal was no problem and the second seemed well within range as he sped towards his double century with two straight sixes off Yadav. But having reached 201 he played a tired dab outside the off stump against Kapil Dev and was caught behind. An economical telegram was immediately despatched from Accrington by David Lloyd. It contained one word – 'Nearly'.

Gatting also completed a majestic double hundred and England declared at 652-7. In their second innings India scored 412 thanks to more exotic batting from Amarnath and Azharuddin; Neil Foster captured five more wickets, giving him a haul of 11 in the match but there was still plenty of time for England to knock off the 35 runs required for victory on the final afternoon. The hotel manager of the Taj Coromandel in Madras, who was obviously a batsman, decked the rooms of Gatting and Fowler with flowers, champagne and chocolate. Foster's wickets did not merit a can of beer, but Fowler, at least, was more than ready to share his chocolate with England's bowling hero.

Remarkably Fowler played just one more Test for England, the final game of that tour at Kanpur, a drawn match which ensured that England won the series, 2-1. Just as Fowler feared, Gooch was restored in the summer of 1985, so that he was consigned to spend the rest of his career on the county circuit, a harsh fate for someone who averaged 54 in his final Test series.

Result: England won by nine wickets

India

*S.M. Gavaskar b Foster	17	c Gatting b Foster	3
K. Srikkanth c Downton b Cowans	0	c Cowdrey b Foster	16
D.B. Vengsarkar c Lamb b Foster	17	c Downton b Foster	2
M. Amarnath c Downton b Foster	78	c Cowans b Foster	95
M. Azharuddin b Cowdrey	48	c Gower b Pocock	105
R.J. Shastri c Downton b Foster	2	c Cowdrey b Edmonds	33
Kapil Dev c Cowans b Cowdrey	53	c Gatting b Cowans	49
†S. M. H. Kirmani not out	30	c Lamb b Edmonds	75
N.S. Yadav b Foster	2	c Downton b Cowans	5
L. Sivaramkrishnan c Cowdrey b Foster	13	lbw b Foster	5
C. Sharma c Lamb b Cowans	5	not out	17
Extras (LB 3, NB 4)	7	(B 1, LB4, NB 2)	7

1/17 2/17 3/45 4/155   **272**   1/17 2/19 3/22   **412**
5/167 6/167 7/241 8/243 9/263   4/212 5/259 6/259 7/341
8/350 9/361

Bowling: *First Innings* – Cowans 12.5-3-39-2; Foster 23-2-104-6; Edmonds 6-1-33-0; Cowdrey 19-1-65-2; Pocock 7-1-28-0. *Second Innings* – Cowans 15-1-73-2; Foster 28-8-59-5; Edmonds 41.5-13-119-2; Cowdrey 5-0-26-0; Pocock 33-8-130-1.

England

G. Fowler c Kirmani b Kapil Dev	201	c Kirmani b Sivaramakrishnan	2
R.T. Robinson c Kirmani b Sivaramakrishnan	74	not out	21
M.W. Gatting c sub b Shastri	207	not out	10
A.J. Lamb b Amarnath	62		
P.H. Edmonds lbw b Shastri	36		
N.A. Foster b Amarnath	5		
*D.I. Gower b Kapil Dev	18		
C.S. Cowdrey not out	3		
†P. R. Downton not out	3		
P.I. Pocock and N. G. Cowans did not bat			
Extras (B 7, LB 19, NB 17)	43	(LB 1, W 1)	2

1/178 2/419 3/563   (7 wkts dec.) **652**   1/7   **35**
4/599 5/604 6/640 7/646

Bowling: *First Innings* – Kapil Dev 36-5-131-2; Sharma 18-0-95-0; Sivaramakrishnan 44-6-145-1; Yadav 23-4-76-0; Shastri 42-7-143-2; Amarnath 12-1-36-2. *Second Innings* – Kapil Dev 3-0-20-0; Sivaramakrishan 4-0-12-1; Shastri 1-0-2-0.

David Gower

The Oval, 29, 30, 31 August, 2 September 1985

Born at Tunbridge Wells on 1 April 1957, David Gower made his debut for Leicestershire in 1975. He captained Leicestershire in 1984-6 and again in 1988-9, before moving to Hampshire for the last four years of his career. He was capped 117 times for England and was captain for 32 matches, too many of which were against the West Indies. He was briefly the highest English runscorer in Test cricket with 8,231 before being overtaken by Graham Gooch in 1993. An elegant left-hander, Gower was a dreadful off spinner, with a dubious action, though no batsman ever complained. He enjoys wildlife photography, winter sports and Bollinger and dislikes cross country running. Upon retirement he became cricket correspondent of The Sunday Express *and a commentator for SKY television.*

1993 was the gloomiest of years for English cricket. Thrashed by India and – much worse – humiliated by the Australians, the romantics among us were thrown into further despair by the decision of David Gower to retire from first-class cricket at the tender age of 36. Gower, blessed with a matchless sense of timing at the crease, withdrew gracefully in November, but he could not time his departure to perfection. Not for him the glorious farewell of Hadlee or Richards in front of a packed stadium of grateful admirers; instead a mild autumnal exclusive in a Sunday paper.

The decision was almost made for him. The England selectors finally bolted the door to Test cricket by declining to pick him during the 1993 Ashes series despite their batsmen's torment at the hands of Warne and Hughes. Once the faintest sniff of Test cricket had been eradicated there was little point in Gower carrying on. Moreover Hampshire, his adopted county, did not appear to be devastated by his decision to retire for Gower, the county cricketer, has rarely been regarded as indispensable (county captains have spent longer plotting the downfall of Tim Curtis); this only applied in Test cricket – until Graham Gooch took over the England captaincy. Gower will be remembered almost exclusively for his Test career, which began and ended against Pakistan. Liaquat Ali's prime claim to cricketing fame is that he propelled Gower's first ball in Test cricket in 1978, which was pulled effortlessly to the Tavern boundary at Lord's. In 1992 the last ball he received was delivered by Waqar Younis at the Oval. Gower, aberrating, shouldered arms and was bowled. In between he delighted, infuriated and mesmerised allcomers; his apparent frailties merely enhanced the spell since we knew that a Gower innings could be a fleeting pleasure.

Gower's 'attitude' was cited as a reason for his exclusion from England teams in the '90s. That noted wit and housewife, Frances Edmonds, once said of him that 'it would be difficult for him to be more laid-back without being comatose' – a remark that might provoke a rare disagreement in the Edmonds household. For anyone who has actually played Test cricket knows that 8,231 Test runs do not materialise without strain. The problem was he made it look so easy. Gower always seemed to be dismissed by a casual shot rather than an unplayable ball.

Although labelled a 'rebel' in the Gooch regime (there's an irony) Gower seldom uttered a seditious word. His declarations of independence were delivered via grand gestures rather than by word of mouth. Back in the '70s having been chided by captain Illingworth for his standard of dress, he pitched up at Grace Road in evening dress for a Sunday league game; everyone chuckled. When his captaincy of England was under threat in 1986 he donned the 'I'm in Charge' T-shirt, which was soon ceremoniously handed over to Gatting (it didn't fit, of course) and we were mildly amused. But that Tiger Moth incident in 1991, when he hired a plane to salute a Robin Smith century in a run-of-the-mill state game in Queensland, enraged those that mattered, whose hysterical reaction confirmed Gower's worst fears. Thereafter Gooch and Gower were never properly reconciled and they should have been. Latterly Gower's talents were tragically wasted.

So much for the wrangles of the '90s. Gower, reflecting without bitterness on his completed career, went back to the uncomplicated summer of 1985 for the match of his life. Leicestershire, under his captaincy, won the Benson and Hedges Cup in July but the pinnacle of that year was the Oval Test against the Australians. 'That match,' says Gower, 'sealed a perfect summer.' England under Gower's captaincy led 2-1 in the series and needed to avoid defeat against Allan Border's side to regain the Ashes. Gower had already been in vintage form. At Edgbaston in the fourth Test he had struck a double century as well as holding a freakish catch, which undermined Australia's resistance – a controversial ricochet off Allan Lamb's boot.

At the Oval the sun shone, the wicket was true and fast and Gower unhesitatingly chose to bat. With the score on 20 Craig McDermott bowled Tim Robinson and Gower joined Gooch. 351 runs later, amassed at a rate of 4.6 per over, they were parted and the Ashes were secure. Together they destroyed the Australian attack; Gooch standing tall thumped them around Kennington, while Gower, after a statutory escape over the slips off McDermott, caressed the ball square of the wicket. Such a partnership should have been a feature of the '90s as well as the '80s. Gower recalls that it was 'simply glorious', a rare moment when sublime form and the crucial occasion were in conjunction. Even though Paul Downton with 16 was the next highest scorer, England had the ballast of a first innings total of 464.

England's motley collection of swingers – Ian Botham, Les Taylor and Richard Ellison, abetted by the two spinners – Gower always preferred a balanced attack where possible – dismissed the tourists for 241 in their first innings. Following on they succumbed meekly for 129 on the

Monday and Gower was soon photographed hoisting a replica of the Ashes urn into the sky, before retreating to the bowels of the pavilion to crack open a few cans – and bottles – with the players of both sides. Meanwhile Border prepared to return home for countless post-mortems – including suggestions that he had been far too friendly towards the Englishmen.

So all was well with the world glimpsed from under those golden locks – or so it seemed. Yet within nine months Gower had been deposed as England captain – he had, of course, led an expedition to the Caribbean in the meantime. The triumphs of 1985 were soon forgotten, though not by Allan Border. When he returned with his Australians in 1989 he displayed a ruthlessness towards his own players and a hostility towards his opponents, not evident in 1985. Those traditional dressing room get-togethers were now disdained – much to Gower's regret.

This time Gower, recalled by Ted Dexter to bring some style back to English cricket, was the hapless victim of the media inquest, as England capitulated, 4-0. Gower may not have been the most complete leader; his *laissez-faire* attitude was incapable of arresting a decline and as a tactician he was methodical rather than intuitive. But he remained the most brilliant and enchanting of batsmen, worthy of an England place right until the sad day he decided to retire.

Result: England won by an innings and 94 runs

England

G.A. Gooch c&b McDermott 196
R.T. Robinson b McDermott 3
*D. I. Gower c Bennett b McDermott . 157
M.W. Gatting c Border b Bennett 4
J.E. Emburey c Wellham b Lawson 9
A.J. Lamb c McDermott b Lawson 1
I.T. Botham c Phillips b Lawson 12
†P.R. Downton b McDermott 16
R.M. Ellison c Phillips b Gilbert 3
P.H. Edmonds lbw b Lawson 12
L.B. Taylor not out 1
Extras (B 13, LB 11, NB 26) 50
1/10 2/371 3/376 4/403   464
5/405 6/418 7/425 8/447 9/452

Bowling: Lawson 29.2-6-101-4; McDermott 31-2-108-4; Gilbert 21-2-96-1; Bennett 32-8-111-1; Border 2-0-8-0; Wessels 3-0-16-0.

Australia

G.M. Wood lbw b Botham	22	b Botham	6
A.M.J. Hilditch c Gooch b Botham	17	c Gower b Taylor	9
K.C. Wessels b Emburey	12	c Downton b Botham	7
*A.R. Border b Edmonds	38	c Botham b Ellison	58
D.M. Wellham c Downton b Ellison	13	lbw b Ellison	5
G.M. Ritchie not out	64	c Downton b Ellison	6
†W.B. Phillips b Edmonds	18	c Downton b Botham	10
M.J. Bennett c Robinson b Ellison	12	c&b Taylor	11
G.F. Lawson c Botham b Taylor	14	c Downton b Ellison	7
C.J. McDermott run out	25	c Botham b Ellison	2
D.R. Gilbert b Botham	1	not out	0
Extras (LB 3, W 2)	5	(B 4, NB 4)	8
1/35 2/52 3/56 4/101	241	1/13 2/16 3/37	129
5/109 6/144 7/171 8/192 9/235		4/51 5/71 6/96 7/114 8/127	
		9/129	

Bowling: *First Innings* – Botham 20-3-64-3; Taylor 13-1-39-1; Ellison 18-5-32-2; Emburey 19-7-48-1; Edmonds 14-2-52-2. *Second Innings* – Botham 17-3-44-3; Taylor 11.3-1-34-2; Ellison 17-3-46-5; Emburey 1-0-1-0.

Tony Greig

Calcutta, 1, 2, 3, 5, 6 January 1977

Born in Queenstown on 6 October 1946, Anthony William Greig was the son of a Scot who settled in South Africa after being stationed there in the RAF. Elder brother of Ian, who also played for England, Tony's first-class career began with Border and Eastern Province. At 6'7", he was never going to go unnoticed and possessed the all-round talent to match his imposing stature. Even before the Springboks were banned from Test cricket, he was making his name in England, and eventually rose from Sussex Seconds to captain his adopted country. A dashing Number 6 batsman, he was a brilliant fielder (especially at slip) and could bowl either medium-fast seamers or brisk off-spin, making the most of his considerable bounce. A natural leader, he was at his best when the odds were against him. Courageous against fast bowling, he relished the challenge of Test matches where he averaged almost 10 runs an innings more than in other first-class games. He played in 58 consecutive Tests, making 3,599 runs, taking 141 wickets and 87 catches. He led England to victory in India, took 13 wickets with his off-spinners in Port of Spain and hit a 100 off Thomson and Lillee at the Gabba. Although he was loved by his players, he was liable to serious errors of judgment both on and off the field. In the eyes of Lord's, his cardinal sin was to leave the bridge of HMS England for the pirate ship of Kerry Packer, but Greig survived to become a noted commentator in Australia.

India evokes mixed emotions in cricketers of other countries; batsmen think more of sickbeds than featherbeds, while fast bowlers tend to regard it as a graveyard. For the fastidious and xenophobic, neither jet travel nor five star hotels have softened the sub-continent's reputation as the place where survival depends on treating the umpires like Maharajahs and the curries like the plague. Although still to produce a bowler of terrifying pace, India can reduce the stoutest batsman to a gibbering wreck, and it is claimed that if the 'Delhi-belly' doesn't confine you to the pavilion, the spinners soon will. Robin Smith once said: 'I just want to get in the middle and get the right sort of runs.' Some famous names have dined on tinned baked beans in their rooms while Phil Tufnell quipped: 'Done the elephants, done the poverty, now I'm off home.' Among the minority who regard an Indian tour as a life-enriching experience you would not expect to find a man whose country of birth was still an unmentionable pariah and whose Cape-rich accent could be sliced with a diamond-cutter. To his everlasting credit, however, Tony Greig is one of them. Having toured in

1972/73, he developed a deep love for the place and its people. To the teeming millions, the tall, blond South African-born all-rounder became an unlikely cult figure while for England, in 1976/77, he was a hero who led from the front.

'I always knew that the Calcutta Test would be decisive,' says Greig, 'and I had painful memories of the previous tour under Tony Lewis. We had started that one well, winning the first Test but then we went down at Eden Gardens and eventually lost the series. So I knew this was a big challenge and was determined that the same thing wouldn't happen again.' History, however, was against him: England had yet to win a Test in Calcutta and a series in India since the Raj. Indeed, it was perhaps no coincidence that the last successful skipper was the vice-regal Douglas Jardine. Under Greig, England ruthlessly captured the first Test in Delhi where Dennis Amiss batted for eight and a half hours to score 179 and John Lever swung a responsive old ball to take seven for 46. 'But,' insists the skipper, 'the foundation for our success was laid with the selection of the party. I knew that we had to counter the Indian spinners so we chose Derek Randall in the middle order and Roger Tolchard as Number 2 wicket-keeper — he was also a great player of slow bowling.' Besides including both men (Tolchard as a batsman) for the second Test, Greig chose a full array of seamers, well aware that the mists from the Hooghly River offered a rare chance of assistance. 'We were keen for Willis, Lever and Old to play,' he recalls, 'and with Underwood and myself, were quite well-equipped to take advantage. We knew we had to get them out for a low score but it was still up to us to counter Bedi, Chandra and Prasanna who must have been the best spin combination in the world.'

That task became immeasurably more difficult when the players arrived at the ground to see the last blades of grass being wire-brushed from the wicket. No group of religious zealots could have scrubbed harder had they been removing graffiti from the Taj Mahal, but Greig took it all in his massive stride. He was just glad to be there. 'Getting to the ground was one of the major hurdles of my life,' he chuckles. 'There were tens of thousands of peoples lining the streets and most of them were either trying to get to the game or get in our bus.' Some succeeded at both but, mercifully, they were policemen who had found the perfect way around the ticket shortage. 'Calcutta is my favourite ground in the world,' says Greig. 'There were about 80,000 people in at the start of play and that's the way it stayed. Even when there was nothing much happening, they were at fever pitch.' But soon Indian wickets began to fall and by lunch on the second day, England had bowled the home side out for 155, Willis taking five for 27. It was not the sort of total that Bedi, who won the toss, had in mind but he was unmoved, barely giving his turban a tug. 'As soon as they were all out,' remembers Greig, 'the wire brushes came out again.'

After losing Brearley and Barlow for 14, England battled to 136 for four at the close with Greig 19 not out. Unlike Randall, who had made a fighting 37, and Tolchard, his partner, the skipper was not a great player of spin. Indeed, his early attempts to deal with it had been embarrassing and now he relied on an exaggerated backlift and a concentration that was absolutely total. To play the long innings that England needed, he would have to be at his best. But that night, he was also at fever pitch – the wrong sort of fever.

'I hardly slept, had a temperature and soaked the sheets with sweat,' he recalls, 'but Bernie Thomas (England's masseur) gave me some tablets and I was able to bat.' Was he in pain? 'No,' says Greig, 'I just concentrated so hard that I didn't feel much at all. I felt weak, of course, as I hadn't eaten that day but I just got on with the job. What helped as much as the tablets was having Kenny Barrington position himself behind the bowler's arm and sit there watching every ball. He never moved and it was a great incentive for me to have him watch me play the spinners for about seven hours. I was more conscious of him than my fever.'

So Greig overcame not only a debilitating illness but his natural inclination to attack. 86 overs were wheeled down by the Indian spin trio and just 149 runs were eked out in a long, hot, exhausting day. Tolchard was finally bowled by Bedi for 67 but Old provided staunch support with 52. Greig made only 75 runs in the day, a monumental vigil of self-denial which might have irked the crowd had he not punctuated his defiance with moments of pure showmanship. When the masses began to let off fireworks, throw rubbish or chant for 'Chandra', the towering figure at the crease would pull away and call for calm, but always in a way calculated to enchant not inflame. Not out 94 overnight, Greig used the rest day to rebuild his strength in order to capitalise on a score of 285 for six. He duly reached three figures but fell lbw to Prasanna shortly afterwards. It was the longest innings of his career and he had survived the heat, the noise, the fever, the finest spinners in the world and a cluster of close fieldmen for almost seven hours. 'I was a great lunger and couldn't play spin to save myself,' he said, 'But every time I looked up, there was Kenny and he seemed to be willing me on.'

Once Gavaskar went early in the Indian second innings, the rest struggled as Underwood and Old each took three wickets. Greig chipped in with two for 27 but it was his batting that had been the pivotal performance of the match and the series. The Indian spin mystery had been, if not unravelled, at least blunted by a display that was genuinely heroic. India were broken, requiring 21 to make England bat again with just three wickets standing. No matter, 50,000 turned up for the formality of defeat on the final morning – a tribute to Greig's finest 414 minutes at the crease. Fittingly for a man who loves India, he had made the right sort of runs.

Result: England won by 10 wickets

India

S.M. Gavaskar c Old b Willis	0	b Underwood	18
A.D. Gaekwad b Lever	32	c Tolchard b Greig	8
P. Sharma c Greig b Lever	9	c Knott b Willis	20
G.R. Viswanath c Tolchard b Underwood	35	c Lever b Greig	3
B.P. Patel hit wkt b Willis	21	lbw b Old	56
E.D. Solkar c Greig b Willis	2	c Knott b Willis	3
Madan Lal c Knott b Old	17	c Brearley b Old	16
†S. M. H. Kirmani not out	25	b Old	0
E.A.S. Prasanna b Willis	2	c Brearley b Underwood	13
*B.S. Bedi c Lever b Old	1	b Underwood	18
B.S. Chandrasekhar b Willis	1	not out	4
Extras (LB 2, NB 8)	10	(B 2, LB 4, NB 16)	22
1/1 2/23 3/65 4/92	155	1/31 2/33 3/36 4/60	181
5/99 6/106 7/136 8/147 9/149		5/70 6/97 7/97 8/146 9/171	

Bowling: *First Innings* – Willis 20-3-27-5; Lever 22-2-57-2; Underwood 13-5-24-1; Old 20-5-37-2. *Second Innings* – Willis 13-1-32-2; 3-0-12-0; Lever 3-0-12-0; Underwood 32.5-18-50-3; Old 12-4-38-3; Greig 10-0-27-2.

England

D.L. Amiss c Kirmani b Prasanna	35	not out	7
G.D. Barlow c Kirmani b Madan Lal	4	not out	7
J.M. Brearley c Solkar b Bedi	5		
D.W. Randall lbw b Prasanna	37		
R.W. Tolchard b Bedi	67		
*A.W. Greig lbw b Prasanna	103		
†A.P.E. Knott c Gavaskar b Bedi	2		
C.M. Old c Madan Lal b Prasanna	52		
J.K. Lever c Gavaskar b Bedi	2		
D.L. Underwood c Gavaskar b Bedi	4		
R.G.D. Willis not out	0		
Extras (B 5, LB 5)	10	(LB 1, NB 1)	2
1/7 2/14 3/81 4/90	321	(0 wkts)	16
5/232 6/234 7/298 8/307 9/321			

Bowling: *First Innings* – Madan Lal 17-4-25-1; Solkar 6-1-15-0; Bedi 64-25-110-5; Chandrasekhar 33-9-66-0; Prasanna 57.4-16-93-4; Sharma 1-0-2-0. *Second Innings* – Madan Lal 1-0-3-0; Bedi 14-0-6-0; Prasanna 1-0-5-0.

Sir Richard Hadlee

AUSTRALIA V NEW ZEALAND

Brisbane, 8-12 December 1985

Born in Christchurch on 3 July 1951, Richard John Hadlee chose a family with impeccable cricketing credentials. His father, Walter, captained New Zealand on its tour to England in 1949 and two of his three elder brothers also wore the silver fern; Dayle playing in 26 Tests. Even Richard's wife, Karen, played for the national women's team. Once a tearaway fast bowler and useful tailender for Canterbury, Hadlee cut his run-up and developed into one of the greatest all-rounders of all time. A blistering lower-middle order batsman, he achieved a metronomic efficiency with the ball: in 86 Tests, he took 431 wickets at a niggardly 22.29. It was a world record tally until Kapil Dev (in his 130th Test) overtook it in 1994. Although very much his own man, Hadlee transformed both New Zealand and Nottinghamshire, his adopted county, into formidable sides. Pre-Hadlee, the Kiwis had won just seven out of 102 Tests and none against the Big Three – Australia, England and West Indies. During Hadlee's pomp, they not only won Tests against this trio but whole series. And in an outstanding decade at Trent Bridge, he and Clive Rice inspired Notts. to two County Championship pennants and two one-day trophy successes. But perhaps 'Paddles's' finest personal achievement in England was to do the double in 1984, a feat thought impossible since the first-class programme was slashed in 1969. Not bad for a man who claimed the most valuable item in his kit was a motivation card.

'In one's sporting career,' says Sir Richard Hadlee, 'you look for the near-perfect Test. The match at the Gabba in the 1985/86 series was it. We did everything right from winning the toss, bowling well in helpful conditions and holding nearly 100 per cent of our catches.' A perfectionist to his size 11 boots, Hadlee did not have the fast bowler's classic build but possessed his action and inner rage. Wiry, saturnine and calculating, he could look as tormented as his victims yet was the most lethal bowler of the 1980s. Off a dozen quietly smouldering paces, he induced the fear of the dentist on piecework. Batsmen would await the inevitable extraction as if strapped in the chair but Hadlee was a chilling sight even when his back was turned. With his left hand on knee, right raised to the heavens, he did not appeal to the umpire, he implored him. Not the fastest bowler of his day, nor the most robust but just look at his record and the remarks of those who faced him. Graham Gooch once said of the New Zealand bowling: 'It was like facing the World XI at one end and Ilford Seconds at the other'; Peter Roebuck always felt as if he'd 'gone into the headmaster's study', while Simon Hughes compared batting against him to 'an interrogation'.

With his outward calm, fierce sense of duty and manically determined glare, Hadlee would have made a ruthless inquisitor. But it was perfection he sought and perfection that he came closer to finding than any other modern paceman. Sir Donald Bradman said of him: 'No bowler I've ever seen had better control of seam and swing.' For all that, Hadlee was the man that Australian crowds loved to hate. A couple of contretemps in his early days were blown out of proportion and the yobbo element never forgave him. Suffice to say that this lack of appreciation only served to harden his innate Kiwi resolve to topple the neighbours. Indeed, when Hadlee talks of 'the near-perfect Test,' the near-perfect setting, if not his home at Lancaster Park or his beloved Trent Bridge, would be in Australia, where he could 'extract' Australian batsmen in their own burnt backyard – and exact a tad of revenge for what New Zealanders consider to be a patronising attitude to their cricket for the best part of four decades.

The Kiwis had been emerging as a potent force for a few years, with the brilliance of Martin Crowe and solidity of John Wright giving Hadlee the breathing space he required on the scoreboard. England had recently been vanquished and even the West Indies were edged out in an acrimonious series. Although Australia had finally lost a Test to the Shaky Isles, they had still to do so at home. That, however, was of little comfort when they surveyed the wreckage of their recent mauling by England and the defections to South Africa. Whatever defiant statements they made to the contrary, Australia were there for the taking. Yes, perhaps for the only time in their history, by New Zealand.

That feeling heightened when Hadlee surveyed the Gabba wicket on that fateful November morning and saw shades of Trent Bridge's greensward. Why, there were even grey skies and were it not for the obvious discrepancy in temperature, the Aussies might have suspected they were about too face Notts. instead of New Zealand. Hadlee acknowledges that he had done 'nothing wonderful in the lead-up' but he also writes in his autobiography *Rhythm and Swing*: 'I'd never known a Test when we had prepared so thoroughly. The atmospheric conditions were clammy, humid and there was low cloud and the threat of showers; my fingers were twitching.' All that was needed was to win the toss and when skipper Coney obliged, the insertion was made and the Australian batsmen soon found themselves struck by Kiwi lightning.

First to go was 'the unhappy hooker', Andrew Hilditch, who was well held by Chatfield off the fifth ball of the match – on the long-leg boundary. After that progress was slow, Wessels and Boon adding 69 defiant runs before Boon was caught by Coney, also off Hadlee, shortly before lunch. With his first ball after the break, Hadlee had Border held at cover for a duck. Two rain interruptions did not stop him grabbing New Zealand's and his own fourth victim when Ritchie was brilliantly snared by Crowe at slip to leave the home side on 146 for four at stumps. As Hadlee said, the Kiwis had done 'everything right'.

Five overs into the second morning, Hadlee removed the stubborn Wessels for a dour 70 and, bowling with even more venom than the day before, ripped through the tail. Passing five wickets in an innings for the 20th time, he used his full repertoire of pace, seam, swing and deadly accuracy to become just about unplayable. The fielding was faultless, too, and once Matthews, hit off the previous delivery, had gone, resistance crumbled. Australia were all out for 179. Hadlee admits 'the ball talked,' and only by holding a tremendous running catch, himself, to remove Geoff Lawson and give Vaughan Brown his only Test wicket, was he prevented from taking all 10. Not quite perfect but near enough: nine for 52 was the fourth best bowling analysis in Test history.

If Australia thought they might wreak similar havoc in the New Zealand innings, they soon had to think again: a magnificent third wicket stand of 224 between Reid and Crowe putting the visitors in total command. Crowe, carrying on from where Hadlee had left off, went on to compile a career-best 188. Hadlee, inevitably, chipped in with a furious half-century, hitting four sixes in little over an hour. So when Coney ended the torment at 553 for six, he was able to give his men two days to bowl the Australians out. With bright sunshine greeting Remembrance Day and the gremlins finally disappearing from the pitch, Australia must have hoped for a respite when they began their second innings . . . 374 behind. But Boon and Wessels went in the first half hour, the only difference being that it was Chatfield, not Hadlee, who did the damage. At 11 a.m., there was a minute's silence but Hadlee admits in his autobiography that he showed 'a lack of courtesy' during those 60 seconds by saying: 'Think Hilditch, think bouncer, think hook, think catch, think out!' And sure enough, the hapless opener obliged, caught by Chatfield off the very first ball after the break. Australia were 16 for three and had limped to 67 for five by lunch.

In the afternoon, Border and Matthews produced some belated Digger resistance with a stand of 199 to ensure the game entered a final day. But Hadlee had Matthews, who made 115, caught by Coney just before the close and there was no way back from there. When Hadlee bowled Bob Holland to dismiss Australia for 333, New Zealand had won by an innings and 41 runs. Hadlee had taken 15 in the match for 123. A despairing Border, who had been left not out on 152, said: 'I don't know what to say to the blokes and I don't know what to do from here.' The final word, however, must go to Hadlee: 'Whilst I had great success,' he writes, 'it was a great team effort that allowed us to win by an innings. It was a significant match in the history of New Zealand cricket because it was the first time we had beaten Australia in Australia. We eventually won the series so the tour proved a great success.' Near-perfect.

Result: New Zealand won by an innings and 41 runs

Australia

K.C. Wessels lbw b Hadlee	70	(2) c Brown b Chatfield	3
A.M.J. Hilditch c Chatfield b Hadlee	0	(1) c Chatfield b Hadlee	12
D.C. Boon c Coney b Hadlee	31	c Smith b Chatfield	1
*A.R. Border c Edgar b Hadlee	1	not out	152
G.M. Ritchie c M. D. Crowe b Hadlee	8	c Coney b Snedden	20
†W.B. Phillips b Hadlee	34	b Hadlee	2
G.R.J. Matthews b Hadlee	2	c Coney b Hadlee	115
G.F. Lawson c Hadlee b Brown	8	(9) c Brown b Chatfield	7
C.J. McDermott c Coney b Hadlee	9	(8) c and b Hadlee	5
D.R. Gilbert not out	0	c Chatfield b Hadlee	10
R.G. Holland c Brown b Hadlee	0	b Hadlee	0
Extras (B 9, LB 5, NB 2)	16	(LB 3, NB 3)	6
1/1 2/70 3/72 4/82 5/148	**179**	1/14 2/16 3/16 4/47	**333**
6/150 7/159 8/175 9/179		5/67 6/264 7/272 8/291 9/333	

Bowling: *First Innings* – Hadlee 23.4-4-52-9; Chatfield 18-6-29-0; Snedden 11-1-45-0; M.D. Crowe 5-0-14-0; Brown 12-5-17-1; Coney 7-5-8-0. *Second Innings* – Hadlee 28.5-9-71-6; Chatfield 32-9-75-3; Snedden 19-3-66-1; M.D. Crowe 9-2-19-0; Brown 25-5-96-0; Coney 3-1-3-0.

New Zealand

B.A. Edgar c Phillips b Gilbert 17
J.G. Wright lbw b Matthews 46
J.F. Reid c Border b Gilbert 108
M.D. Crowe b Matthews 188
*J.V. Coney c Phillips b Lawson 22
J.J. Crowe c Holland b Matthews 35
V.R. Brown not out 36
R.J. Hadlee c Phillips b McDermott . 54
†I.D.S. Smith not out 2
M.C. Snedden
E.J. Chatfield
Extras (B 2, LB 11, NB 32) 45
1/36 2/85 3/309   (7 wkts dec.) 553
4/362 5/427 6/471 7/549

Bowling: Lawson 36.5-8-96-1; McDermott 31-3-119-1; Gilbert 39-9-102-2; Matthews 31-5-110-3; Holland 22-3-106-0; Border 0.1-0-0-0; Wessels 1-0-7-0.

Umpires: A. R. Crafter and R. A. French

Neil Harvey

SOUTH AFRICA V AUSTRALIA

Durban, 20, 21, 23, 24 January 1950

Born in the Melbourne suburb of Fitzroy on 8 October 1928, Robert Neil Harvey was the second youngest of six cricket-playing brothers, three of whom played for Victoria, two for Australia. Neil, the only left-hander, was the most gifted and by the time he retired in 1963, had amassed 6,149 Test runs – a total exceeded only by Bradman. Exuding total confidence and a rare mastery at a tender age, 'Ninna', as he became known, hit 100s on his debuts for both club and state before scoring a famous 112 in his first Ashes Test in 1948. He was 19. Very much the baby of Bradman's 'Invincibles', Harvey toured England four times but it was on the Springboks that he made the biggest impression: on the 1949/50 tour, he scored eight centuries, in 1952/53, he hit four more and then married a South African. An electrical fitter and turner by trade, his eyesight failed him in later years but he remained a marvellous fielder either at slip or in the covers. An all-round sportsman, he was selected for Australia at baseball and played high-grade rules football. He moved to Sydney in 1958 and signed off with a flourish – hitting 231, his highest first-class score, for New South Wales, and 154 against England in his farewell season, 1962/63.

Patsy Hendren compared him to Clem Hill, Sir Neville Cardus to Mozart, while the most grudging observer would have to place him among the greatest left-handers of all time. But perhaps the most apposite tribute to Neil Harvey came from *The Times* which simply stated that he was 'a player who never grew old.' Whether dancing down the track to hit against the spin or darting in from cover to save a single, the dapper Victorian exuded the jauntiness of youth – even in his dotage. And to those who followed his career from cobbled lane to hallowed turf, he never lost his back-street hunger for runs. Indeed, whether heaving Laker over the mid-wicket fence or holding a thrilling catch 'baseball-style' above his head, he never forgot the habits of his classic education. For it was on the jagged blue-stone of a back alley in north Melbourne that the young Harvey learned his craft. Playing with a tennis ball and kerosene can 'wicket', he coped with bounce that was at best irrational and turn that was positively schizophrenic. After a downpour during the third Test in Durban in 1950, the circumstances were very different but the ball behaved with similar mischief – the bowlers being two of the finest spinners in the world. Survival itself would have been a major triumph, but victory? Only South Africans harboured such thoughts . . .

Having established himself on the tour of England, Harvey cemented his reputation on the Veld, his weight of runs at least partly offsetting the chasm caused by Bradman's retirement. Lindsay Hassett became Australia's captain and immediately impressed with his shrewdness. If Bradman's loss to Australian cricket was akin to Britain losing India, this pair could not have done more to conceal it. Inevitably, Harvey became the first in a distinguished but unfortunate line to be dubbed 'the new Bradman' and with a Test average of 132.00 at the end of his first South African series, he perhaps came closer to emulating the great man than any subsequent pretender. A teetotaller, non-smoker and just 5'8" and 10st 7lb, Harvey would hurry to the wicket with short, business-like strides, always capless, his dark, wavy hair neatly combed and an eager look on his face. With a complete range of strokes and sparkling footwork, he was indeed 'impossible' to bowl at in his early years.

After winning the first Test in Johannesburg by an innings, Australia took hold of the series with an eight-wicket win in Cape Town, where Harvey made a swashbuckling 178. In spite of the mauling South Africa were getting, a big crowd turned up in sub-tropical Durban on the first day of the third Test – and they could not have asked for more. Not only did Dudley Nourse and Eric Rowan lay a solid foundation by reaching stumps at 240 for two, overnight rain convinced many that it was already a match-winning total. 'After that,' recalls Harvey, 'it was a real battle of tactics.'

In Hassett, Australia had the ideal skipper for the occasion. Even when he had to bow to umpires who insisted upon a resumption that was too soon for his tastes on a rain-sodden pitch, he was always in command. 'Our tactics were to keep them in as long as possible and not do anything with the ball,' says Harvey, still barely able to supress a chuckle some 44 years later. Rowan went on to make 143 and South Africa, oblivious to the bluff until it was too late, were all out for 311. It should still have been enough but skipper Nourse knew that valuable time had been wasted.

In a further effort to keep the South Africans guessing and shield his top batsmen from the wiles of Tayfield and 'Tufty' Mann, Hassett promoted tailenders Johnston and Saggers to open the innings. But when Australia lurched to 63 for nine at the end of the second day, it looked as if Hassett's deception had been in vain. However, when the last wicket fell at 75 on the third morning, Nourse did not enforce the follow-on and lunched contentedly with his side at 85 for three in the second innings. With the pitch still a minefield, Johnston and Johnson wrapped up the remaining seven wickets for just 14 runs in an hour and not even Hassett could put the brakes on, South Africa crashing to 99 all out. But the visiting skipper was smiling through clenched teeth: the target was 336 and there was still a day and a half to go.

The wicket now looked as if a herd of wildebeest had spent the night on it. 'It was full of divots, ball-marks and was a real turner,' remembers Harvey. 'And it wasn't just because it was unplayable that we were concerned, it was because they had as good a pair of spinners as any in the game.' The strip's behaviour was not unlike that of the cobbled lane in Fitzroy and when Harvey joined Morris at 59 for three, he was soon springing lightly down to the pitch of the ball, smothering the spin and frustrating 'Toey' and 'Tufty' as he once had his elder brothers. Australia reached 80 for three at the close, still requiring 251 and very much at the mercy of the weather. Harvey admits: 'One or two of the boys thought it was a lost cause but I remember Sam Loxton saying: "We'll win this match".' As for Harvey? 'I always believed in playing my natural game and when we resumed on the final morning, we neither played for a draw nor a win. We just treated each ball on its merits.' The trouble was, each ball demanded the utmost respect and Morris spent two and half hours making 44. Harvey, too, was uncharacteristically subdued but 'time', he reminds you, 'was the least of our worries and I did not forget to hit the bad ball.'

As understatements go, that takes some beating for Harvey was playing one of the game's great knocks. Once joined by his pal Loxton, the super optimist, Harvey upped the tempo and at last runs began to come. With the bowlers blunted, the wicket losing its venom and Loxton determined to confound the sceptics in his own team, Australian hopes rose. A catch went down, too, at fine leg and South African heads dropped. Nourse looked a worried man. The Victorian pair won a moral victory when Nourse, now at his wit's end for a wicket, took the new ball. But still the breakthrough did not come. In three hours, 135 runs had been added to shift the psychological balance. Loxton eventually fell to Mann but Harvey, whose 100 had taken almost four hours, was in total command. And besides batting in a way that Cardus claimed 'defied statistical assessment,' he had another worthy partner. Colin McCool knew a thing or two about spin and carried on where Loxton had left off. At tea, the score was 269 for five with 67 still wanted in two hours. It could hardly have been more tantalisingly poised and Harvey recalls: 'A few fingernails were bitten in our dressing room.'

Harvey's were not among them as he and McCool confidently reached the target with 25 minutes to spare, the left-hander a magnificent 151 not out. He had not given a chance and had defied two of cricket's most lethal spinners for five and a half hours on a pitch that had been made for them. 'Yes, I think it was probably as good an innings as I've played,' he acknowledges. 'It was very satisfying but I had some good allies.' That night in a Hollywood-style tribute, a tree was planted in Harvey's honour. Sadly, it has now made way for redevelopment of the Kingsmead ground but the memory of that masterly innings will last forever.
Result: Australia won by five wickets

South Africa

	First Innings		Second Innings	
E.A.B. Rowan c Johnston b Miller	143	c Saggers b Lindwall	4
O.E. Wynne b Johnston	18	b Johnson	29
J.D. Nel c and b Johnson	14	lbw b Johnston	20
*A.D. Nourse c Saggers b Johnston	66	c McCool b Johnson	27
†W.W. Wade b Lindwall	24	b Johnston	0
N.B.F. Mann b Johnston	9	(9) lbw b Johnson	0
J.E. Cheetham c Hassett b Johnston	4	(6) c Hassett b Johnson	1
J.C. Watkins b Lindwall	5	(7) st Saggers b Johnson	2
H.J. Tayfield run out	15	(8) b Johnston	3
V.I. Smith b Lindwall	1	b Johnston	4
C.N. McCarthy not out	0	not out	2
Extras (B 3, LB 7, NB 2)	12	(B 5, LB 1, NB 1)	7
1/32 2/75 3/242 4/264	**311**	1/9 2/51 3/85 4/85	**99**
5/283 6/289 7/293 8/304 9/308		5/88 6/90 7/93 8/93 9/93	

Bowling: *First Innings* – Lindwall 19-3-47-3; Miller 24-5-73-1; McCool 13-3-35-0; Johnston 31.2-5-75-4; Loxton 6-1-31-0; Johnson 16-5-38-1. *Second Innings* – Lindwall 4-1-7-1; Miller 7-0-12-0; Johnston 18.2-6-39-4; Johnson 17-2-34-5.

Australia

	First Innings		Second Innings	
A.R. Morris c Smith b Tayfield	25	hit wkt b Tayfield	44
J. Moroney b Tayfield	10	lbw b Tayfield	10
I.W. Johnson lbw b Tayfield	2		
K.R. Miller b Tayfield	2	(3) lbw b Mann	10
*A.L. Hassett lbw b Tayfield	2	(4) lbw b Mann	11
†R.A. Saggers c Cheetham b Mann	2		
C.L. McCool lbw b Mann	1	not out	39
R.R. Lindwall b Mann	7		
R.N. Harvey c and b Tayfield	2	(5) not out	151
S.J.E. Loxton c Cheetham b Tayfield	16	(6) b Mann	51
W.A. Johnston not out	2		
Extras (B 3, LB 1)	4	(B 7, LB 9, NB 1)	17
1/31 2/35 3/37 4/39 5/42	**75**	1/41 2/33 3/59 4/95	**336**
6/45 7/46 8/53 9/63		5/230	

Bowling: *First Innings* – McCarthy 6-2-8-0; Watkins 4-1-9-0; Mann 10-1-31-3; Tayfield 8.4-1-23-7. *Second Innings* – McCarthy 12-3-32-0; Watkins 6-2-10-0; Mann 51.6-13-101-3; Tayfield 49-5-144-2; Smith 5-0-32-0.

Merv Hughes

Old Trafford, 27, 28, 29, 31 July, 1 August 1989

Born in Euroa, Victoria, on 23 November 1961, Mervyn Gregory Hughes grew up in Werribee, west of Melbourne, addicted to team games. An excellent Aussie Rules player, he made 95 appearances in the Victoria Football League besides winning an Esso cricket scholarship to England. An unlikely Essex Man, he took 60 wickets for that county's Seconds in 1983. After becoming the mainstay of the Victorian attack, he made a disastrous Test debut against India, taking one for 123 and getting a duck. Typically, he fought back and his magnificent 13 wicket haul (including a hat-trick) against the West Indies in 1987 confirmed this school-master's son as a class act. With the look of a larrikin and heart of a lion, he rapidly achieved cult figure status, his boundary callisthenics being aped by thousands in the stands. Shrewdly exploiting his opponents' tendency to under-rate him, he became only the seventh Australian to take 200 Test wickets during his second tour of England in 1993.

Whether you call him 'fruit fly' or 'sumo', mincing or menacing, thinker or oaf; whether he's bowling a fearsome bouncer or a gentle leg-break, defending stoutly or hitting hugely, is on the wagon or on the booze, Merv Hughes is a larger-than-life enigma. A diligent wearer of zinc cream under grey English skies, a workhorse with wonky knees, a Michelin man who loosens up like an Olympic gymnast, he sledges a batsman at the crease and buys him a beer at stumps . . . But the paradox that most appeals is that of 'impostor' and unsung hero. It took only one Test for Merv to earn the critics' wrath but years of back-bending to win them over. His girth and gait didn't help and Frank Keating, in an otherwise positive piece, once wrote: 'his mincing, falling-forward approach to the wicket resembles someone in an unfamiliar tight skirt late for his cue on drag-show beginners' night.' But smirking at Merv can be costly, for no Test bowler has taken as many wickets with the force of his personality. And for a charismatic individual, he is also a quintessential team man.

Asked what his own contribution was to Australia's nine-wicket win over England at Old Trafford in 1989, Hughes's reply was an unprintable version of negligible. For the record, it was two wickets and three runs as Terry Alderman and Geoff Lawson routed England's hapless batsmen yet again. Hughes merely filled a supporting role. No matter, 'this is the match for me,' he insists. 'Winning the Ashes after being written off as the worst Australian side ever to go to England . . . you can never top that.'

Not the 13 wickets against the Windies? 'Nah, I'm not interested in personal stuff. Nothing will beat the feeling we had when Boonie hit the winning runs in Manchester that day.'

If Hughes's choice raises eyebrows, it is nothing to what the celebrations in the Australian dressing room did. Suffice to say, the air was still blue with blasphemous Antipodean delight and the walls were dripping with amber nectar hours after the mythical urn had changed hands. To appreciate Australia's delirium, you need to think of the despair they had felt in recent years – defeat by Mike Gatting's England, defeat by Pakistan, a thrashing by the West Indies. They had won only five of the 30 Tests since losing 3-1 to Gower's side on the previous tour to England and were described as 'pussy-cats' by Tony Greig. 'Then,' says Hughes, 'we lost to Worcester in the first county game of the tour.' The tourists failed to take the match into a third day. As for Hughes, a late choice when the arguably more deserving Mike Whitney was mysteriously left out, many considered him fortunate to be there at all. In *Australian Cricket – From Bradman to Border,* Jack Pollard observed: 'Judged on his fitness, team-spirit and gutsy end-of-the-day displays, Whitney could not be faulted, whereas Hughes appeared a wayward clown of a bowler, more intent on luring crowds into mimicking his warm-up exercises than taking wickets.'

It was in the opening Test at Headingley that he had his first chance to prove the critics wrong and he fairly hustled to the wicket with Australia 441 for six. Expected to play second fiddle as Steve Waugh guided his country past 500, Merv got off the mark with a six! He bludgeoned 71 runs before Border declared at 601 for seven. Alderman, dubbed 'straight up and down' by Greig, took 10 wickets to spearhead the 210-run victory. Hughes chipped in by finishing off the tail. At Lords, Hughes contributed a vital 30 and took six wickets in a six-wicket triumph, removing Gower (106) when the England skipper looked capable of salvaging a draw. With mean eyebrows and a mo that threatened to trip the batsman at the non-striker's end, Hughes bristled with raw animal aggression. 'Name a Test bowler with a bigger ticker,' says Bob Simpson. 'Why the English seem oblivious to his talents is totally beyond us.' Already two-nil up and with the third Test ruined by rain, Australia had an aura of invincibility about them based on meticulous preparation and admirable professionalism – qualities epitomised by the 'wayward clown'.

With the old enemy in disarray, Australia tuned up for the decisive fourth Test at Old Trafford with a relaxing trip to Scotland followed by a draw with Hampshire and a crushing win over Gloucestershire. More important, however, was that key players either maintained or found their form. Waugh and Boon hit tons at Southampton, Taylor and Jones at Bristol where, crucially, Lawson grabbed a match haul of 10 for 77. On a Manchester track that was compared to 'a piece of Stilton, little veins running through it in the form of cracks,' Gower won what might have been an Ashes-saving toss and batted. But at 56 for three, it was a familiar tale of English woe, the only difference being that Lawson was the destroyer. Gower joined Smith but at 132, the captain was trapped lbw by leg-spinner Trevor Hohns and Smith waged a lone battle, making a magnificent 143 out of 260 before Hughes had him caught by Hohns.

Lawson finished with six for 72. The ruthless machine that the

Australian team had become then set about amassing an Ashes-winning total, Taylor and Marsh laying the perfect foundation with their first century partnership of the series. For once no one went on to make a hundred and the ultimate total of 447 might have disappointed Border, who batted five and a quarter hours for 80. But the Australians need not have worried – England's hapless batsmen were always likely to help them out. Indeed, so pathetic were the top order attempts to cope with Alderman and a rejuvenated Lawson that Hughes was cast in the supporting role. It was even greater carnage than in the first innings: 28 for four, 38 for five, 59 for six! Only the redoubtable Jack Russell and the inimitable John Emburey resisted and their 142-run seventh wicket partnership at least made Australia bat again. The tourists lost three wickets in knocking off the 81 runs required. And then the celebrations began.

'It was a tremendous release of all the pressure that had built up,' says Hughes. 'To start the tour with such a poor reputation and to get beaten in two days . . . it just added to the pressure. It was nowhere near my best game but when I've finished playing, I'm sure I'll look back on the team efforts with more satsifaction than individual performances. And this just meant so much. A fantastic amount of work had gone into it – especially from Bob Simpson and A.B. – and to play so consistently well for the whole series was . . .'

Border thus became only the second Australian skipper this century to regain the Ashes in England, Bill Woodful (in 1930 and 1934) being the other. It was a marvellous triumph for the Australians who were denied the credit their overwhelming superiority deserved by the immediate announcement of a mass exodus of English players to South Africa. With *The Sun* screeching 'Good riddance – we won't miss any of this lot,' Alan Lee in *The Times* declared: 'England's ineptitude has unfairly upstaged Australia's authority throughout this remarkable summer.' But Border could still hardly believe that he had won the Ashes so easily. 'I always felt it was going to be a very tight series,' he said. 'To be 3-0 after four Tests is beyond my wildest dreams.' As for Merv, he became an even better bowler after this tour and played a greater role in the 1993 tour. He says: 'But nothing I will do can take away the memory of that day in Manchester.' A team of 'no-hopers' and its chief 'impostor' had arrived.

Result: Australia won by nine wickets

England

G.A. Gooch b Lawson	11	c Alderman b Lawson	13
T.S. Curtis b Lawson	22	c Boon b Alderman	0
R.T. Robinson lbw b Lawson	0	lbw b Lawson	12
R.A. Smith c Hohns b Hughes	143	c Healy b Alderman	1
*D.I. Gower lbw b Hohns	35	c Marsh b Lawson	15
I.T. Botham b Hohns	0	lbw b Alderman	4
†R.C. Russell lbw b Lawson	1	not out	128
J.E. Emburey lbw b Hohns	5	b Alderman	64
N.A. Foster c Border b Lawson	39	b Alderman	6
A.R.C. Fraser lbw b Lawson	2	c Marsh b Hohns	3
N.G.B. Cook not out	0	c Healy b Hughes	5
Extras (LB 2)	2	(LB 6, NB 5, W 2)	13

1/23 2/23 3/57 4/132 5/140   260   1/10 2/25 3/27 4/28 5/38   264
6/147 7/158 8/232 9/252   6/59 7/201 8/223 9/255

Bowling: *First Innings* – Alderman 25-13-49-0; Lawson 33-11-72-6; Hughes 17-6-55-1; Hohns 22-7-59-3; Waugh 6-1-23-0. *Second Innings* – Lawson 31-8-81-3; Alderman 27-7-66-5; Hohns 26-15-37-1; Hughes 14.4-2-45-1; Border 8-2-12-0; Waugh 4-0-17-0.

Australia

M.A. Taylor st Russell b Emburey	85	(2) not out	37
G.R. Marsh c Russell b Botham	47	(1) c Robinson b Emburey	31
D.C. Boon b Fraser	12	not out	10
A.R. Border* c Russell b Foster	80		
D.M. Jones b Botham	69		
S.R. Waugh c Curtis b Fraser	92		
I.A. Healy+ lbw b Foster	0		
T.V. Hohns c Gower b Cook	17		
M.G. Hughes b Cook	3		
G.F. Lawson b Fraser	17		
T.M. Alderman not out	6		
Extras (B 5, LB 7, N B6, W 1)	19	(NB 3)	3

1/135 2/143 3/154 4/274 5/362   447   1/62   (1 wkt) 81
6/362 7/413 8/423 9/423

Bowling: *First Innings* – Foster 34-12-74-2; Fraser 36.5-4-95-3; Emburey 45-9-118-1; Cook 28-6-85-2; Botham 24-6-63-2. *Second Innings* – Foster 5-2-5-0; Fraser 10-0-28-0; Emburey 13-3-30-1; Cook 4.5-0-18-0.

Umpires: J.H. Hampshire and B.J. Meyer

Alan Knott

Headingley, 10, 11, 12, 14, 15 July 1969

Born 9 April 1946, Alan Knott kept wicket for Kent from 1964 until his retirement in 1985. He played 95 Tests for England and he would have played many more if he had not signed for Kerry Packer as well as the South African rebels, led by Graham Gooch, in 1981. In Test cricket he claimed 269 victims in between all those stretching exercises. He was a genuine allrounder thanks to his innovative batting style which was often touched with genius. Against spin bowling he was capable of sweeping every ball; against pace he mastered the 'upper cut'; he finished with a Test batting average of 32. He is now one of the TCCB's band of expert coaches.

Thank heavens for Derek Underwood. Before he evolved as a freakish left-arm spinner, Kent were flirting with the idea of employing the young Alan Knott as an off spinner who could bat a bit. Even Les Ames thought this was a good idea. Fortunately it was decided that Underwood, who began his cricketing life as an opening bowler, might fulfil the spinner's role a little more effectively and Knott was left to concentrate on his keeping.

The two names were thereafter inseparably linked and became part of cricket's folklore. 'Ct Knott b Underwood' cropped up in our newspapers even more frequently than 'ct Marsh b Lillee' or 'lbw b Alderman'. Knott came to know Underwood's bowling intimately. 'Early on it infuriated Deadly (Underwood) that I could tell what he was going to bowl as he ran up to the wicket since he reasoned the batsman must know as well. As a result he changed his run up so that he was partially hidden by the umpire. We talked constantly during his spells, usually about the pace he was bowling. We had a simple sign system as well. If I felt a slower ball was a good idea, I lifted my head in the air; if I wanted a quicker one my gloves pointed to the base of the stumps. He was a challenge for any wicketkeeper, not just because of his unusual pace, but also his amazing accuracy. I once kept to him at Lahore for two hours without taking a ball and yet I had to expect every one.'

Underwood had a crucial role in the match chosen by Knott – the Headingley Test of 1969 against the West Indies. As usual this was a difficult selection to make. At county level Knott considered a game against Leicestershire at Maidstone in 1977 when everything 'went perfectly' – a century plus nine victims. His most memorable innings was a matchsaving 73 in the West Indies in 1968 on his first tour, though there were later five Test centuries – usually in adversity – to rival that performance. But he says 'in 1969 technically I was at my peak as a keeper, especially when standing up at the wicket. Later on I had to take some technical short cuts because I was not as mobile' – not that any of us outside the keeper's union noticed.

In 1969 England, 1-0 up in a three match series when they arrived at Headingley, were led by Ray Illingworth in his first summer as captain and Knott's account of the match focusses on the excellence of his leadership. 'Illingworth was the best captain I've ever played under' – quite a commendation when you consider that Knott played with Brearley, Cowdrey and Greig. 'He knew everything about the game and the techniques of his opponents and he thrived on pressure, as bowler, batsman and captain. We always knew that he wouldn't panic and that the opposition might.' This was certainly the case at Headingley.

The weather was damp, overcast and ideal for seam and swing bowlers when England batted. Only Edrich, D'Oliveira and Knott could cope as England struggled against Vanburn Holder and John Shepherd to a modest total of 223. The West Indies fared worse in their first innings. Against an all seam attack they plummetted to 161 all out; as ever the vital wicket was that of Gary Sobers, caught at first slip by Phil Sharpe off Barry Knight, whose skidding seamers tormented the West Indian captain throughout the series.

England's second innings of 240 was a dour affair. It lasted 130 overs and everyone reached double figures except Boycott. Knott batted for 130 minutes for his 31 before edging Sobers to the keeper for the second time in the match and a last wicket partnership of 37 between Snow and Brown gave England a vital fillip. So West Indies required 303 to win; after the rest day the pitch had dried out and the sun was shining, creating the best batting conditions of the match. Snow removed Roy Fredericks cheaply when he skied an attempted hook. Sharpe running back from slip held the catch; Knott recalls impishly: 'he robbed me of one of my victims; it was well within my reach and normally I would have expected to take the catch since I had the gloves on, but he called out with such authority – and he was such a good catcher – that I had to leave it to him. But I never let that happen again!'

Camacho, Davis and Butcher restored the West Indian innings so that with 35 minutes of the fourth day remaining the tourists were well placed at 219-3, Basil Butcher 91 not out. Now the match was transformed with Illingworth juggling his bowlers like a magician as Knott recalls: 'Deadly made the breakthrough; he made one bounce to Butcher, which I thought clipped his glove (Butcher was less convinced). The ball went down after contact so that was a very satisfying catch. At the other end David Brown had been bowling beautifully to Butcher and Clive Lloyd. But with the appearance of Sobers, the last man you would want to see coming to the wicket as an opposition captain, Illy immediately replaced Brown with Knight; he even pushed mid off back to give a single when Lloyd was facing Knight; imagine contriving to get Sobers on strike rather than away from it! Throughout the series Knight had bowled a full length and wide of off stump to Sobers and twice he had dismissed him, caught at slip. This time Sobers over-compensated, got an inside edge as he drove from the crease and he was bowled for a duck.

'Now Illy took Underwood off, even though he had just taken a wicket in his previous over, and bowled himself to the left-handed Lloyd. Sure enough, Lloyd went to cut and got a thick edge and I held it – another good one. After that one over, Illy took himself off immediately and brought back Underwood. Deadly bowled a full length seamer to John Shepherd, who played inside it and I took the catch. Every bowling change had worked perfectly. I know there's always an element of luck, but this was brilliant captaincy under pressure.' It was also high class keeping, though Knott was not at pains to stress this. In the space of 20 minutes West Indies had slumped from 219-3 to 228-7.

The following morning the last three West Indies batsmen lasted 80 minutes against the new ball, but they ended 30 runs short of their target. After the match Knott was voted the man of the series, a rare recognition of the keeper's contribution. 25 years on, England are still seeking another series victory over the West Indies.

Result: England won by 30 runs

England

G. Boycott lbw b Sobers	12	c Findlay b Sobers	0
J.H. Edrich lbw b Shepherd	79	lbw b Sobers	15
P.J. Sharpe Findlay b Holder	6	lbw b Sobers	15
J.H. Hampshire c Findlay b Holder	1	lbw b Shillingford	22
B.L. D'Oliveira c Sobers b Shepherd	48	c Sobers b Davis	39
†A.P.E. Knott c Findlay b Sobers	44	c Findlay b Sobers	31
*R. Illingworth b Shepherd	1	c Lloyd b Holder	19
B.R. Knight c Fredericks b Gibbs	7	c Holder b Gibbs	27
D.L. Underwood c Findlay b Holder	4	b Sobers	16
D.J. Brown b Holder	12	b Shillingford	34
J.A. Snow not out	1	not out	15
Extras (B 4, LB 3, NB 1)	8	(LB 5, W 1, NB 1)	7
1/30 2/52 3/64 4/140	223	1/0 2/23 3/42 4/58	240
5/165 6/167 7/182 8/199 9/217		5/102 6/147 7/147 8/171 9/203	

Bowling: *First Innings* – Sobers 21-1-68-2; Holder 26-7-48-4; Shillingford 7-0-21-0; Gibbs 19-6-33-1; Shepherd 24-8-43-4; Davis 1-0-2-0. *Second Innings* – Sobers 40-18-42-5; Holder 33-13-66-1; Shillingford 20.4-4-56-2; Gibbs 21-6-42-1; Davis 17-8-27-1.

West Indies

R.C. Fredericks lbw b Knight	11	c Sharpe b Snow 6
G.S. Camacho c Knott b Knight	4	c Hampshire
		b Underwood 71
C.A. Davis c Underwood b Knight	18	c&b Underwood 29
B.F. Butcher b Snow	35	c Knott b Underwood 91
*G.S. Sobers c Sharpe b Knight	13	b Knight 0
C.H. Lloyd c Snow b Brown	27	c Knott b Illingworth 23
†T.M. Findlay lbw b D'Oliveira	1	lbw b Knight 16
V.A. Holder b Snow	35	c Sharpe b Brown 13
L.R. Gibbs not out	6	c Knott b Brown 4
G.C. Shillingford c Knott b Brown	3	not out 5
J.N. Shepherd absent hurt	0	c Knott b Underwood 0
Extras (LB 7, NB 1)	8	(LB 11, NB 3) 14

1/17 2/37 3/46 4/80 5/88	**161**	1/8 2/69 3/177 4/219 **272**
6/91 7/151 8/153 9/161		5/224 6/228 7/228 8/251
		9/255

Bowling: *First Innings* – Snow 20-4-50-2; Brown 7.3-2-13-2; Knight 22-5-63-4; D'Oliveira 15-8-27-1. *Second Innings* – Snow 21-7-43-1; Brown 21-8-53-2; Knight 18.2-4-47-2; D'Oliveira 10-3-22-0; Illingworth 14-5-38-1; Underwood 22-12-55-4.

Harold Larwood

Sydney, 23, 24, 25, 27, 28 February 1933

Born in Nuncargate, Nottinghamshire, on 14 November 1904, Harold Larwood was a miner's son. At 14 he, too, was working on the coal face, 'crawling in them tunnels,' but it was not the only place where he bent his back. The scourge of village batsmen, he was taken by Joe Harstaff Snr. for a trial at Trent Bridge, where the Notts. committee were as amazed by his sickly appearance (pale and just 5'4" tall) as his speed. Batsmen tended to look just as ashen after facing him and Notts. offered him daylight and '30 bob a week'. He cleaned the boots of visiting players, including those of his hero, Maurice Tate, whom he was soon to join in the England side. After making his Test debut against Australia in 1926, Larwood was a member of Percy Chapman's party that won the Ashes in 1928/29. But he did not reach his peak until the infamous Bodyline tour four years later. With 33 wickets at 19.51 apiece, he reduced Bradman to a mere mortal and won back the ancient urn. A hero in English eyes, he never played for his country again – a craven Lords making him the scapegoat for 'Mr Jardine's leg theory.' Although he had been vilified on tour, he was warmly welcomed when he settled in Australia in 1950. His haul of 78 wickets was a paltry reward for a legend among legends.

Friends – he had many but few were batsmen – called him 'Lol'; 'enemies' preferred 'Killer', 'Wrecker' or 'Murder on Tip-Toe'. Even Sir Neville Cardus claimed: 'A breed of Larwoods, armed with eight or so fieldsmen on the legside, would no doubt put an end to cricket altogether.' A pit-pony boy who nearly split an empire, his action was worthy of ancient Greece, his delivery of modern warfare. He could hit a thrupenny bit at 100mph and terrorised a generation; he even cut Bradman's average in half. When he set off on that run of his, there was an expectant hush as awed spectators held their breath, batsmen retreated to square-leg, slips to third man. It was poetry that chilled. Of the 1932/33 series, Bill Bowes wrote: 'To have seen Larwood in Australia is to have witnessed one of the greatest of all sporting occasions.'

Yet on Bodyline his lips are sealed. 'I'm not going to talk about it,' he says in an accent still thick with Nottinghamshire coal dust after more than four decades in the Sydney sunshine. He made it a condition of being in the book and once that jaw is set, there's nowt that can shift it. After all, even Lord's couldn't get him to change his mind once he'd stood up to their shameful hypocrisy over Bodyline. No, he would not apologise and even the end of his Test career wouldn't budge him. Fortunately for us and for England, he could bat so it is his epic 98 as nightwatchman in his last Test that we agreed upon. But had it been dominoes in the sheds, he still would have been included.

The Ashes were already wrapped in Jardine's Harlequin cap by the time the teams returned to Sydney for the fifth and final Test of cricket's most notorious campaign. England led 3-1 with Australia's only win coming at Melbourne where Bradman made 103 not out. That levelled the series after Larwood's 10 wickets had put England one up at the first SCG game. It had been the third Test at Adelaide that was decisive and which had all but torn the two nations asunder. After Larwood had struck Woodfull a fearful blow above the heart and broken Oldfield's skull, England prevailed by 338 runs, going on to clinch the Ashes with a six-wicket triumph at Brisbane.

The second Sydney match may have been dead but the atmosphere was still more like a bull-ring than a cricket ground when Woodfull won the toss for the fourth time in the series and batted. The mood of the crowd was not improved when Richardson was out for a duck in the first over – caught Jardine bowled Larwood. With three men – including Bradman – out for 64, it looked ominous for Australia but the home side rallied to reach 435, their highest of the series. There was some spirited middle and lower order batting but they owed much to the profligacy of the English fielders. Larwood ended with four for 98 but had 'half a dozen' catches spilled.

The crowd had more to cheer when England batted, Jardine falling for 18 but Hammond joined Sutcliffe to take the score to 153 before the Yorkshireman was caught off O'Reilly with just 10 minutes of play remaining. Larwood recalls: 'Mr Jardine had already called out: "Harold, put the pads on." But I was a bit annoyed because I'd just bowled 32 overs. Then there was a roar when the wicket fell and Mr Jardine said: "Righto, Harold. Go in." As I walked out, I told the others to get ready because I thought I was going to get out.' But having been entrusted with an entirely different role – survival against the wily 'Tiger' and the charging Bull – the Notts. Express did not let his skipper down. 'I could hear the crowd yelling for Bull Alexander, their fast bowler, to give me some of my own back as he came charging in. I just stood there,' he adds.

The next morning England resumed at 159 for two with Hammond on 72, Larwood on five. 'I remember Wally saying to me: "Just settle down," and it did me good to have such a great player at the other end.' Still, Australia fancied an early breakthrough and kept the pressure on the junior partner. But Larwood's confidence grew as he kept the strike, taking singles off O'Reilly and boundaries off O'Brien and Alexander. 'He bowled so short, I could see them coming a mile off and just pulled and hooked and cut them,' Larwood says. Hammond then pulled O'Reilly for four to take the stand to 52 in 54 minutes, Larwood having made 34 of them. Breakthrough? This was fast becoming an irritation. The Aussies were well aware of Hammond, but Larwood? He had made a first-class 100 not out for his county and the more informed among them would have recalled his 70 and 37 at Brisbane on the previous tour, but they weren't prepared for him to dominate a partnership with England's greatest batsman!

Scoring mainly on the on-side, Larwood revealed a pleasing range of strokes, splicing judicious defence with powerful pulls and drives. The new ball held no terrors for him and he completed a superb half-century in 77 minutes, receiving generous applause. As ever, the crowd were rallying to the underdog, which is how nightwatchmen are always perceived, and no matter that it was the opposition, no matter that it was one of the main villains of the piece, the Sydney spectators were appreciating the knock. 'The Australians love a fighter,' says Larwood, 'and I think they could see I was fightin' that day.' Having been almost caught for 50, the Nottinghamshire hero simply carried on as if nothing had happened, hooking with rare relish and glancing deftly with only the occasional mis-hit. It was a stunning performance which to some extent overshadowed Hammond's century. 'Settle down?' Larwood, chuckles "e were out before me!'

When Hammond was lbw to Lee for 101, Leyland joined Larwood with England still 190 behind. The nightwatchman's role long since forgotten, England's makeshift number 4 consolidated their position before bringing what would have been an unforgettable century within sight. Slamming 14 off the first four balls of Lee's over, the wiry paceman brought the crowd to their feet with a blazing straight six. Few on the ground would have begrudged him two more runs and many were willing him to get them. The ground buzzed as Lee came in and there were as many groans as cheers when Larwood lifted an intended drive to mid-off. He had the misfortune to be caught by Ironmonger, supposedly the worse fielder in the game. Indeed, the general reaction was sheer disbelief that 50-year-old 'Dainty' had held it.

Larwood headed for the pavilion and the crowd rose as one. The *Sydney Morning Herald* wrote: 'Had Larwood made his score on his home ground at Nottingham he could not have received a greater ovation than the Sydney crowd gave him.' Larwood will never forget it even if it took a while to sink in: 'I'd been barracked so much on the tour I thought they were cheering because I was out,' he recalls. 'But it kept on until I got to the pavilion and then the members rose. Only then did I realise they were cheering *me*. It were a wonderful reception.' Did he regret missing the 100? 'If I'd got the two runs, it would have been pushed under the carpet and forgotten. I think it's remembered more because I didn't get them. And I've had a lot more sympathy.' As to the reaction of his teammates, he says; 'They just said "Well, done." There were no kissin' and cuddlin' like there is today. . .'

England went on to make 454 and won the match by eight wickets after Australia (182) collapsed to Verity (five for 33) in their second innings. Larwood made the breakthrough but broke down himself as Bradman appeared. 'My foot went and I was in agony,' he recalls. 'I asked Mr Jardine if I could go off but he whispered: "Not until the little bastard's out." I stayed on in agony until Bradman was bowled by Hedley [Verity]. Mr Jardine immediately ordered me to go and Bradman and I walked off side by side, neither saying a word.' For the Don there were to be many more innings but for Larwood it was the end of the tunnel. He was not prepared to do that other kind of crawling.
Result: England won by eight wickets

Australia

V.Y. Richardson c Jardine b Larwood	0	c Allen b Larwood	0
*W.M. Woodfull b Larwood	14	b Allen	67
D.G. Bradman b Larwood	48	b Verity	71
L.P.J. O'Brien c Larwood b Voce	61	c Verity b Voce	5
S.J. McCabe c Hammond b Verity	73	c Jardine b Voce	4
L.S. Darling b Verity	85	c Wyatt b Verity	7
†W.A.S. Oldfield run out	52	c Wyatt b Verity	5
P.K. Lee c Jardine b Verity	42	b Allen	15
W.J. O'Reilly b Allen	19	b Verity	1
H.H. Alexander not out	17	lbw b Verity	0
H. Ironmonger b Larwood	1	not out	0
Extras (B 13, LB 9, W 1)	23	(B 4, NB 3)	7

1/0 2/59 3/64 4/163 5/244   435   1/0 2/115 3/135 4/139   182
6/328 7/385 8/414 9/430   5/148 6/161 7/177 8/178
                                         9/178

Bowling: *First Innings* – Larwood 32.2-10-98-4; Voce 24-4-80-1; Allen 25-1-128-1; Hammond 8-0-32-0; Verity 17-3-62-3; Wyatt 2-0-12-0. *Second Innings* – Larwood 11-0-44-1; Allen 11. 4-2-54-2; Hammond 3-0-10-0; Voce 10-0-34-2; Verity 19-9-33-5.

England

*D.R. Jardine c Oldfield b O'Reilly	18	c Richardson b Ironmonger	24
H. Sutcliffe c Richardson b O'Reilly	56		
W.R. Hammond lbw b Lee	101	(4) not out	75
H. Larwood c Ironmonger b Lee	98		
M. Leyland run out	42	(3) b Ironmonger	0
R.E.S. Wyatt c Ironmonger b O'Reilly	51	(2) not out	61
†L.E.G. Ames run out	4		
E. Paynter b Lee	9		
G.O.B. Allen c Bradman b Lee	48		
H. Verity c Oldfield b Alexander	4		
W. Voce not out	7		
Extras (B 7, LB 7, NB 2)	16	(B 6, LB 1, NB 1)	8

1/31 2/153 3/245 4/310 5/330   454   1/43 2/43   (2 wkts) 168
6/349 7/374 8/418 9/434

Bowling: *First Innings* – Alexander 35-1-129-1; McCabe 12-1-27-0; O'Reilly 45-7-100-3; Ironmonger 31-13-64-0; Lee 40.2-11-111-4; Darling 7-5-3-0; Bradman 1-0-4-0. *Second Innings* – Alexander 11-2-25-0; O'Reilly 15-5-32-0; Ironmonger 26-12-34-2; Lee 12.2-3-52-0; McCabe 5-2-10-0; Darling 2-0-7-0.

Umpires: E.G. Borwick and G.Hele

Bill Lawry

Old Trafford, 27, 28, 29, 31 July & 1 August 1961

Born in the Melbourne suburb of Thornbury on 11 February 1937, William Morris Lawry takes his cricket very seriously – in spite of being nicknamed 'Phantom' for his liking of the comic character. Even at school he could bat for a week and made his debut for Victoria the day before his 19th birthday. An apprentice plumber and pigeon-fancier, he became one of the game's most immovable sheet anchors. A knock of 266 against New South Wales earned him a berth on the 1961 Ashes tour when he became only the third Australian since World War II to pass 2,000 runs in an English season. Centuries at Lord's and Old Trafford were the first major landmarks in a Test career that brought him 5,234 runs including a highest of 210 (in a partnership of 382 with Bob Simpson) against the West Indies. He assumed the Australian captaincy in 1967 but was unfortunate in leading non-vintage sides. After being unceremoniously sacked before the final Test during England's 1970/71 visit, he gamely tried to regain his place but retired when overlooked for the 1972 tour to England. Since then he has become a commentator with a style in marked contrast to his batting.

Bill Lawry's gum-chewing obstinacy evoked purple prose from the critics. Among the more celebrated epithets were Brian Scovell's 'Pinnochio' and Ian Wooldridge's 'corpse with pads on', while the man, himself, recalls such labels as 'a rheumatic rhino' and 'a cricketing scrooge'. Realising his own limitations, eliminating every vestige of risk and accumulating runs like a flannelled Micawber totting up his farthings, the tall, angular Victorian epitomised the defiant and courageous – as befits a man whose biography is entitled *Run Digger*. But the most irresistible description of his batting came from John Arlott who wrote: 'Gaunt and gawky as an electric pylon, Lawry never had a chance to become a stylist. He settled for results. Spectators in England may walk out on him; Hillites in Sydney may jeer. He is consoled by his run account. Bill Lawry is a one-man army of occupation, exacting endless toll from the enemy. Such men as Kanhai or O'Neill or Barber play precariously exciting innings; runs settle on Bill Lawry like barnacles on an old ship.'

On their tour of England in 1961, the Australians were well-endowed with top-order batsmen, McDonald, Simpson, Harvey, O'Neill and Burge seemingly bankers for the Test side. Lawry, who had been earmarked for the role of reserve opener, looked to have a challenge to avoid being one of the forgotten men that all tours produce. It was not the kind of task Bill relished – he preferred the stiffer one of breaking into the Test team. An endless run-harvest later, *Wisden* made him one of its Five Cricketers of the Year.

It will amaze no one that Lawry was forthright in choosing his greatest game: nor will it surprise that he opted for a team performance rather than an individual one (though he did contribute substantially). But it may raise an eyebrow or two that the game he chose from an 18,734-run career is universally known as 'Benaud's match'. However, when the significance of the occasion is recalled along with Lawry's own two knocks, he could hardly pick anything else. 'There's no doubt at all,' he says, 'that the game was one of the great Test matches. As well as being exciting throughout, it was where we won the Ashes after looking as if we were going to lose them. When we went up to Manchester, it was one-Test all with one drawn and one more still to play so there was always a very good chance that this match would decide the series. People remember the final afternoon but there were twists and turns early on and a very big last-wicket partnership. Every day had something and I, personally, had a good match. It is still vivid in the memory and meant so much to the experienced guys who had lost in '53 and '56.'

The '61 Australians were the last to go to England and back by sea and, after the epic series with the West Indies and the recent chucking controversy, the old country did not quite know what to expect when the *Himalaya* docked at Tilbury on 21 April. At Worcester, Benaud injured his shoulder and did not regain full fitness on the tour. But there was a truce on chucking and two evenly-matched teams drew the first Test at Edgbaston where Lawry made a resolute 57 out of 516. At Lords, he defied Trueman, Statham, Flavell and the infamous 'Ridge' with a heroic 130 to set up a five-wicket win. At Leeds, a Trueman-inspired England levelled, the hosts holding the upper hand for most of the fourth Test. Only Lawry (74) and Booth (46) offered much resistance as Australia tumbled to 190 all out. When Lawry reached 50, it was the twelfth time had made a half-century in 28 innings on the tour and yet another example of his resourcefulness. Writing in the *Sydney Morning Herald*, Tom Goodman called Lawry: 'A tremendous find and one who picked the ball to hit.' As the rampant English pacemen sought to exploit the lively wicket, the Victorian remained as steadfast at the Rock of Gibraltar in a hurricane.

On the first day at Manchester, there was no respite for the Australian batsmen. O'Neill was hit three times in one over by Flavell before being controversially given out 'hit wicket' after falling on his stumps to Trueman. At lunch Australia had staggered to 99 for three with Lawry's 50 not out the ballast that kept the innings together. When he was eventually trapped leg before by the accurate Statham, Goodman claimed: 'The pugnacious, well-controlled and thoroughly admirable innings of the young Melbourne plumber, left-hander Bill Lawry, shone vividly among the ruins.'

But it looked a vain effort as England, although having to fight for every run, fashioned a lead of 177 before a 25,000 crowd. When Lawry and Simpson began Australia's second innings, few in the large crowd doubted that a home victory would come. Even when Lawry was dropped by Subba Row at 25, there was no panic but there should have been – giving 'Phanto' a let-off was like giving Houdini bail. And, sure enough, the 'twin pillars of Hercules' added 113 for the first wicket to gradually haul Australia back into the match. Harvey and O'Neill gave valuable support but it was Lawry who provided the backbone. When he reached 100, it was the eighth time he'd got to three figures on the tour but he never looked secure against Allen who finally snared him in the leg trap for 102. The 24-year-old was disgusted with himself but received a standing ovation from the packed crowd. The visitors slid from 331 for six to 334 for nine, Allen taking three for none in 15 balls and once again it looked as if the Phantom's efforts would be undone by his teammates. A home win looked certain when McKenzie joined Davidson with Australia's lead just 157. But the great all-rounder belted Allen for 20 in one over, including two massive sixes, and out of the attack. 'That over was a big turning point,' recalls Lawry, 'as the man who had done the damage was smashed out of the ground.' Indeed, in one of the great last wicket stands of Ashes history, the two added 98. It was gold dust.

England now required 256 in 230 minutes but, in yet another turn, seized the initiative through Dexter who, in lordly mode, threatened to win the game in a haughty canter. With Subba Row as the anchor, Lord Ted raced to 76 out of 110 in 84 minutes before Benaud decided to meet fire with fire. 'The only way out of this,' he told vice-captain Harvey, 'is to win.' And the Australian skipper began bowling around the wicket into Trueman's footmarks. In 20 devastating minutes, he turned the match and the series. Dexter edged to Grout and then, to the crowd's horror, May was bowled around his legs second ball. Close, in for the indisposed Cowdrey, attempted to hit England home but perished ignominiously and then, just before tea, Subba Row was yorked. Suddenly, it was Australia who were in charge and it was all down to Benaud – the skipper had taken four for nine in 19 balls but even those figures did scant justice to the boldness of his tactics. After the break, England's cause was lost when Barrington, who might have held out for a draw, was lbw to Mackay. In another daring move, Benaud, who had both Murray and Allen brilliantly held by Simpson at slip, brought on the slipper to have Trueman caught before Davidson wrapped up an astonishing win by bowling Statham. The Australians leapt like salmon when it was all over and Lawry cannot recall a more joyous occasion. Benaud finished with six for 70 and Australia won by 54 runs with 20 minutes to spare. England had lost nine wickets for 51 runs and even Sir Neville Cardus thought Benaud 'lucky'. More gracious was Arlott who said: 'Had the scores been reversed, every England supporter would have hailed it as one of the most glorious victories in the history of Test cricket – and it was, in truth, nothing less than that.' And the Phantom was a real hero.

Result: Australia won by 54 runs

Australia

W.M. Lawry lbw b Statham 74	c Trueman b Allen 102
R.B. Simpson c Murray b Statham 4	c Murray b Flavell 51
R.N. Harvey c Subba Row b Statham ... 19	c Murray b Dexter 35
N.C. O'Neill hit wkt b Trueman 11	c Murray b Statham 67
P.J.P. Burge b Flavell 15	c Murray b Dexter 23
B.C. Booth c Close b Statham 46	lbw b Dexter 9
K.D. Mackay c Murray b Statham 11	c Close b Allen 18
A.K. Davidson c Barrington b Dexter ... 0	not out 77
*R. Benaud b Dexter 2	lbw b Allen 1
†A.T.W. Grout c Murray b Dexter 2	c Statham b Allen 0
G.D. McKenzie not out 1	b Flavell 32
Extras (B 4, LB 1) 5	(B 6, LB 9, W 2) 17
1/8 2/51 3/89 4/106 5/150 190	1/113 2/175 3/210 4/274 432
6/174 7/185 8/185 9/189	5/290 6/296 7/332 8/334
	9/334

Bowling: *First Innings* – Trueman 14-1-55-1; Statham 21-3-53-5; Flavell 22-8-61-1; Dexter 6.4-2-16-3. *Second Innings* – Statham 44-9-106-1; Trueman 32-6-92-0; Flavell 29.4-4-65-2; Allen 38-25-58-4; Dexter 20-4-61-3; Close 8-1-33-0.

England

G. Pullar b Davidson 63	c O'Neill b Davidson 26
R. Subba Row c Simpson b Davidson 2	b Benaud 49
E.R. Dexter c Davidson b McKenzie 16	c Grout b Benaud 76
*P.B.H. May c Simpson b Davidson 95	b Benaud 0
D.B. Close lbw b McKenzie 33	c O'Neill b Benaud 8
K.F. Barrington c O'Neill b Simpson ... 78	lbw b Mackay 5
†J.T. Murray c Grout b Mackay 24	c Simpson b Benaud 4
D.A. Allen c Booth b Simpson 42	c Simpson b Benaud 10
F.S. Trueman c Harvey b Simpson 3	c Benaud b Simpson 8
J.B. Statham c Mackay b Simpson 4	b Davidson 8
J.A. Flavell not out 0	not out 0
Extras (B 2, LB 4, W 1) 7	(B 5, W 2) 7
1/3 2/43 3/154 4/212 5/212 367	1/40 2/150 3/150 4/158 201
6/272 7/358 8/362 9/367	5/163 6/171 7/171 8/189
	9/193

Bowling: *First Innings* – Davidson 39-11-70-3; McKenzie 38-11-106-2; Mackay 40-9-71-1; Benaud 35-15-80-0; Simpson 11.4-4-23-4. *Second Innings* – Davidson 14.4-1-50-2; McKenzie 4-1-20-0; Benaud 32-11-70-6; Simpson 8-4-21-1; Mackay 13-7-33-1.

Umpires: J.G. Langridge and W.E. Phillipson

Dennis Lillee

Adelaide, 29, 30 January, 1, 2 & 3 February 1971

Born in Subiaco, Perth, on 18 July 1949, the 101st anniversary of W.G. Grace's birth, Dennis Keith Lillee looked and bowled like a reincarnated Spofforth. Once he'd marked out his run 'from the neighbour's lawn,' Lillee was destined to become a demon bowler. A tearaway in his youth, he mellowed to deliver equally deadly fast-medium, losing pace but none of his effectiveness in 14 years at the top. Arguably the most complete fast bowler of all time, he would surely have approached 500 Test wickets but for serious back trouble and the Packer hiatus. As it is, he managed 355 from just 70 Tests with five in his first, 11 in the Centenary Test and eight for 29 against the Rest of the World among the highlights. As fiery on the field as he was affable off it, Lillee became a cult figure in the '70s. He raced in like a thorough-bred to the cries of 'Lillee . . . Lillee,' once used an aluminium bat, aimed a kick at Javed Miandad, won a celebrated bet against his own team and made no bones about his loathing for batsmen. 'I try to hit a batsman in the rib-cage when I bowl a purposeful bouncer,' he wrote in his autobiography. 'And I want it to hurt so much that the batsman doesn't want to face me any more.' He had total mastery of his art, was a great competitor and if injudicious at times, was forgiven for his courage and commitment. He would get the new ball in the mythical all-time XI.

Clive Lloyd once said 'There is no batsman on earth who goes out to meet Lillee and Thomson with a smile on his face.' With his Zapata headband, Mephistophelean moustache and Sonny Liston glare, Lillee was a forbidding sight – even in the changing room. Tony Greig observed: 'You felt intimidated by the presence of the man before he bowled a ball to you.' And when he did, whether it was a snorting leg-cutter that ripped out off-stump, an ankle-breaking yorker or a hair-parting bouncer, you had to agree with Ray Lindwall who said, 'He's possibly the best fast bowler the game has seen.' As a youth, he tore in to bowl with fire-breathing malevolence but could be wild. Western Australian captain Tony Lock once told him that he was bowling like 'a flippin' old tart', and the label stuck.

When Illingworth's England toured Australia in 1970/71, Lillee was just making his name in Perth as John Snow tore the heart out of the home batsmen. With Garth McKenzie past his best and eventually dropped, Australia, trailing 1-0 and the Ashes all but lost, scoured the length and breadth of the wide, brown land for someone who could meet fire with fire. Eventually, they found him and England would discover that the judgment of their former spinner was not to be trusted.

When asked to choose the game of his life, Lillee said: 'Well, there's the Centenary Test – a magnificent, never-to-be-forgotten match. The Oval Test in 1972 – heralding a new era in Australian cricket – and then there's the first Test I played in. Perhaps not the "greatest" game, but certainly one of the most memorable. Ah, yes, I remember it well . . . 10.55 a.m. 29 January, 1971. I'll never forget striding out on to the Adelaide Oval (I was the last one on to the ground) and marvelling to myself how white all the shirts looked. Like everybody's mum had a Whirlpool. Whiter than white. The selection . . . I was the ninth fast bowler used that summer against the Poms; there was the publicity about a bouncer war; Snowy was giving it to us. The night before the opening day; the chat with The Don. "Just bowl the way you've been bowling," he said. "That's why we've picked you."'

The 21-year-old, who had come to attention by knocking Boycott's cap off in Perth a month earlier, was given a harsh baptism in the realities of Test cricket; Boycott and Edrich putting on yet another century opening partnership for 'the Poms'. Boycott was eventually run out for 58 but did not want to go, believing he had made his ground. Edrich was joined by Fletcher, who ground out his first substantial Test score (80), and England reached an impregnable 276 for two on the first day. Lillee? 'None for plenty,' he remembers. The second day, however, was very different. His first Test victim was the gritty Edrich (caught by Stackpole) and he also removed nightwatchman Alan Knott. But solid middle order batting by D'Oliveira, Hampshire, Illingworth and Snow took England to 470. Lillee came back to bowl both Illingworth and Snow, finishing off the innings when Walters caught Willis. His figures were an impressive five for 84 off 28.3 overs. 'Five for not very many on the second day,' he remembers. Lillee and Alan Thomson had dismissed the last four England batsmen with the new ball for 22 runs and skipper Bill Lawry was pleased with the fightback. He and Stackpole reached 50 without loss by the end of the second day.

Stackpole had made 41 of those, cracking 14 off Snow's first over. It was an assault that would have controversial repercussions. Snow twice asked for the ball to be changed, believing it had gone soft but Lawry felt the England paceman was deliberately indulging in gamesmanship in order to get back the ball used with such effect by Lillee. It was, after all, familiar to both Snow and his skipper, whom the youngster had removed less than an hour earlier. Umpire Tom Brooks agreed with Snow and the balls were changed but it was another reminder of the effectiveness of Lillee, whose bowling evoked memories of the debut of another Sandgroper – Garth McKenzie – at Lord's in 1961.

Apart from Stackpole, who made 87 out of 117, Australia batted poorly and could only total 235 in the first innings. Mindful of the wear and tear on his fast bowlers and the true nature of the pitch, Illingworth did not enforce the follow-on, declaring the second innings at 233 for 4, Boycott not out 119. Lillee? None for 40 off seven. He had the distinction of not bowling a maiden in the match. With 469 to make in 500 minutes, Australia batted more resolutely in their second dig, both Stackpole and Ian Chappell making hundreds and the draw being negotiated with a minimum of discomfort. Lawry had gone in the fourth evening but

Stackpole and Chappell put on 202 for the second wicket.

Illingworth admitted that he'd 'misread the wicket a bit,' but with a groin strain himself, Snow not firing and D'Oliveira also under the weather, the skipper was not too distraught with a draw. Lawry, however, felt that England had come to Australia intent on gaining one win in the series and 'now they've got it, they're going to hang on to it'. The fallacy of this would be proved in the final Test in Sydney when England won by 62 runs but Lawry, alas, was not there to see it. After captaining Australia in 26 of his 68 Tests, the Victorian was replaced by Chappell, hearing about his dismissal on the radio. As Lillee says, not the greatest match but it marked the dawning of a new era – one in which Lillee was a major figure. Of all players, no one has ever bowled less like 'a flippin old tart'.
Result: Match drawn

England

G. Boycott run out	58	not out 119
J.H. Edrich c Stackpole b Lillee	130	b Thomson 40
K.W.R. Fletcher b Thomson	80	b Gleeson 5
†A.P.E. Knott c Redpath b Lillee	7	
B.L. D'Oliveira c Marsh b G.S. Chappell	47	(4) c Walters b Thomson ... 5
J.H. Hampshire c Lillee b G.S. Chappell	55	(5) lbw b Thomson ... 3
*R. Illingworth b Lillee	24	(6) not out 48
J.A. Snow b Lillee	38	
P. Lever b Thomson	5	
D.L. Underwood not out	1	
R.G.D. Willis c Walters b Lillee	4	
Extras (B 1, LB 5, NB 11, W 4)	21	(LB 4, NB 8, W 1) ... 13

1/107 2/276 3/289 4/289 5/385   470   1/103 2/128   (4 wkts dec.) 233
6/402 7/458 8/465 9/465   3/143 4/151

Bowling: *First Innings* – Thomson 29.7-6-94-2; Lillee 28.3-0-84-5; Walters 9-2-29-0; G. S. Chappell 18-1-54-2; Gleeson 19-1-78-0; Mallett 20-1-63-1; Stackpole 12-2-47-0. *Second Innings* – Lilee 7-0-40-0; Thomson 19-2-79-3; Walters 3-0-5-0; G. S. Chappell 5-0-27-0; Gleeson 16-1-69-1; Mallett 1-1-0-0.

Australia

K.R. Stackpole b Underwood	87	b Snow	136
*W.M. Lawry c Knott b Snow	10	c Knott b Willis	21
I.M. Chappell c Knott b Lever	28	c Willis b Underwood	104
I.R. Redpath c Lever b Illingworth	9	not out	21
K.D. Walters c Knott b Lever	8	not out	36
G.S. Chappell c Edrich b Lever	0		
†R.W. Marsh c Knott b Willis	28		
A.A. Mallett c Illingworth b Snow	28		
J.W. Gleeson c Boycott b Willis	16		
D.K. Lillee c Boycott b Lever	10		
A.L. Thomson not out	6		
Extras (LB 2, NB 3)	5	(B 2, LB 3, NB 5)	10
1/61 2/117 3/131 4/141 5/145	235	1/65 2/267 (3 wkts)	328
6/163 7/180 8/219 9/221		3/271	

Bowling: *First Innings* – Snow 21-4-73-2; Lever 17.1-2-49-4; Underwood 21-6-45-1; Willis 12-3-49-2; Illingworth 5-2-14-1. *Second Innings* – Snow 17-3-60-1; Lever 17-4-49-0; Willis 13-1-48-2; Illingworth 14-7-32-0; Underwood 35-7-85-1; D'Oliveira 15-4-28-0; Fletcher 4-0-16-0.

Umpires: T.F. Brooks and M.G. O'Connell

Ray Lindwall

The Oval, 14, 16, 17, 18 August 1948

Born in Sydney on 3 October 1921, Raymond Russell Lindwall lost both his parents at an early age. Of Irish and Swedish extraction, he was educated at a college run by Marist Brothers and became a brilliant all-round sportsman. At rugby league, he was a goal-kicking fullback, playing for St George in the 1947 grand final, but cricket was his forte – especially batting. 'It's easier than bowling,' he once said – but he did not have to face himself. Living near Bill O'Reilly in Hurstville, the young Lindwall tried to impress the great man whenever he walked past the street games, but O'Reilly's head would remain buried in his paper. Had he noticed? You bet. 'He was commissioned by God to be a good athlete,' declared 'Tiger' who eventually told the kid to 'forget batting'. Lindwall played for New South Wales just before the War which he spent in the Signals in Papua New Guinea and the Solomon Islands. His first Test was against New Zealand in 1946 and he soon became his country's spearhead. At his best between 1946 and 1953, he played Test cricket for 15 years, retiring with a record 228 wickets in 1960. At 5'11" and 13 stones, he was one of the all-time great bowlers and with two Test centuries, he had not 'forgotten' his batting, either. As for his action? Sir Pelham Warner summed it up best: 'Poetry, pure poetry.'

Just as a velvet glove can deliver a killer blow, a silken verse can produce a deadly message. And so it was with Ray Lindwall, whose run-up might have been scripted by Wordsworth but whose effect on batsmen came straight from the Krupp factory. Denis Compton admitted to being 'a frequent visitor to the little room off the dressing room,' while Len Hutton's greatest dread was 'falling to the first ball of a Test match bowled in the hush by Lindwall.' Yet it was probably another Englishman who was responsible for the initial 'conversion' of the Australian from promising batsman to legendary fast bowler.

Although he loved making runs, when the 11-year-old Lindwall went with his older brother Jack to the Sydney Test in December 1932, his attention was drawn more to Larwood than to Bradman. 'Larwood's action was the smoothest I'd ever seen,' he said, 'and he bowled so fast that Jack and I couldn't even see the ball after it had left his hand.' Consciously or unconsciously, the Sydneysider developed a run-up that soon bore the chilling hallmarks of the England ace. Although a taller man, the Australian's arm was markedly lower and smoother. The upshot was that Lindwall's pace was deemed 'deceptive', his trajectory lower than average

107

but his effect devastating.

In tandem with Keith Miller, he formed one of the most feared pace partnerships the game has seen – even though the bouncer was used far more judiciously than in recent times – while testimony to Lindwall's laser-like accuracy is that no less than 42.5 per cent of his victims were bowled. (A remarkable proportion when compared to the 12 per cent by Lillee, who was not exactly wayward!) With Hutton as his first English Test victim, a dashing century and a place at the top of the bowling averages after Hammond's tour of 1946/47, Lindwall's place among Bradman's 1948 'Invincibles' was already etched in stone. And long before the end of that series, a generation of schoolboys was running down the street trying to imitate 'the new Larwood'.

Lindwall finished his sojourn through England with 86 wickets at 15.68 apiece, 27 of them in Tests. He had cut a swathe through English batting and – Bradman notwithstanding – had been one of the major differences between the sides. It was by common consent the finest Australian team of all-time but England, with the likes of Hutton, Washbrook, Compton and Edrich, were not exactly mugs with the bat. No, as Hutton recognised, what England lacked was a fast bowler of genuine pace – someone like Lindwall.

After a record-breaking tour, Bradman brought his men to The Oval leading 3-0 in the Tests with one drawn. It was to be his final Test and every day the ground was packed as the English public flocked to bid him farewell. When asked if he felt the emotion surrounding Bradman had overshadowed his own performance in this match, Lindwall quipped: 'We were all overshadowed before the tour started.' You would never have known. Play began an hour late, Norman Yardley having won the toss and elected to bat in a humid atmosphere with the square liberally plastered with sawdust. By the lunch-break, England were 29 for four and staring a fourth defeat squarely in the face. But if lunch was hard to swallow, tea was even less palatable.

Yet Yardley's decision did not look a bad one for the first half-hour when the ball barely rose above the stumps and Hutton, at least, kept both Lindwall and Miller at bay with relative ease. But then Dewes was bowled by Miller and Edrich fell to Johnston. In came Compton but he was badly rattled when a rising ball from Lindwall knocked the bat out of his hands. Soon afterwards, the Middlesex man tried to hook the same bowler but was caught by Morris at square-leg in a well-laid trap. After lunch, Lindwall wrecked England with a spell of five for eight off eight overs. Four batsmen were clean bowled and the defiant Hutton, whose 30 was more than half the total, finally succumbed to a brilliant leg-side catch by Tallon. 'That was a fantastic catch,' recalls Lindwall, 'but I can remember every victim.' Compton was the only one who could complain about the pitch, everyone complained about the bowling – it was unplayable. Lindwall finished with six for 20 off 97 balls and England's 52 was the lowest total they had made in a home Test.

When Morris and Barnes went in, batting looked an altogether different art and the England total was doubled before Hollies had Barnes caught by Evans for 61. Splendidly though he was bowling, the ruddy-faced leg-spinner little knew that he was two balls from immortality as all eyes were focussed on the pavilion and the possible final entrance of the greatest player ever to wield a bat. When Bradman emerged, the whole crowd rose as one and gave him the finest reception any incoming batsman has received. When the all-too-familiar figure reached the crease, Yardley shook Bradman's hand and called for three cheers to which the England players responded in rousing fashion. Hollies, who had only been persuaded to play by the Warwickshire committee after saying he preferred to help his county in their championship chase, prepared to bowl. Bradman played the first ball safely enough where-upon Hollies opted for a googly. To his own, Bradman's and the world's amazement, the great man missed it and was bowled. There was a roar of delight from the crowd and then Bradman, stunned, turned in pin-drop silence to make his way back to the pavilion for the last time in a Test. He departed just four runs short of 7,000 in Tests and an average of exactly 100.

Bradman denied that his mis-reading of the wrong'un was because he was moist-eyed with emotion, but for this unforgettable moment, it may have been known as Lindwall's match. Once Morris had finished flailing the England bowlers to make 196 of Australia's 389, Lindwall set about reclaiming it, breaking the back of England's second innings with three more wickets. The home side had to make 337 to make Australia bat again and when Lindwall yorked Dewes with the score on 20, it looked unlikely that Bradman would get another knock. When he bowled Edrich on the third morning, it was as good as over, although Hutton thought otherwise. He and Compton added 61 before Compton was brilliantly held by Lindwall at slip off Johnston. Shortly after, Lindwall bowled Evans before bad light stopped play, but the game was as good as over.

When Australia wrapped it up the next day, the victory margin was an innings and 149 runs. The story had been Bradman's duck but Morris's 196 and Hollies' five wickets were not forgotten. Nor was 'Killer's' contribution. Although he still insists 'it was a great team effort,' others recognised his match figures of nine for 70. 'It was a blitzkrieg,' said Denzil Batchelor, who added that Lindwall 'induced a Hamlet-like indecisiveness' among England's batsmen. One of them, Compton, perhaps paid him the ultimate compliment by saying: 'He possesses a slow bowler's subtlety.' *Wisden*, which made him one of the five Australians who were 'Cricketers of the Year', said: 'By whatever standard he is judged, Raymond Lindwall must be placed permanently in the gallery of great fast bowlers.' But the final word must go to Middlesex paceman and raconteur John Warr who said his last cricketing wish would be 'to see Lindwall from the Nursery End.'

Result: Australia won by an innings and 149 runs

England

	First Innings		Second Innings	
L. Hutton	c Tallon b Lindwall	30	c Tallon b Miller	64
J.G. Dewes	b Miller	1	b Lindwall	10
W.J. Edrich	c Hassett b Johnston	3	b Lindwall	28
D.C.S. Compton	c Morris b Lindwall	4	c Lindwall b Johnston	39
J.F. Crapp	c Tallon b Miller	0	b Miller	9
*N.W.D. Yardley	b Lindwall	7	c Miller b Johnston	9
A.J. Watkins	lbw b Johnston	0	c Hassett b Ring	2
†T.G. Evans	b Lindwall	1	b Lindwall	8
A.V. Bedser	b Lindwall	0	b Johnston	0
J.A. Young	b Lindwall	0	not out	3
W. E. Hollies	not out	0	c Morris b Johnston	0
	Extras (B 6)	6	(B 9, LB 4, NB 3)	16
	1/2 2/10 3/17 4/23 5/35	52	1/20 2/64 3/125 4/153	188
	6/42 7/45 8/45 9/47		5/164 6/167 7/178 8/181	
			9/188	

Bowling: *First Innings* – Lindwall 16.1-5-20-6; Miller 8-5-5-2; Johnston 16-4-20-2; Loxton 2-1-1-0. *Second Innings* – Lindwall 25-3-50-3; Miller 15-6-22-2; Johnston 27.3-12-40-4; Loxton 10-2-16-0; Ring 28-13-44-1.

Australia

S.G. Barnes	c Evans b Hollies	61
A.R. Morris	run out	196
*D.G. Bradman	b Hollies	0
A.L. Hassett	lbw b Young	37
K.R. Miller	st Evans b Hollies	5
R.N. Harvey	c Young b Hollies	17
S.J.E. Loxton	c Evans b Edrich	15
R.R. Lindwall	c Edrich b Young	9
†D. Tallon	c Crapp b Hollies	31
D.T. Ring	c Crapp b Bedser	9
W.A. Johnston	not out	0
	Extras (B 4, LB 2, NB 3)	9
	1/117 2/117 3/226 4/243 5/265	389
	6/304 7/332 8/359 9/389	

Bowling: Bedser 31.2-9-61-1; Watkins 4-1-19-0; Young 51-16-118-2; Hollies 56-14-131-5; Compton 2-0-6-0; Edrich 9-1-38-1; Yardley 5-1-7-0.

Umpires: H.G. Baldwin and D. Davies

Vic Marks

Gillette Cup semi-final, Taunton, 16 August 1978

Born on 25 June 1955 in Somerset, Vic Marks was a sparkling, graceful right-handed batsman and a luckless purveyor of fizzing off-spinners. Scandalously limited to just six Tests for England – when everybody else was banned for going to South Africa – this underestimated, modest cricketer now scratches a living writing for The Observer.

'I now realise that the simple task of plucking out one memorable match is not as straightforward as it first appears. Even though I am not so overburdened with alternatives as the majority of subjects in this book, it has been an agonising exercise. A few one day internationals sprang to mind as well as the unusual experience of scoring important runs for England in a Test match in Lahore, but in the end I went back to Somerset and 1978.

'This was a time of innocence and high ambition at Taunton. Brian Close had just retired to be succeeded by the rather more phlegmatic Brian Rose. His side was young and gifted: Viv Richards was nearing his awesome peak; Botham, just one year since becoming an England player, was on the ascendant; Garner had been spotted from the Lancashire League. In addition there was a flowering of home-grown talent – the likes of Peter Denning, growling amiably in the corner of the dressing room, Peter Roebuck just down from Cambridge University and Colin Dredge from Frome. All of them sensed that this team could win something and were utterly committed to this goal, yet in the same breath they were haunted by the fact that Somerset in 103 years had never won anything.

'Only one other club was in the same position – Essex – a team of gifted, rapidly improving clowns led by Keith Fletcher. In 1978 these two sides were drawn together in the semi-final of the Gillette Cup. Somerset's progress to the semi-final had been spectacular. Thanks to a vintage Richards century, they had overtaken Warwickshire's 292 with 17 balls to spare; against Glamorgan they rattled up 330 as Denning carved (he never 'stroked') a magnificent 145.

'On 16 August, however, Denning was grumpy – I have a team photograph to prove it – since he had failed a fitness test. These were the days before the Taylor report imposed careful restrictions on the crowd capacity, yet by 10.30 a.m. the ground was packed and the gates were locked until the Club Chairman, Herbie Hoskins, a local farmer, who understood that you have to make hay when the sun shines – opened them again. Hundreds of spectators could barely see the middle, yet they didn't seem to mind. Just being there was enough.

'Rose surprised his team by choosing to bat; usually we preferred chasing runs – our batting was stronger – but this was a semi-final, an occasion more taut even than a Lord's showpiece. He wanted runs on the board and to let Essex do the fretting in the cavern of a visitor's dressing room in the old pavilion at Taunton.

'Somerset started nervously. Denning's replacement, Phil Slocombe, was lbw to Norbert Phillip's first ball and both Rose and Richards were dropped by Kenny McEwan in the slips; at one point Rose played five consecutive maidens from seamer Stuart Turner. Yet the innings soon gained momentum because of Richards. He was in ferocious rather than calculating mood. John Lever was whipped through mid-wicket from outside off stump and was clearly saddened by the injustice of it all.

'The departure of Rose for an unusually scratchy 26 scarcely mattered. Peter Roebuck was soon a reliable ally. After Richards had clubbed Keith Pont over mid on by sheer brute force, Roebuck recalls advising him to "cool it". The next ball flashed over cover, the next was cracked over the bowler's head. Ah well, it was just a thought. Against the left arm spin of East, Richards took an outrageous step to the legside and cracked him over extra cover for six. He sailed past his century and when he was dismissed for 116, brilliantly caught by Denness at mid-wicket, Somerset were on 189-3. Botham was soon bowled by an East lob, which he tried to crack over extra-cover even harder and further than Richards. Now I made a minor contribution to the game – a scuttling, bustling innings of 33 in the final overs, which I had imagined to be full of strokes of grace and delicacy . . . until I saw the highlights on television.

'Somerset's 287 was a formidable score – especially in a semi-final, but the Taunton boundaries are notoriously short, the outfield fast. After losing Denness in the second over, Essex advanced steadily. Whenever a wicket fell the new batsman seemed able to maintain the momentum immediately. Gooch flexed his blacksmith's forearms, Fletcher improvised delicately, McEwan drove imperiously. I suppose I must mention that I bowled one disastrous over to Gooch just before tea, being swept for 13 runs (in those days I think I was picked for my batting). Rose was forced to recall Garner prematurely and he managed to dismiss Gooch, but with Essex 246-4 we were struggling.

'Now Botham finally entered the fray, first by brilliantly running out Keith Pont and then by catching Keith Fletcher off his own bowling. Next, Phillip suffered a rare mode of dismissal – run out by a direct hit from Marks at mid-wicket. Suddenly it was 248-7 and we had some breathing space. But not for long.

'Turner struck two consecutive boundaries off Botham before he was bowled with Essex needing 23 off three overs. Garner bowled his final over cheaply, leaving Colin Dredge, the whole-hearted, unassuming 'Demon of Frome' to bowl the sixtieth, Essex needing 12 to win with two wickets in hand. In those days there were no restrictions on the number of boundary fielders so Rose despatched most of us to the ropes.

'The first ball went for a single, the second for four, but the third knocked back Ray East's middle stump. The fourth to Lever was a disaster; a no-ball followed by overthrows, yielding three runs. Four were needed off three balls and Essex were favourites again . . . To the next Smith swung and missed . . . Somerset became favourites. Then a single, so that three were needed off the last ball if Essex, rather than Somerset, were to go to Lord's.

'By now everyone was on the boundary. I was at deep mid-wicket, a prime target area for late-order batsmen and praying that it would go elsewhere. It did. Fittingly it sped to Rose, the captain, at deep point. He seemed to lose it for a while against the backdrop of scurrying white bodies in the distance. Eventually he located it and sent it back to Derek Taylor the wicketkeeper, who dived at the stumps. By now the Essex keeper, Neil Smith, was no more than two feet from the crease.

'Afterwards, everyone collapsed for a while; it had all been so draining that raucous celebration was scorned. Even the crowd was subdued – they too were exhausted. The Essex players gallantly came to our dressing room to share some champagne before the long trek up the motorway.

'But we never did win anything in 1978. Maybe we had not recovered from that game by the time we went to Lord's for the final. In any event we played limply against Sussex and lost easily. But in 1979, by happy coincidence, Somerset and Essex shared all the domestic trophies.'
Result: Somerset won with scores level, having lost fewer wickets

Somerset

*B.C. Rose c East b Pont 24
P.A. Slocombe lbw b Phillip 0
I.V.A. Richards c Denness b Gooch .. 116
P.M. Roebuck c Lever b Phillip 57
I.T. Botham b East 7
V.J. Marks not out 33
G.I. Burgess b Lever 5
D. Breakwell not out 17
Extras: (B 10, LB 14, W 1, NB 3) 28
1/2 2/86 3/189   (6 wkts) 287
4/208 5/247 6/255
Did not bat: †D.J.S. Taylor, J. Garner and C.H. Dredge

Bowling: Lever 12-0-61-1; Phillip 11-1-56-2; Turner 8-6-22-0; Pont 12-0-42-1; Gooch 12-0-42-1; East 11-1-43-1.

Essex

M.H. Denness c Marks b Dredge 3
G.A. Gooch c Taylor b Garner 61
K.S. McEwan b Burgess 37
K.W.R. Fletcher c&b Botham 67
B.R. Hardie run out 21
K.R. Pont run out 39
N. Phillip run out 1
S. Turner b Botham 12
R.E. East b Dredge 10
†N. Smith run out 6
J. K. Lever not out 5
    Extras: (B 14, LB 9, NB 2) 25
1/9 2/70 3/127 4/166   287
5/246 6/248 7/266 8/281

Bowling: Garner 12-1-46-1; Dredge 12-0-60-2; Botham 12-1-48-2; Burgess 12-1-43-1; Breakwell 2-0-11-0; Marks 1-0-13-0; Richards 9-1-41-0.

Rod Marsh

Centenary Test, Melbourne, 12, 13, 14, 16 & 17 March 1977

Rodney William Marsh was born in Armadale, Western Australia, on 11 November, 1947. To weak-kneed batsmen, it may come as a relief to know that he was not hewn from some outback monolith, fed lumps of raw kangaroo meat to chew on and grenades to catch. Ian Chappell said that Marsh is the bloke he'd want next to him in the trenches – and not because he'd dive in front of him. A Digger to his boot-straps, Marsh would snare a live shell in front of first slip and then square-cut his way out of the ambush. To him, cricket was about mateship and he once said: 'Who cares if you personally get 100 or take five wickets, but the team loses the game?' Younger brother of Graham, who became a world-class golfer, Rod was primarily a batsman in his youth and gave notice of his combativeness with 104 on his first-class debut – against Hall and Griffith. 15 stones and dubbed 'Iron Gloves' when he first kept for Australia in 1970/71, he honed himself into a lethal accomplice to Lillee and Thomson – and a Number 7 batsman of some clout. Standing well back to the pace duo, he hurled himself about like a demented gymnast – and held everything. Besides taking the most (28) dismissals in a series (all caught) against England in 1982/83 and becoming the first Australian 'keeper to score a Test century, he claimed a record 355 victims (95 off Lillee) in all. The iron had long since turned to Superglue.

The mid-1970s was no time to bat against Australia. Roaring in to bowl was that fearsome creature 'Lillian Thomson' and, if you somehow survived and were checking your anatomy and then your wicket, you got no sympathy from behind the stumps. For there crouched the intimidating, gum-chewing presence of a man who dived for snicks as if his life was at stake; and if the delivery hadn't terrified you, the roar of the appeal certainly would. And yet this was the fellah who would be first into your dressing room with a tinnie afterwards and who said of the Centenary Test: 'Every time you go into the hotel you see 200 blokes who are better cricketers than you.' 200? Come off it, Rod. When it comes to standing back, only a couple of 'keepers compare with you. Marsh's modesty reflected the imposing nature of the guest list. Bradman, O'Reilly, Larwood, Hutton, Lindwall, Miller, Compton ... no less than 244 survivors of Ashes Tests assembled to fulfil a dream of Hans Ebeling and commemorate the first match that had started this whole peculiar business 100 years ago. John Arlott wrote: 'The cumulative effect of all these men under the same roof, dining, lunching, watching the play, reminiscing, recalling old triumphs – and failures – across 40 or 50 years produced an atmosphere of almost unbelievable nostalgia.' No modern player wanted to miss out, yet many had their doubts. Marsh was one of them: 'I thought there was no way the game could live up to all the hype,' he said.

The pomp and circumstance of the opening pageant was worthy of the Raj yet Bay 13 roared its approval – even for the Bodyline 'villains' Larwood and Voce. Anglo-Australian cricket's greying gods graced the game's finest arena once more, anthems were played by massed bands, the sun shone and 61,316 paid homage. 'This was, without doubt,' said Sir Len Hutton, 'the greatest cricket scene I have ever seen.' Yet Marsh's fears soon looked justified. 'When one side gets bowled out on the first day,' he says, 'you don't expect the game to last until after tea on the fifth.' Indeed, it all went horribly wrong for the hosts from the moment England's skipper Tony Greig won the toss (of a specially minted coin) and asked Australia to bat. With five wickets down at lunch and Rick McCosker in hospital with a broken jaw, the visitors had shown little gratitude for the hospitality.

Rising marvellously to the occasion, Willis, Old and Underwood had Australia on the back foot – a ball from Willis lifting from just short of a length to hit McCosker on the hand, then jaw, then stumps. At 51 for five, Marsh joined Greg Chappell, who was in charge for the first time against England, and the carnage came to a temporary halt. The pair represented Australia's last chance of respectability and although they doubled the score, it was still nowhere near enough, the innings eventually subsiding to 138 all out. Marsh made a defiant 28 and Chappell a 237-minute 40, causing Bill O'Reilly to remark: 'Australia batted as though the original XI from 1877 had been specially resurrected for the job.'

With the Queen and Duke of Edinburgh due on the fifth day, there was talk of arranging a one-day game if the main attraction did not last. This idea gathered momentum when England, who ended the first day at 29 for the loss of Woolmer, crashed to the even greater ignominy of 95 all out. Lillee, roared on by a vociferous crowd and ably supported by Walker, did most of the damage with six for 26. Marsh took four catches including Randall, who had unwisely doffed his hat after a Lillee bouncer, only to edge the next ball to those now non-ferrous gloves. Marsh overtook Wally Grout's record number of dismissals for an Australian 'keeper but that was only one reason he would always remember this match.

'The drama was unbelievable,' he recalls, 'and it was an amazing game. There were so many twists and turns and the catching of both sides was really memorable.' When Australia batted a second time, England, aggressively led by Greig, soon had them pegged at 53 for three but gradually the home batsmen took control with Doug Walters and David Hookes smashing half-centuries and finally Marsh playing the knock of his life. 'With five down, the wicket playing easier and McCosker's jaw wired up, it was vital that I made a few,' he says. Although, the afore-mentioned batsmen had tilted the game even more in favour of the home side, it was a game of such fluctuating fortunes that everyone present suspected that an England fightback was probably part of the script. So even though a lead of 230 did not call for trench warfare, Marsh's appearance was, as ever, a reassuring sight.

Moustache bristling, shirt billowing open to reveal a hairy, barrel chest, the West Australian came in when Walters fell just after lunch. At the other end, Hookes, the 21-year-old Adelaide PE student who was making his debut, raised the tempo dramatically with five fours off successive balls from Greig. He went soon afterwards but in Jack Fingleton's words 'had been the best thing to happen to this match.' Until that fateful over, the batsmen of both sides had played as if inhibited by the watching legends. But now the batting had come alive and it was up to Marsh to put the game beyond England's reach. He did not disappoint. After being almost bowled by Underwood for five, he set about the English bowlers with a judicious mix of powerful hitting and impenetrable defence. His half-century came with a glorious straight-drive for four off Old – just one shot in his repertoire that reminded us of his pedigree. He had, after all, scored 236 for Western Australia against Pakistan in 1972/73 and his Test average was in the high thirties. And now, in his stands first with Hookes, then Gilmour, his alter ego Lillee and, finally, with the courageous McCosker, he made sure that it would not be forgotten. As England held themselves together in the final session, ensuring that the match did not run totally beyond their grasp, Marsh became bogged down, adding only 14 in the last 75 minutes as a restless crowd urged him to complete his century before the close. Playing as ever for the team, he ignored them, ground relentlessly on and duly reached his third Test 100 on the fourth morning. He was undefeated on 110 when Chappell declared at noon, setting England 463 to win in 650 minutes.

When Woolmer and Brearley walked to the wicket to begin the chase – or was it the quest for survival? – a good many observers were still wondering whether the match would go the distance. The initiative, so aggressively seized by Greig on the first day, had well and truly been wrestled back by Australia while none of the watching luminaries had managed such a fourth innings feat in their prime. 'It might have been 1,000,' wrote Alex Bannister in the *Daily Mail* but by the close England were 191 for two with Randall 87 not out. 'I have never seen Derek bat better,' said a delighted and still hopeful Greig. According to Bannister, the Nottinghamshire batsman 'had laid bare the Australian secret that they are virtually a two-man bowling side.' With Amiss and later Greig, Randall threatened to defy history and wrest this now fascinating game back England's way once more.

But Marsh would not be left out of the game for long – even if his next intervention was memorable for its chivalry. Having made 161, a tiring Randall edged Chappell to the 'keeper who appeared to take one of his customary diving catches. But no sooner had 'Iron Gloves' rolled over and a crestfallen Randall left the crease than Marsh ran down the wicket to say the ball had hit the ground. Randall was recalled and the knights nodded approvingly. But Randall soon perished for an epic 174 and Lillee swept Australia to victory – by 45 runs, which, as every schoolboy knows, is the margin they won by 100 years ago. Randall was made man of the match in spite of Lillee's 11 wickets, but Marsh has more reasons to remember it. And no one else will forget his catches record, his fighting century or his chivalry.

117

Result: Australia won by 45 runs

Australia

I.C. Davis lbw b Lever	5	c Knott b Greig	68
R.B. McCosker b Willis	4	(10)c Greig b Old	25
G.J. Cosier c Fletcher b Lever	10	(4)c Knott b Lever	4
*G.S. Chappell b Underwood	40	(3)b Old	2
D.W. Hookes c Greig b Old	17	(6)c Fletcher b Underwood	56
K.D. Walters c Greig b Willis	4	(5)c Knott b Greig	66
†R.W. Marsh c Knott b Old	28	not out	110
G.J. Gilmour c Greig b Old	4	b Lever	16
K.J. O'Keeffe c Brearley b Underwood	0	(2)c Willis b Old	14
D.K. Lillee not out	10	(9)c Amiss b Old	25
M.H.N. Walker b Underwood	2	not out	8
Extras (B 4, LB 2, NB 8)	14	(LB 10, NB 15)	25

1/11 2/13 3/23 4/45 5/51   138
6/102 7/114 8/117 9/136

1/33 2/40   (9 wkts dec.) 419
3/53 4/132 5/187 6/244 7/277
8/353 9/407

Bowling: *First Innings* – Lever 12-1-36-2; Willis 8-0-33-2; Old 12-4-39-3; Underwood 11.6-2-16-3. *Second Innings* – Lever 21-1-95-2; Willis 22-0-91-0; Old 27.6-2-104-4; Greig 14-3-66-2; Underwood 12-2-38-1.

England

R.A. Woolmer c Chappell b Lillee	9	lbw b Walker	12
J.M. Brearley c Hookes b Lillee	12	lbw b Lillee	43
D.L. Underwood c Chappell b Walker	7	(10)b Lillee	7
D.W. Randall c Marsh b Lillee	4	(3)c Cosier b O'Keeffe	174
D.L. Amiss c O'Keeffe b Walker	4	(4)b Chappell	64
K.W.R. Fletcher c Marsh b Walker	4	(5)c Marsh b Lillee	1
*A.W. Greig b Walker	18	(6)c Cosier b O'Keeffe	41
†A.P.E. Knott lbw b Lillee	15	(7)lbw b Lillee	42
C.M. Old c Marsh b Lillee	3	(8)c Chappell b Lillee	2
J.K. Lever c Marsh b Lillee	11	(9)lbw b O'Keeffe	4
R.G.D. Willis not out	1	not out	5
Extras (B 2, LB 2, NB 2, W 1)	7	(B 8, LB 4, NB 7, W 3)	22

1/19 2/30 3/34 4/40 5/40   95
6/61 7/65 8/78 9/86

1/28 2/113 3/279 4/290 417
5/346 6/369 7/380 8/385 9/410

Bowling: *First Innings* Lillee 13.3-2-26-6; Walker 15-3-54-4; O'Keeffe 1-0-4-0; Gilmour 5-3-4-0. *Second Innings* – Lillee 34.4-7-139-5; Walker 22-4-83-1; Gilmour 4-0-29-0; Chappell 16-7-29-1; O'Keeffe 33-6-108-3; Walters 3-2-7-0.

Umpires: T. F. Brooks and M. G. O'Connell

Bob Massie

AUSTRALIA V REST OF THE WORLD

Sydney, 8-13 January 1972

Born in Subiaco, Western Australia, on 14 April, 1947, Robert Arnold Lockyer Massie was the ultimate shooting star of Australian cricket. Indeed, it is impossible to imagine a more meteoric rise than his beyond the pages of Boys' Own *– just as it is difficult to believe that it all ended so suddenly. Massie, whose father came from Scotland, chose an unusual route to the top via Kilmarnock, but in a region better known for its long links and wee drams, he found an atmosphere made for his medium-pace swing. He once took 10 for 34 and was offered a trial by Northants in 1970. But after claiming just three wickets for 165 in two 2nd XI matches, he was not offered a contract. However, he persevered, returning to Perth where he worked as a labourer on the W.A.C.A. ground. He made the Australian XI that played the Rest of the World and earned a place on the 1972 tour of England by dint of one amazing spell of 6-27. His 16-wicket Test debut at Lord's will be etched on his tombstone but it proved an impossible act to follow, with just seven more wickets in the three remaining Tests of the series. He went to the West Indies in 1973 but suffice to say that his haul in a six-Test career was just 31 wickets. Never able to recapture that prodigious swing, he soon lost his place in the State side. Disillusioned, he retired while his side-kick in the Lords 'massacre', Dennis Lillee, was taking his tally to 355.*

Never has a cricketer been, like Cromwell, so 'damned by everlasting fame.' The mere mention of Bob Massie's name in the contents list would have convinced every reader that this page would be recalling that overcast scene at Lord's in 1972. For that was Massie's match like nobody had ever claimed a match before – as much as Old Trafford belonged to Jim Laker in 1956 or The Oval to Len Hutton in 1938. Or Don Bradman at . . . But those legends had other matches and Lord's was, after all, Massie's debut! Roy of the Rovers would at least have waited until later in the series . . .

But the West Australian also had another match and as he refused to talk about Lord's, we must be grateful for Sydney, earlier that year. 'That's where I made the tour,' he says, 'and it could have been a lot better than seven for 79 as I had a catch dropped when it was six for 27.' Okay, okay, but . . . 'No, I don't want to discuss it. I'm sick of it. It is so well-documented . . .' But? 'I'm sick and tired of it.' Yet he once said: 'I have no regrets.' A touch less convincing than Edith Piaf, perhaps. More understandable was his reticence to discuss his demise and that, too, is well documented, if unexplained. Greg Chappell said: 'It [Lord's] was the worst thing that ever happened to him.' Maybe. Lord's apart, Massie was co-operative. He even said: 'I enjoyed my success while it lasted.' But not any more, it seems.

Massie emerged in the 1971/72 season in Australia, a season when the South Africans should have toured but didn't. But Massie still claimed Graeme Pollock among his scalps, the Australian Cricket board wisely deciding to cancel the Springbok tour, inviting a Rest of the World team instead. Cynics who thought the public were in for exhibition stuff had to think again as the likes of Sobers, Lloyd, Kanhai, Gavaskar, the Pollock brothers and Bedi were not content merely to parade their skills, they played to win. And they played hard. Australia, under Ian Chappell, knew no other way. But the 'series' began inauspiciously with rain ruining the first international in Brisbane. The match was not without incident, however; Lillee cracking Kanhai a fearful blow to the ribs, but the West Indian still made a 100, as did South African opener Hylton Ackerman. Chappell reached three figures in each innings. It was a taste of things to come.

With Lillee at his incandescent best, Australia won the second match in Perth by an innings and 111 runs, the great man taking eight for 29 in the first innings and 12 for 92 in the match. The third match in Melbourne was rated by many as the finest international since the tied Test of 1960, with Sobers scoring a wondrous 254 to help the visitors to victory by 97 runs. Massie, playing in his first game for Australia, made little impression. And so to Sydney with the surprisingly full-blooded series intriguingly poised at one-all. Bill Jacobs, who managed the World XI, claimed that his men sustained 35 injuries, the most serious of which was Lloyd who flew back to England with two crushed vertebrae and his career in jeopardy. For Australia, Graeme Watson had to have heart massage and 40 pints of blood after being hit by a beamer from Greig. Stocky opener Keith Stackpole propped up the Australian innings with his second 100 of the series but his only support came from John Benaud and Rod Marsh, the innings subsiding to Bedi and Intikhab for a modest 312. Enter Massie. The West Australian had Ackerman brilliantly caught by John Inverarity in the gully in his first over and the home side left the ground in better spirits. That, too, was a taste of things to come.

The next morning Massie resumed from the Randwick End, bowling into a north-easterly breeze. It helped as he swung the ball in both directions and in his second over he had the Pakistani Asif Masood caught at mid-on and then Zaheer Abbas held by Stackpole at slip. Eight for three, Massie three for none. The crowd, many of whom had not heard of this six-foot Sandgroper, was open-mouthed. But in strode Graeme Pollock to join Gavaskar. Sanity, surely, would be restored. But when the Indian master groped nervously and edged Massie to slip for just six, the fans had mixed emotions. They had come to watch the world's finest batsmen display their wares yet most of them were now back in the pavilion, victims of an unknown! Many wanted the carnage to stop – and they thought the rare sight of Sobers and Pollock together, a West Indian and a white South African, and arguably the two best left-handers to have graced the game, would be enough to ensure that. Massie, playing only his 16th first class match, had other ideas.

'I realised I had to do something today,' he said in the dressing room later. 'You have to succeed when they pick you or they'll pick someone else who will. At the start of the season I was working as a labourer and I'd only been married a few months. I wondered if it was all worthwhile. I decided to work for the eastern tour with the State side and if I'd failed, I probably would have given the game away.' Having returned from Scotland with a 'beer belt' from quenching his thirst in Killie, he hardly looked like a man who could shove aside either Lillee or 'Garth' McKenzie for Western Australia. But 13 wickets in two games gave him his chance – with Australia.

Slanting the ball away from Sobers, he had the great man caught by Marsh and, 10 minutes later, ruined the entertainment by having Pollock gleefully pouched by Stackpole. It was 68 for six, a nightmare for a 28,000 crowd but undisguised delirium for Massie. Ever modest, he says: 'There was nothing wrong with the pitch but the breeze really helped. There was a lot of construction going on at the SCG at the time and there were some gaps in the stands. This breeze came through one of them and was just perfect.' A bit like the Westerlies off Ayrshire, perhaps? Massie's morning was not quite perfect, however, as, having set a leg-trap for Engineer and lured him into it, Inverarity spilled the catch. It would have given Massie seven for 27 and reduced the World XI to 68 for seven. Massie eventually took his seventh wicket but by then the visitors had added 200 runs; Engineer making 36, Greig 70 and Intikhab 73 not out. They were all out for 277.

In Australia's monumental second dig, Stackpole made 95, Ian Chappell 119 and brother Greg a massive 197 not out in a total of 546. With the Aussie spinners licking their lips at the prospect of dismissing the World XI, rain intervened and no play was possible on the final day, the match petering out to a draw. But Massie had booked his ticket to England. Bill O'Reilly said: 'He mounted a wonderful in-swing onslaught – grand bowling, in-swing at its very best.' It wasn't quite, of course, but that is another story.

Result: Match drawn

Australia

K. Stackpole b Bedi	104	b Sobers ... 95
J. Inverarity c G. Pollock b Cunis	12	b Cunis ... 9
I. Chappell b Bedi	17	c Engineer b Masood ... 119
J. Benaud c & b Intikhab	54	c Ackerman b Bedi ... 17
G. Chappell b Bedi	0	not out ... 197
D. Walters c G. Pollock b Masood	8	b Intikhab ... 4
R. Marsh not out	77	c Gavaskar b Masood ... 22
K. O'Keeffe run out	20	st Engineer b Bedi ... 54
T. Jenner c Engineer b Bedi	7	c Sobers b Intikhab ... 14
R. Massie b Intikhab	1	c Ackerman b Intikhab ... 0
D. Lillee c Cunis b Intikhab	5	b Intikhab ... 2
Extras	7	... 13
1/55 2/101 3/145 4/148 5/163	312	1/32 2/185 3/207 4/294 546
6/232 7/269 8/281 9/306		5/301 6/350 7/484 8/541 9/546

Bowling: *First Innings* – Sobers 6-1-33-0, Masood 8-0-36-1; Cunis 9-0-48-1; Greig 6-1-28-0; Bedi 20-3-85-4; Intikhab 20.2-1-75-3. *Second Innings* – Masood 13-0-84-2; Cunis 15-1-80-1; Sobers 13-0-63-1; Bedi 29-2-144-2; Greig 8-2-30-0; Intikhab 24. 4-1-132-4.

Rest of the World

H. Ackerman c Inverarity b Massie 1	c I. Chappell b Inverarity .. 87
S. Gavaskar c Stackpole b Massie 6	not out 68
A. Masood c Lillee b Massie 0	
Z. Abbas c Stackpole b Massie 0	b O'Keeffe 1
G. Pollock c Stackpole b Massie 37	c Inverarity b O'Keeffe 0
G. Sobers c Marsh b Massie 15	b Inverarity 2
A. Greig c Marsh b Lillee 70	
F. Engineer c Inverarity b Jenner 36	c Stackpole b O'Keeffe 2
Intikhab Alam not out 73	not out 1
R. Cunis c Marsh b Inverarity 6	
B. Bedi c O'Keeffe b Massie 19	
Extras 14	 12

1/6 2/6 3/8 4/21 5/61   277   1/155 2/156   (5 wkts) 173
6/88 7/134 8/216 9/230   3/156 4/159 5/164

Bowling: *First Innings* – Lillee 19-4-70-1; Massie 20.6-5-76-7; G. Chappell 3-0-17-0; Jenner 18-2-69-1; O'Keeffe 7-2-25-0; Inverarity 2-0-6-1. *Second Innings* – Lillee 7-2-28-0; Massie 4-1-19-0; G. Chappell 5-1-29-0; Jenner 6-1-20-0; Inverarity: 14-6-31-2; O'Keeffe: 12-1-34-3.

Javed Miandad

Austral-Asia Cup final, Sharjah, 18 April 1986

Born in Karachi on 6 June 1957, Javed Miandad brings to the crease the courage and cunning of a street-fighter and the mastery of an all-time great. One of seven children to Noor Mohammed Miandad, a first-class cricketer in India before Partition, Javed made his first-class debut at 16. He scored 311 for Karachi Whites as a 17-year-old and 163 in his first Test two years later. He then became the youngest Test player to hit a double century (19 years and four months) and before his 22nd birthday, had compiled no less than six Test 100s. Hailed as a genius, his record-breaking feats have been frequently interspersed with controversy. He brandished a bat at Dennis Lillee, conspicuously failed to play 'Henry Kissinger' in Mike Gatting's row with Shakoor Rana, and was not given out lbw in Pakistan until his 35th home Test! Javed regarded it as a compliment when Keith Miller said: 'He becomes the eye of every storm in the cricket world.' Pilloried as 'the world's most hated batsman' for his incorrigible cussedness, to many opponents even his smile seems like that of the moneychanger. Besides being married to a millionairess, he has a wealth of runs; 8,832 at 52.57 in 124 Tests putting him third on the all-time list before he retired briefly early in 1994. A troublesome back and tempestuous cricket politics conspired to dull his appetite and it took Prime Minister Benazir Bhutto to persuade him to come back.

Of all the unlikely corners where leather has been whacked by willow, none has seemed more improbable or intrinsically alien at first glance than Sharjah, the oil-rich emirate on the Persian Gulf. Although once one of the Trucial States, there had been no great colonial legacy and the egg and tomato ties of Lord's were aflutter at the prospect of dishdashed umpires, 'dust-storm stopped play' and third man patrolling the Straits of Hormuz. But the cricket-loving Pakistani businessman Abdul Rahman Bukhatir knew what he was doing when he dug up the sand and turned his sprinklers on. With hundreds of thousands of resident Pakistanis and Indians, guaranteed sunshine and a brightness that had Dickie Bird's light meter bleeping for mercy, Bukhatir knew that Sharjah was a potential hotbed for the game. So he brought couch from the subcontinent, desalinated water from the Gulf and set about creating his cricket oasis. A Pakistani groundsman was hired, stands were built and canopied, lounges were air-conditioned, seats cushioned with velvet and V.I.P.s transported like royal caravans. All that was needed were the players, but millions of dirhams brought five sceptical countries to the inaugural

Austral-Asia Cup. Lords of the desert? With the turf-loving Sheikhs in attendance, it was more like Ascot. And what better place for a batsman who, like Ranji, is said to have 'never played a Christian shot?'

Javed Miandad is unequivocal. Indeed, of all the 50 contributors to these pages, he is the most certain just which was his 'greatest game' – and this is a man with two decades of top-flight encounters (including more than 200 one-day matches) to choose from. But, for him, Test double centuries and five World Cups pale compared to one desert storm in 1986. It was the final of the Austral-Asia Cup and his 96th one day international. 'I choose this match for three reasons,' he says, 'It was the first trophy which Pakistan won, it was a great game of cricket and it was my best innings. You know, there are so many one-day games that it is difficult to remember most of them, but that one was something special.' Indeed, that innings has long since passed into Pakistani folklore as it turned them into a formidable one-day side. And it put Sharjah firmly on the world cricket map.

Run as part of the Cricketers' Benefit Fund Series, the event had a complicated format. As winners of the Asia Cup, Sri Lanka were given a bye into the semi-finals where they were joined by India and Pakistan, the first-round winners, and New Zealand who qualified as first-round losers with the lesser margin of defeat! Of the five participating nations, only Australia missed out. In the semis, India edged Sri Lanka by three wickets, Gavaskar making 71, while Pakistan crushed New Zealand (all out 64) by 10 wickets. Pakistan reached the final without Javed having made it to the crease, but when his turn finally came, he faced a forbidding task.

He reflects: 'When one-day cricket started, nobody knew how to play the game. You would bowl with a couple of slips throughout the innings and the batsmen would have a go as soon as they went in. But now, it's much more scientific with batsmen content to take singles off every ball to get six runs an over instead of slogging, while bowlers rely more on accuracy than getting people out.' A marvellous improviser who could be devilishly difficult to contain, Javed has caused bowlers to complain that they never know whether he was making them look good to bring in the field or bad to have them taken off. But on this occasion he had little room for manoeuvre. 'When the fourth wicket went down, he says, 'we needed about 10 an over and I was the only recognised batsman left.'

Although a number 7 by the name of Imran Khan may disagree, the gist of Javed's recollections are accurate. Chasing a formidable 246 to win (Gavaskar had made 92 and Srikkanth 75 of India's 245 for seven) Pakistan began badly. Javed came in at 39 for two but when Salim Malik was run out at 110 for four, they were way behind the run rate. But they were thankful that the Indians had not capitalised on a magnificent start to their innings. An opening stand of 117 had been followed by another of 99 for the second wicket. But Imran and Wasim had pegged back the Indian middle order and the target was at least attainable. But when Pakistan batted and Abdul Qadir came in, the odds were very much on India.

'I still managed to bat the way I wanted,' insists Javed. 'I enjoyed myself and played shots that were far more innovative than any I would dare play in a Test. I did not slog but kept the scoreboard ticking and the bowlers were tiring. But I shall never forget the crowd: the ground was full of Pakistanis and Indians – our rivalry is like that of England and Australia – and they were cheering wildly. The atmosphere was more tense than anything I can remember. But that day I was really in control, playing well but not slogging, and the runs kept coming.'

The original target of five an over had risen to nine off each of the last 10 overs and wickets were tumbling. For all Javed's thrilling improvisation and 'scared rabbit' running between the wickets, Pakistan looked like falling tantalisingly short of their goal when Qadir, after making a brave 34 in a stand of 71, was caught off Kapil Dev and Imran was bowled by Madan Lal. Then Manzoor Elahi was caught off Chetan Sharma and at 215 for seven, the vital wicket of Wasim fell when the big-hitter was run out for three. Everything now depended on Javed.

'When I reached my century, the crowd went crazy but I knew I still had a lot of work to do,' he says. 'I still had to score very quickly but the pressure to keep it up at that rate was terrible. In fact, the tension was so great that several people died in Pakistan watching it on television.' Javed, himself, 'died' a thousand deaths when the ninth wicket fell at 241 and four were still needed off the last ball. The field was scattered around the boundary when Chetan Sharma steamed in. As a subcontinent held its breath, Javed hit it for six and the ground erupted. Parties went on all night in Pakistan but the hero, himself, had the most to celebrate. He has never been specific about it but reliable sources say that he was given a Merc and 100,000 dirhams (US$25,000), plus a camel train of gold and jewellery. It became known as 'the six that made a million' and even the Arabs were impressed. That last, lusty belt could in no way be described as a Christian shot.

Result: Pakistan won by one wicket

India

K. Srikkanth c Wasim b Qadir	75
S.M. Gavaskar b Imran	92
D.B. Vengsarkar b Wasim	50
K. Azad b Wasim	0
*Kapil Dev b Imran	8
Chetan Sharma run out	10
R.J. Shastri b Wasim	1
†C S. Pandit not out	0
LB 6, W 2, NB 1	9

1/117 2/216 (7 wkts, 50 overs) 245
3/216 4/229 5/242 6/245 7/245

M. Azharuddin, Madan Lal and Maninder Singh did not bat.

Bowling: Imran 10-2-40-2; Wasim 10-1-42-3; Manzoor 5-0-33-0; Mudassar 5-0-32-0; Qadir 10-2-49-1; Tauseef 10-1-43-0.

Pakistan

Mudassar Nazar lbw b Chetan 5
Mohsin Khan b Madan Lal 36
Ramiz Raja b Maninder 10
Javed Miandad not out 116
Salim Malik run out 21
Abdul Qadir c sub (R. Lamba) 34
  b Kapil Dev
*Imran Khan b Madan Lal 7
Manzoor Elahi c Shastri b Chetan 4
Wasim Akram run out 3
†Zulqarnain b Chetan 0
Tauseef Ahmed not out 1
LB 11 11
1/9 2/39 3/61   (9 wkts, 50 overs) 248
4/110 5/181 6/209 7/215 8/235 9/241

Bowling: Kapil Dev 10-1-45-1; Chetan 9-0-51-3; Madan Lal 10-0-53-2; Maninder 10-0-36-1; Shastri 9-0-38-0; Azharuddin 2-0-14-0.

Umpires: D. M. Archer and A. Gaynor

Keith Miller

Lord's, 25, 27 28 August 1945

Born in a place called Sunshine (a Melbourne suburb) on 28 November 1919, and named after aviation pioneers, Keith Ross Miller was destined for life in the stratosphere. Sir Neville Cardus called him 'an Australian in excelsis', while Sir Robert Menzies hung a photo of him in his Canberra office, claiming his cover drive 'would have provoked immense joy in ancient Athens.' He was once dubbed 'the Byron of cricket', but was better known as 'the Nugget' whom Wisden *felt 'would have enriched even the Golden Age.' As a boy, he was small enough to think seriously of becoming a jockey, but grew one foot in a year to emerge as one of cricket's greatest all-rounders as well as a fine Australian Rules footballer. Primarily a batsman in his youth, he developed from a net bowler to a lethal new ball partner for Ray Lindwall. The War came just after he'd broken into the Victorian side – he moved to New South Wales in 1947 – but when he emerged from the cockpit, smoothing his hair, it was not only cricket-lovers who found him irresistible. He was not just a dashing batsman with film-star looks, a fiery fast-bowler and a brilliant fielder, he was a hero as well! His hitting in the Victory series endeared him to two grateful nations for the next decade and he totalled 2,958 runs and 170 wickets in his 55 Tests. But such stats can never convey the thrill that lesser mortals felt when he ran his hand through that dark mane of his and strode to the wicket.*

Keith Miller could unite an empire with a toss of his head: small boys wanted to be like him, women swooned over him, gnarled sages lauded him – in England and Australia. Tall and handsome in what Cardus called 'a sun-stained, windswept way,' Miller was a heart-throb on both sides of the world – in both senses. A swashbuckling fighter-pilot, he could crash-land a burning plane before breakfast and make a hundred before lunch. The afternoon? He would spend it at the race track given half a chance, while evenings might last until the start of the next morning's play which he often attended still wearing his dinner suit. As brilliant as he was unpredictable, he once reached the S.C.G. in a dishevelled state after celebrating the arrival of his first born child – and then bowled out South Australia for 27. He took seven for 12, still the best figures in the Sheffield Shield, but cricket stats meant less to him than the form guide. Under his captaincy, the 12th man placed the bets before he brought the drinks, while his field-setting owed more to laissez-faire than little black books or slide-rules. Players recall being told simply to 'scatter', while, on the famous occasion that New South Wales took the field with 12 men, Miller's solution was to utter the immortal line: 'I say, would one of you chaps piss off?'

Interviewing him has been compared to facing him on the field: either as a bowler of darting leg breaks off a long run, rearing bumpers off a short one or as a batsman who could belt your best effort from the blockhole to kingdom come. Asked to name his greatest match, his response was characteristically cavalier: 'Pick one yourself,' he said, 'I'm sure you'll do a better job than I would . . .' No, he didn't want to talk about his 145 not out and four for 37 at Sydney in 1951, nor his 10 wickets at Lord's in 1956; and he seemed bored at the mere mention of countless other match-winning performances that made him a giant in the game. 'I'll leave it to you,' he insisted and proceeded to talk of his old pal Denis Compton and old skipper, Sir Donald Bradman, whom he admires more than their on-field tiffs suggested. And he was, of course, totally charming. But how to do him justice?

Hearing how much he revelled in the Victory Tests and that he was sometimes disenchanted with the seriousness of the real McCoy, knowing how much his spirit lifted the war-weary public in the summer of 1945 and that he never quite realised what John Arlott claimed was 'the potential to become the best batsman, best bowler and best fielder in the world,' but had fun instead, the task suddenly became easier. 'Test cricket was a bloody picnic to me,' he said. 'I used to play to win but mainly for enjoyment.' So if the essential Keith Miller is to be captured in one innings, what better than his unforgettable assault on the Lord's pavilion in 1945?

'Those were the days,' he smiles. 'The Aussies were a make-shift bunch and we played an England team that had men like Hammond, Hutton and Compton. Everyone wanted to enjoy themselves – they were so happy the War was over – so we tried to make it entertaining, everyone-having-a-go type of cricket and the crowds loved it.' After six years of facing some awkward deliveries from the Germans, Londoners flocked to Lord's to witness a barrage that put the place in greater danger than it had ever been from the Luftwaffe – from a Flying Officer in the RAAF! Admitting that his first sight of the famous ground had been a disappointment – 'compared to Melbourne and Sydney, it seemed a dingy little place' – he grew to love it and had some of his finest hours on its famous slope. There would be none finer than during the match between a Commonwealth XI and England after the Victory series with Australia had ended.

The Dominions, captained by Leary Constantine in the absence of the indisposed Lindsay Hassett, made 307 all out on the first day, thanks largely to a splendid century from the New Zealand left-hander Martin Donnelly. Miller made just 26 and the England XI were 28 for three by the close. A masterly 121 by skipper Wally Hammond was the main contribution to their eventual total of 287 and, maintaining the brisk tempo, the Dominions had reached 145 for three at the end of the second day. Miller made 61 not out – relatively sedately, by his standards. But when he resumed his innings the next morning, he enquired of umpire Archie Fowler: 'Is it true that the only player to hit a ball over the pavilion

Merv Hughes is triumphant as he snares Test victim number 200.

Bob Simpson (left) and Bill Lawry about to open yet another innings. The most effective opening partnership Australia ever had, they piled on 382 against the West Indies at Bridgetown in 1965.

Dennis Lillee following through with fire-breathing malevolence. The Australian is probably the greatest fast-bowler of all time, taking 355 wickets in just 70 Tests.

What Rod Marsh is not saying is: 'Missing by a mile, umpire,' as he gently coaxes an affirmative. The victim here is Geoff Boycott.

A mischievous smile about to break out from the great improvisor Javed Miandad as he revels in another ferocious dispatch to the fence.

Keith Miller, according to **Wisden,** *'would have enriched the Golden Age.' Known as 'the Nugget', he was one of the all-time great all-rounders, fast-bowler, big-hitter and hero.*

Norman O'Neill: a marvellously-gifted all-round sportsman who could have made it at golf, baseball or swimming were it not for an even greater talent as a batsman.

Sonny Ramadhin was the ultimate mystery spinner. Reading him was like trying to decipher Sanskrit as 158 Test wickets testify.

Indian all-rounder 'Polly' Umrigar was a penetrative bowler and imperious strokemaker during his country's formative Test years.

Oh the power, the majesty. A bearded Viv Richards in lordly, helmetless mode.

Taking a breather: West Indies' skipper Richie Richardson is down but not out.

was Albert Trott [another Australian] in 1899?' When Fowler confirmed the fact, Miller declared: 'Well, Archie, I'm going to clear it this morning.'

He did not quite make it but the grand old pile wobbled under a sustained bombardment that had some older members thinking they were back in the trenches. Seven times the ball sailed into their serried ranks, many of whom were unsure whether to rise to the batsman or dive under their seats for cover. Most observers agree that the biggest of these 'mortar shells' would have cleared the pavilion had it not clattered into the BBC commentary box which was perched at the top – it had not been there in Trott's day. It was murderous, yes, but magnificent, majestic and *Wisden* called it 'one of the most masterly innings seen for a generation.' *The Times* wrote: 'We were beginning to wonder whether Lord's is big enough to take such terrific hitting,' while Miller, himself, acknowledged: 'Everyone loved it, the ground was packed and it felt great.' Sir Pelham Warner went as far as to say: 'In 60 years I have never seen such hitting.' After a two and a quarter hour innings, seven sixes and 13 fours, Miller was caught in the deep for 185. *The Times* wrote: 'It will be remembered for all time by those who saw it.' The Dominions soon folded to 336 all out, leaving the England XI a target of 357. Hammond made his second hundred of the match but, apart from Davies, had little support and the home side fell 45 runs short when they were all out with just 10 minutes remaining.

Miller had already topped the batting averages for Australia in the Victory Tests and it was during this summer that he began to bowl seriously. 'There was no one else,' is his explanation, 'and I was asked if I would give it a go.' As a fielder, he would think nothing of taking slip catches while doing acrobatics or putting the ball in his pocket and pretending it had gone for four. Indeed, he would have been made for the one-day game – Alan McGilvray maintains that 'he would have been the best ever' – and, with his personality allied to modern marketing, would have been a millionaire in no time. Typically, he has no regrets. 'They're professionals now and they deserve it,' he says. 'Flying across the world in an economy seat, off the plane jet-lagged and straight on to the field . . . I wouldn't want to do that.' No, for Keith Ross Miller, only first-class would do – on Concorde with a glass of champagne in one hand and a copy of the *Sporting Life* in the other.
Result: Dominions won by 45 runs

The Dominions

	First Innings		Second Innings
D.R. Fell c Griffith b Wright	12	b Davies	28
H.S. Craig c Davies b Phillipson	56	c Hammond b Davies	32
J. Pettiford b Davies	1	b Wright	6
K.R. Miller lbw b Hollies	26	c Langridge b Wright	185
M.P. Donnelly c b Hollies	133	b Wright	29
L.N. Constantine c Hollies b Wright	5	c Fishlock b Hollies	40
C.G. Pepper c Hammond b Wright	51	c Robertson b Hollies	1
D.R. Cristofani lbw b Edrich	6	b Wright	5
R.G. Williams lbw b Wright	11	c Hammond b Wright	0
R.S. Ellis b Wright	0	st Griffiths b Hollies	0
C.D. Bremner not out	1	not out	0
Extras (LB 3, W 2)	5	(B 6, LB 8, NB 1)	10
Total	307		336

Bowling: *First Innings* – Phillipson 16-2-40-1; Edrich 9-1-19-1; Wright 30-2-90-5; Davies 22-9-43-1; Hollies 20.2-3-86-2; Langridge 6-1-24-0. *Second Innings* – Phillipson 2-1-1-0; Edrich 3-0-13-0; Hollies 29-8-115-3; Wright 30.1-6-105-5; Davies 13-3-35-2; Langridge 8-0-57-0

England

	First Innings		Second Innings
L.B. Fishlock c Pettiford b Ellis	12	run out	7
J.D. Robertson lbw b Constantine	4	c Fell, b Pettiford	5
James Langridge lbw b Cristofani	28	b Pepper	15
W.I. Phillipson b Pepper	0	run out	14
S.C. Griffith c Bremner b Williams	15	c Pepper b Pettiford	36
W.R. Hammond st Bremner b Pepper	121	st Bremner b Cristofani	102
H. Gimblett c Pettiford b Cristofani	11	b Pepper	30
W.J. Edrich c Pepper b Cristofani	78	c Pepper b Ellis	31
J.G.W. Davies lbw b Pepper	1	b Pepper	56
D.V.P. Wright lbw b Pepper	0	b Cristofani	0
I. Hollies not out	0	not out	0
Extras (B 7, LB 6, W 2, NB 2)	17	(B 6, LB 5, NB 4)	15
Total	287		311

Bowling: *First Innings* – Miller 1-0-2-0; Ellis 4-1-4-1; Williams 22-4-49-1; Cristofani 23-34-82-4; Constantine 15-2-53-1; Pettiford 5-0-23-0; Pepper 18-3-57-4. *Second Innings* – Williams 2-0-11-0; Constantine 6-0-27-0; Pepper 33-13-67-3; Cristofani 21.3-1-64-2; Ellis 2-4-54-1; Pettiford 14-3-45-2; Miller 5-0-28-0.

Norman O'Neill

AUSTRALIA V WEST INDIES

Brisbane, 9, 10, 12, 13, 14 December 1960

Born in Sydney on 19 February 1937, Norman Clifford O'Neill was sickeningly talented as a teenager. Besides being brilliant at golf, tennis and swimming, he was named in the Australian baseball team for the 1956 Olympics. Cricket? After being barred from the Melbourne Games for receiving £6 a day expenses on a tour with New South Wales, he turned down a £2,000 signing-on fee from the New York Yankees – to concentrate on cricket. Well, he was hailed as 'the new Bradman' . . . A sensation in the 1957/8 season, O'Neill amassed 1,005 runs (av. 83.75) including a memorable 233 in 244 minutes against Victoria. In his first Test series against England, he averaged 56.40, was a star in India and then in England, but bowlers eventually sussed that he was a nervous starter and he began to fade. His knees also gave him trouble and in 1967 – just after his 30th birthday – he bowed out. To those who witnessed what Jack Fingleton called his strokes of 'masterly beauty', the memory will never dim and it is a measure of the massive expectation he carried that his early promise was largely unfulfilled – even with a first class average of over 50!

If, as American sportsmen disparagingly claim, 'a draw is like kissing your sister,' just what are we to make of the first Test of the 1960/61 Australia-West Indies series at the Gabba? Gloriously upholding the pledges of rival captains Richie Benaud and Frank Worrell to play positively, it is universally acclaimed as the greatest Test of all time. Yet when Joe Solomon ran out Ian Meckiff with one ball remaining, an unimaginable climax left thousands of people wondering who had won – including several players on both sides!

Only a sport with the eccentric complexities of cricket could have contrived a tie after five days of fluctuating drama that even a flannelled Hitchcock would have hesitated to script. 'It was a marvellous game throughout but sitting in the changing room at the end not knowing who had won was what I remember most,' says O'Neill. 'There was just total confusion and Ian Meckiff was inconsolable – he was sure we had lost.' The crowd poured on to the pitch and many West Indians were dancing with joy, sure they had won. There was pandemonium: umpires and scorers conferred, players and spectators held their breath, runs were counted. And then it was announced: 'It's a tie, it's a tie.' Meckiff recalls: 'I suddenly felt 100 per cent better.' Rohan Kanhai asked: 'Has there ever been such drama?' Everywhere there was chaos and congratulations, and

131

as *both* sides celebrated, everyone agreed: 'No one deserved to lose.' Indeed, Sir Don Bradman said: 'It was the greatest Test of all time.'

Cricket needed it. Interest in the game was flagging in Australia after Burke and Bailey had bored the pants off everyone during the previous Ashes series. Then there were rows about chucking and dragging, while the Australian team, itself, was in the doldrums. So the first Test, the 500th in all, began before an understandably small crowd in Brisbane. Those who *did* bother to go on the first day were treated to a masterpiece. 'The game got off to a cracking start,' recalls O'Neill, 'with Gary Sobers making a brilliant 132 [in 174 minutes].' After the West Indies had lost three wickets for 65 to Alan Davidson, Sobers, then aged 24, savaged the bowling to help his team to a healthy 359 for seven at stumps. The Australian press labelled it a 'golden' innings, one of the greatest ever played. Even Benaud thought it 'amazing' while Worrell rated it 'Sobers' best'. The West Indies eventually reached 453 all out, Davidson taking five for 135.

The scene was set for a response in kind and O'Neill was considered the Australian batsman most capable of matching the Caribbean cut-and-thrust. Broad-shouldered and just over six feet, his strokes had a majestic grandeur that earned accolades from the greats. Bill O'Reilly rated him 'the second Bradman — a blind man can see it,' while Wally Hammond thought he was 'the most brilliant post-War batsman.' Ted Dexter even filmed his square cut in slow motion, calling the stroke 'an elephant-gun to the peashooter of lesser players.' But on this occasion, O'Neill curbed his natural ebullience and dropped anchor. 'It was vital that we got up to their total,' recalls the New South Welshman. 'In spite of all the talk of attractive cricket, both captains badly wanted to win the first Test.' Dropped at 47 and 54, O'Neill dug in but no partner was able to stay with him for long. 'People kept getting out which upset my momentum,' he recalls. 'And big Wes [Hall] was sending 'em down at my ribs . . . But we were pretty satisfied to be 52 in front.' O'Neill, forcing the pace as wickets fell, eventually skied Hall into the hands of Valentine for 181, hitting 22 fours in a six and a half hour stay. It was his highest Test score in a total of 505 and only Simpson (92) and McDonald (57) of the other batsmen topped fifty.

Frank Worrell, Kanhai and Solomon steadied the West Indies' second innings in the face of fiery fast bowling from Davidson, whose seven for 93 gave him 12 wickets in the match. But a total of 284 did not look enough until Australia lost half their side for 57 runs in the second innings. The target of 233 in 310 minutes had looked decidedly attainable but once Hall had worked himself up, the home side was tottering and defeat looked imminent. Coming in at seven for two, O'Neill had steered them past 50 but perished attempting another square cut off Hall. Ken 'Slasher' Mackay stayed 78 minutes scoring 28 before playing on (92 for six), which brought Benaud in to join Davidson. In a ferocious, fighting performance, the magnificent Hall had taken four of the wickets and, in the opinion of several hundred spectators who headed for the exits, would rip through the Australian tail. To the eternal regret of the departees, Davidson and Benaud decided otherwise.

Batting like heroes, running like hares, the pair took on the West Indies attack. Davidson, who had a stupendous match, became the first player to score 100 runs and take 10 wickets in a Test. Thrillingly, in the face of a bumper barrage from Hall, the pair raced towards the target, splicing attacking strokes with judicious defence, Davidson unforgettably hooking the fast bowler for four off a ball seemingly destined for his temple! The fielding fell apart in the face of the Australian counter-attack and only the competitiveness of Hall and calmness of Worrell held the visitors together. With 12 minutes remaining, Australia wanted seven runs for victory and had four wickets in hand. No one left the ground now as they waited for the formality of a home victory.

Off the fourth ball of the penultimate over, bowled by Sobers, Davidson attempted one single too many and was run out by a direct throw from Solomon. He and Benaud had put on 134 to bring Australia to within seven runs of the target. The incoming Wally Grout scampered for a single off the seventh ball and then faced Hall, steaming in for the fateful final over. Australia were 227 for seven. The clock above the scoreboard showed 5.55 p.m. This is how the epic events unfolded.

First ball: Grout, hit on the pad, somehow scrambles a leg bye – 228 for seven.

Second ball: a bouncer which Benaud tries to hook. He edges and is caught behind. It is 228 for eight. Five runs wanted, six balls left, and two wickets in hand.

Third ball: Hall, long, loping strides full of menace, arms whirling, storms in. Ian Meckiff manages to fend it to safety.

Fourth ball: A searing, lifting delivery flies past Meckiff to the 'keeper. Grout races for an amazing bye. Four balls left, four runs needed.

Fifth ball: Grout skies it on the leg side. It's Kanhai's catch but Hall and a posse of fielders converge. The batsmen cross. Hall reaches for the catch . . . and drops it. A single. 230 for eight.

Sixth ball: Meckiff swings high to square leg. The batsmen cross twice as the ball nears the boundary. But as Grout belts for the third, Hunte's arrow-like throw from the fence lands in the 'keeper's gloves. Grout dives . . . but doesn't make it – by inches. 232 for nine. The scores level.

Seventh ball: Kline, weakened by the flu, pushes to leg and both batsmen set of instinctively for the winning run. Meckiff charges down to the keeper's end but Solomon gathers coolly and, with one stump to aim out, throws down the wicket. Meckiff is out of his ground and the first Test match in 500 ends in a tie!

Result: Match tied

West Indies

C.C. Hunte c Benaud b Davidson	24	c Simpson b Mackay	39
C.W. Smith c Grout b Davidson	7	c O'Neill b Davidson	6
R.B. Kanhai c Grout b Davidson	15	c Grout b Davidson	54
G.S. Sobers c Kline b Meckiff	132	b Davidson	14
*F.M.M. Worrell c Grout b Davidson	65	c Grout b Davidson	65
J.S. Solomon hit wkt b Simpson	65	lbw b Simpson	47
P.D. Lashley c Grout b Kline	19	b Davidson	0
†F.C.M. Alexander c Davidson b Kline	60	b Benaud	5
S. Ramadhin c Harvey b Davidson	12	c Harvey b Simpson	6
W.W. Hall st Grout b Kline	50	b Davidson	18
A.L. Valentine not out	0	not out	7
Extras (LB 3, W 1)	4	(B 14, LB 7, W 2)	23

1/23 2/42 3/65 4/239 5/243 6/283   453
7/347 8/366 9/452

1/13 2/88 3/114 4/127   284
5/210 6/210 7/241 8/250
9/253

Bowling: *First Innings* – Davidson 30-2-135-5; Meckiff 18-0-129-1; Mackay 3-0-15-0; Benaud 24-3-93-0; Simpson 8-0-25-1; Kline 17.6-6-52-3. *Second Innings* – Davidson 24. 6-4-87-6; Meckiff 4-1-19-0; Benaud 31-6-69-1; Mackay 21-7-52-1; Kline 4-0-14-0; Simpson 7-2-18-2; O'Neill 1-0-2-0.

Australia

C.C. McDonald c Hunte b Sobers	57	b Worrell	16
R.B. Simpson b Ramadhin	92	c sub (L. R. Gibbs) b Hall	0
R.N. Harvey b Valentine	15	c Sobers b Hall	5
N.C. O'Neill c Valentine b Hall	181	c Alexander b Hall	26
L.E. Flavell run out	45	c Solomon b Hall	7
K.D. Mackay b Sobers	35	b Ramadhin	28
A.K. Davidson c Alexander b Hall	44	run out	80
*R. Benaud lbw b Hall	10	c Alexander b Hall	52
†A.T.W. Grout lbw b Hall	4	run out	2
I. Meckiff run out	4	run out	2
L.F. Kline not out	3	not out	0
Extras (B 2, LB 8, NB 4, W 1)	15	(B 2, LB 9, NB 3)	14

1/84 2/138 3/194 4/278 5/381   505
6/469 7/484 8/489 9/496

1/1 2/7 3/49 4/49 5/57   232
6/92 7/226 8/228 9/232

Bowling: *First Innings* – Hall 29.3-1-140-4; Worrell 30-0-93-0; Sobers 32-0-115-2; Valentine 24-6-82-1; Ramadhin 15-1-60-1. *Second Innings* – Hall 17.7-3-63-5; Worrell 16-3-41-1; Sobers 8-0-30-0; Valentine 10-4-27-0; Ramadhin 17-3-57-1.

Umpires: C. J. Egar and C. Hoy

Graeme Pollock

Trent Bridge, 5, 6, 7, 9 August 1965

Born in Durban on 27 February 1944, Robert Graeme Pollock's only rival as the best left-hander of all time is Sir Garfield Sobers, yet his mother tried to make him bat right-handed when he was three. The second son of a Scottish-born newspaper editor, who kept wicket for Orange Free State, Graeme learned the game in furious backyard 'tests' with brother Peter. The young Graeme was also a quick bowler, taking 10 for 25 and scoring 117 not out in the same school match. He was nine years old. Peter went on to open the bowling for South Africa but Graeme turned to leg-spin. And carried on batting. After excelling in all sports at high school, he became the youngest Currie Cup player at 16 and a year later was 'Cricketer of the Year'. At 19 he was the youngest South African to score a first-class double century and notched three Test centuries before he was 21. His hero was Neil Harvey, whom he had watched in his home town of Port Elizabeth, but the strapping 6'2" South African looked even better. After stunning Australia in 1963/64, he helped to win the 1965 series in England but took an even greater liking to Aussie bowlers, slamming a double century off the 1966/67 Australians and a monumental 274 in 1969/70. Only Sir Donald Bradman had a better Test average when the sports boycott nipped his career in the bud. Pollock batted on, of course, and was still murdering attacks in the Currie Cup, with the International Cavaliers and in World Series cricket in Australia. He retired at 43 and even at that age was hitting notes good enough to give him a first-class average in the mid-fifties. Test cricket now knows what music lost when Mozart died aged 34.

Like all legends, Pollock had a huge basket of riches from which to choose his 'greatest game'. Among the leading candidates were his 274 off Bill Lawry's men in Durban; his 175 in Adelaide when he shared a South African all-wicket record partnership of 341 with Eddie Barlow (while still in his teens); his 209 against Bobby Simpson's side; 137 and 77 not out off England on his home patch at Port Elizabeth; or the 127 not out in Perth when Sir Donald Bradman told him: 'If you ever score a century like that again, I hope I'm there to see it.' 'But I go for Trent Bridge,' he says, 'for a number of reasons. It was my first Test 100 in England, the wicket was not conducive to stroke-play and it was a low-scoring match. We also won the Test and went on to win the series, my brother Peter took 10 wickets in the match and it was my mother's birthday!' Pollock's own contribution was a mere 125 in the first innings and 59 in the second. It was a far cry from the golden summers of the southern hemisphere: the sky was grey, the ground less than full, but to have witnessed Graeme Pollock bat that day was to have glimpsed a god.

The South Africans had not arrived in England until mid-June, sharing a split summer with New Zealand, and they had lost to Derbyshire in their first first-class match. England had won the winter's five-Test series on the Veldt 1-0 and the first Test at Lord's was drawn. There had been whispers about the batting of Pollock but nothing prepared England or the Nottingham crowd for what was to come when the 21-year-old strode to the middle with South Africa perilously placed at 16 for two. That old master of swing, Tom Cartwright, included for his only Test of the summer, had removed Lance and Lindsay, and was quite unplayable from the Pavilion End. He drew gasps from the members as the ball veered dramatically, giving Parks a thorough examination behind the stumps. The batsmen, brought up on the burnt backyards of the Cape, could hardly lay a bat on him. The carnage continued as Barlow, Bland and then Bacher followed. Shortly after lunch, South Africa were 80 for five. But the lunchtime chatter was as much about the comfort and surety of touch displayed by Pollock as it was about the swing of Cartwright. Tall, broad-shouldered, with his feet wide apart, his bottom hand low on the handle, the young South African did not have the most elegant stance. Nor did he have a reputation for grafting. He began by treating Cartwright with respect but was in no trouble, picking the balls to hit, which he did with consummate ease. At the interval, he had reached 34 not out. It was a mere appetiser.

The crowd were soon gasping again but not at the prodigious swing of the ball: now it was the sheer majesty of the batting. Launching into cover drives off front and back foot, Pollock was suddenly contemptuous of even Cartwright, piercing the field at will, rattling the pickets with an awesome, effortless power. Only his skipper, van der Merwe, offered any support as the youngster raced to his 100 with a mastery that was being compared favourably to Frank Woolley. E. W. Swanton wrote: 'An innings was played here today by Graeme Pollock which in point of style and power, of ease and beauty of execution, is fit to rank with anything in the annals of the game.' *The Times* suggested that 'not since McCabe made 232 on this same ground in 1938 has a batsman held such sway over an England attack', adding, 'It is the sure sign of greatness to stand alone as Pollock did. He held dominion where others foundered.'

Such was his command that he might have reached his double century by tea had not Cartwright finally found the edge but he was surprised to be given out when Cowdrey pouched him at slip. The crowd stood as one to salute a genius, sad to a man that it had ended. He had smote 125 in two hours and 20 minutes, the last 91 out of 102 in 70 minutes! He had hit 21 fours and the buzz around the ground lasted the season. Pollock was out at 178 and the tail managed to wag for a final total of 269. That looked a lot more after 35 minutes of the England innings, Boycott and Barrington both falling to Peter Pollock. Never have two brothers so dominated a day's play. But neither of them had finished yet.

Night-watchman Titmus helped Barber to put on 55 for England's third wicket the next morning, but after that only Cowdrey, with a patient 105, looked anywhere near comfortable. When skipper Mike Smith was with him, Cowdrey looked as if he might shepherd England to a first innings lead but Peter Pollock took the new ball to put paid to that and complete a remarkable fraternal mastery. In the home side's 240, he had taken five for 53 off 23 overs of sustained hostility. The intriguing match took another turn when South Africa again made a bad start. They were reduced to 35 for two when Pollock strode to the crease for the second time. Crucially, however, his was not a lone hand this time, Barlow (76) giving pugnacious support and, perhaps just as vitally, Cartwright was taking no further part having broken his right thumb stopping a hard return in the first innings. Pollock's 59 was not quite as memorable as his first innings blitz but ensured that England would have to bat better in the second innings to win. And when Bacher chipped in with a doughty 67, a fourth-innings target of over 300 already looked beyond them.

By Saturday night, England had again subsided to Peter Pollock's initial onslaught and the use of two night-watchmen meant that the batsmen would always be up against it. A weekend 10 for two was soon 10 for three and 41 for five, but after Smith (24) had ensured against a total rout, Parfitt and Parks rallied. Their spirited eighth-wicket stand of 97 even conjured hopes of the impossible but Pollock senior would not be denied a second five-wicket haul and a famous South African victory. For England it was Smith's first defeat in 15 Tests as skipper but the final word must be on Graeme Pollock. Sir Donald Bradman said of him: 'It is one of the great tragedies of sporting history that cricket lovers outside South Africa were denied the opportunity of watching such a marvellous player during a period when he undoubtedly would have been at the height of his powers.' Those at Trent Bridge that first day know how lucky they were.

Result: South Africa won by 94 runs

South Africa

Batsman	First Innings	Score	Second Innings	Score
E.J. Barlow	c Cowdrey b Cartwright	19	b Titmus	76
H. Lance	lbw b Cartwright	7	c Barber b Snow	0
†J. D. Lindsay	c Parks b Cartwright	0	c Cowdrey b Larter	9
R.G. Pollock	c Cowdrey b Cartwright	125	c Titmus b Larter	59
K.C. Bland	st Parks b Titmus	1	b Snow	10
A. Bacher	b Snow	12	lbw b Larter	67
*P.L. van der Merwe	run out	38	c Parfitt b Larter	4
R. Dumbrill	c Parfitt b Cartwright	30	b Snow	13
J.T. Botten	c Parks b Larter	10	b Larter	18
P.M. Pollock	c Larter b Cartwright	15	not out	12
A.H. McKinnon	not out	8	b Titmus	9
Extras	(LB4)	4	B4, LB5, NB3	12
		269		**289**

1/16 2/16 3/42 4/43 5/80 6/178 7/221 8/242 9/252

1/2 2/35 3/134 4/193 5/228 6/232 7/243 8/265 9/269

Bowling: *First Innings* – Larter 17-6-25-1; Snow 22-6-63-1; Cartwright 31.3-9-94-6; Titmus 22-8-44-1; Barber 9-3-39-0. *Second Innings* – Larter 29-7-68-5; Snow 33-6-83-3; Titmus 19.4-5-46-2; Boycott 26-10-60-0; Barber 3-0-20-0.

England

Batsman	First Innings	Score	Second Innings	Score
G. Boycott	c Lance b P. M. Pollock	0	b McKinnon	16
R.W. Barber	b Bacher b Dumbrill	41	c Lindsay b P.M. Pollock	1
K. F. Barrington	b P.M. Pollock	1	c Lindsay b P.M. Pollock	1
F.J. Titmus	c R. G. Pollock b McKinnon	20	c Lindsay b McKinnon	4
M.C. Cowdrey	c Lindsay b Botten	105	st Lindsay b McKinnon	20
P.H. Parfitt	c Dumbrill b P.M. Pollock	18	b P.M. Pollock	86
*M.J.K. Smith	b P.M. Pollock	32	lbw b R.G. Pollock	24
†J. M. Parks	c and b Botten	6	not out	44
J.A. Snow	run out	3	b Botten	0
J.D.F. Larter	b P. M. Pollock	2	c van der Merwe b P.M. Pollock	10
T.W. Cartwright	not out	1	lbw b P.M. Pollock	0
Extras	(B 1, LB 3, W 1, NB 6)	11	(LB 5, W 2, NB 11)	18
		240		**224**

1/0 2/8 3/63 4/67 5/133 6/225 7/229 8/236 9/238

1/1 2/10 3/10 4/13 5/41 6/59 7/114 8/207 9/207

Bowling: *First Innings* – P.M. Pollock 23.5-8-53-5; Botten 23-5-60-2; McKinnon 28-11-54-1; Dumbrill 18-3-60-1; R.G. Pollock 1-0-2-0. *Second Innings* – P.M. Pollock 24-15-34-5; Botten 19-5-58-1; McKinnon 27-12-50-3; Dumbrill 16-4-40-0; Barlow 11-1-20-0; R. G. Pollock 5-2-4-1.

Umpires: C.S. Elliott and J.F. Crapp

Sonny Ramadhin

ENGLAND V WEST INDIES

Lord's, 24, 26, 27, 28 & 29 June, 1950

Born in Esperance Village, Trinidad, on 1 May, 1929, Sonny Ramadhin brought the magic of the East to West Indian cricket. When chosen for the 1950 tour to England, he was as big a mystery to his teammates as he would be to Hutton, Compton & Co. An orphan, he had played in just two first-class matches before becoming the first East Indian to play for the West Indies. In his book, Days at the Cricket, *John Arlott wrote: 'Ramadhin and Valentine were probably the greatest gamble that any touring side had ever taken for a Test series in England.' Just 5'4" tall, Ramadhin trotted in gently and bowled out of the back of his hand, his arms a loose, white windmill of buttoned-down sleeves, his maroon cap often still on his head. Although he looked more like a leg-spinner, he bowled mostly off-spinners with leggies and quicker balls thrown in. Reading him was akin to deciphering Sanskrit, with straight balls leaving even the most literate of campaigners baffled. In all, he took 158 Test wickets but was never the same force after May and Cowdrey had blunted him with their epic stand of 411 at Edgbaston in 1957. After years in the Lancashire Leagues, he represented the county with some success in the 1960s.*

'Facing Ramadhin,' a Derbyshire batsman once claimed, 'was like trying to face a boonch of confetti.' And so it seemed when the little man was unleashed on England's unsuspecting batsmen in the summer of 1950. He and Jamaica's slow-left-armer Alf Valentine made their first Test appearances at Old Trafford and even though Valentine took 11 wickets in the match (including eight in the first innings) and Ramadhin four, England had not perceived the looming threat. A West Indian batting collapse enabled the home side to win by 202 runs – a margin convincing enough to shrug off the batsmen's dyslexia against both the spinners. Indeed, it was all Greek to the groping England batsmen as Ramadhin beat the bat time and again but only ended with four for 167 – match figures so cruel as to be sadistic. So it was on to Lord's with England not heeding the warnings and confident that the injured Compton, Simpson and Bailey would not be missed. Hutton was to resume his opening partnership with Washbrook, Bedser would take the new ball and Parkhouse came into the middle order for his first Test. The crowd was 12 deep on the grass when King George VI was presented to the teams a quarter of an hour before the start and the gates closed on some 30,000. Goddard won the toss and batted; Ramadhin's pulse raced but he would have to wait to weave his magic. 'It was every schoolboy's dream to play at Lord's,' he says, 'and for me it was a very special occasion, being my first tour and me being so inexperienced. It was also quite daunting, West Indies having never won there.'

On a pitch that R. C. Robertson-Glasgow compared to 'a muscular Philistine, hard underneath and soft on top,' Rae and Stollmeyer opened circumspectly, making 37 before Wardle, with his first ball in a Test in England, trapped Stollmeyer lbw. The arrival of Worrell, the first of the three W.s, raised the tempo while Rae was the perfect foil to this middle-order powerhouse. Both Worrell (whose innings Robertson-Glasgow described as 'fierce noon without dawn') and Weekes made brilliant half-centuries, Rae a careful 106. But with Bedser at his niggardly best, the visitors had to be content with 320 for seven at the close. It was not quite total command and when England removed the tail for just six more runs on the second morning, there were those who felt it was perhaps not quite enough. They were sure it wasn't when Hutton and Washbrook had put on 62 for the first wicket, but those watching closely disagreed. The trouble for England was that neither batsman had a clue which way the ball was turning and both were soon out chasing wide ones outside the off-stump. Hutton and Washbrook both stumped? It hardly seems credible and if *they* were frustrated, what chance the rest?

Edrich eschewed all attacking strokes for the soft-handed dab while the rest of the front-line batsmen were simply mesmerised. Skipper Norman Yardley later admitted that the damage was done in the dressing room where incoming batsmen watched in bewilderment. They were no wiser when they batted. Doggart fell lbw sweeping, Parkhouse 'slogged' to a debut duck and then Edrich finally succumbed for just eight in 90 befuddled minutes. Only Wardle's lusty blows threatened to break the spell but England were all out for 151, their lowest total against the West Indies. Ramadhin finished with five for 66, Valentine four for 48 and the first verse of the Cricket Calypso had been written.

As 'those little pals of mine' rested their spinning fingers, it was the turn of that genial giant Clyde 'Jersey Joe' Walcott to put the game beyond England's reach. In spite of the heroic endeavours of Roly Jenkins who single-handedly reduced the visitors to 146 for four, the burly wicket-keeper batsman smashed 168 not out with such power that even his defensive strokes caused stinging hands. His boundaries? Well, Old Father Time was supposed to have been relieved at the declaration . . . It came at 425 for six after Walcott and Gomez had plundered a record sixth-wicket stand of 211. When Bedser had Gomez caught for 70, Goddard asked England to score 601 to win. More correctly, he gave them a day and a half to decipher the hieroglyphics of his spinners.

At the end of the fourth day, England were making a fist of it at 218 for four with the indefatigable Washbrook still in residence. Hutton had perished ignominiously again, offering neither bat nor pad to Valentine's arm ball and Edrich and Doggart had both gone cheaply to Ramadhin for the second time in the match. Parkhouse had batted well for 48 before smashing a Valentine full toss to Goddard at silly mid-off in the final over. According to Alex Bannister in the *Daily Mail,* the pair had done much to erase the blot of the first innings – and to destroy the myth that

'Ramadhin is unplayable.' But had they?

When Washbrook was bowled by Valentine without adding to his overnight 114, any glimmer the home side had of pulling off a victory that would have required history's highest fourth innings total – by some 200 – disappeared. Apart from Wardle's long handle, it was all fairly painless to Goddard's men, the last six wickets crashing for 46 runs, with Ramadhin taking six for 86, Valentine three for 79. The Trinidadian had sent down a staggering 72 overs, 46 of which were maidens. Destroying the myth? By their own admission, England's batsmen hadn't the faintest – and it would stay that way until 1957. Trevor Bailey acknowledged: 'Our failure to play Ramadhin and Valentine was our downfall. We never really got it right during that series.' Ramadhin says: 'That was the greatest time of my career. It was a dream come true to take 11 wickets on the most famous ground in cricket. Frank Worrell was a great help to me as he kept stressing that I should be patient, that the wickets would come.'

E. W. Swanton observed: 'Ramadhin bowled magnificently, using the arts and subtleties of a spinner in a way extraordinary in one who had had not a scrap of experience before this tour.' The most fitting tribute was that thousands of West Indians burst on to the hallowed turf and brought a touch of the Caribbean to St John's Wood with the immortal calypso:

> Cricket, lovely cricket,
> At Lord's where I saw it.
> Yardley tried his best,
> But West Indies won the Test,
> With those little pals of mine,
> Ramadhin and Valentine.

Result: West Indies won by 326 runs

West Indies

A.F. Rae c&b Jenkins	106	b Jenkins	24
J.B. Stollmeyer lbw b Wardle	20	b Jenkins	30
F.M. Worrell b Bedser	52	c Doggart b Jenkins	45
E. Weekes b Bedser	63	run out	63
C.L. Walcott st Evans b Jenkins	14	not out	168
G.E. Gomez st Evans b Jenkins	1	c Edrich b Bedser	70
R.J. Christiani b Bedser	33	not out	5
J.D. Goddard b Wardle	14	c Evans b Jenkins	11
P.E. Jones c Evans b Jenkins	0		
S. Ramadhin not out	1		
A. Valentine c Hutton b Jenkins	5		
Extras (B 10, LB 5, W 1, NB 1)	17	(LB 8, NB 1)	9

1/37 2/128 3/233 4/262 5/273   326   1/48 2/75   (6 wkts dec.) 425
6/274 7/320 8/320 9/320   3/108 4/146 5/199 6/410

Bowling: *First Innings* – Bedser 40-14-60-3; Edrich 16-4-30-0; Jenkins 35.2-6-116-5; Wardle 17-6-46-2; Berry 19-7-45-0; Yardley 4-1-12-0. *Second Innings* – Bedser 44-16-80-1; Edrich 13-2-37-0; Jenkins 59-13-174-4; Wardle 30-10-58-0; Berry 32-15-67-0.

England

Hutton st Walcott b Valentine	35	b Valentine	10
Washbrook st Walcott b Ramadhin	36	b Ramadhin	114
W.J. Edrich c Walcott b Ramadhin	8	c Jones b Ramadhin	8
G.H.G. Doggart lbw b Ramadhin	0	b Ramadhin	25
Parkhouse b Valentine	0	c Goddard b Valentine	48
N.W.D. Yardley b Valentine	16	c Weekes b Valentine	19
Evans b Ramadhin	8	c Rae b Ramadhin	2
Jenkins c Walcott b Valentine	4	b Ramadhin	4
Wardle not out	33	lbw b Worrell	21
Bedser b Ramadhin	5	b Ramadhin	0
Berry c Goddard b Jones	2	not out	0
Extras (B 2, LB 1, W 1)	4	(B 16, LB 7)	23
1/62 2/74 3/74 4/75 5/86	151	1/28 2/57 3/140 4/218	274
6/102 7/110 8/113 9/122		5/228 6/238 7/245 8/258	
		9/258	

Bowling: *First Innings* – Jones 8.4-2-13-1; Worrell 10-4-20-0; Valentine 45-28-48-4; Ramadhin 43-27-66-5. *Second Innings* – Jones 7-1-22-0; Worrell 22.3-9-39-1; Valentine 71-47-79-3; Ramadhin 72-43-86-6; Gomez 13-1-25-0; Goddard 6-6-0-0.

Derek Randall

Sydney, 6, 7, 8, 10, 11 January 1979

Born in Retford on 24 February 1951, Derek Randall made his debut for Nottinghamshire in 1972 and played for the county until his retirement in 1993. During that time he was rarely over-burdened with responsibility – 'I was vice-captain for about five minutes but I failed to deliver one of Clive Rice's messages and I lost the job.' A spectator's delight whether batting in his idiosyncratic style or fielding in the deep. His 174 in the Centenary Test made him an automatic choice as one of Wisden's *Five Cricketers of the Year in 1978. He played 47 Tests, but his apparent frailty and nervousness meant that he was often the first to be dropped after a disappointing English performance. In 1994 he played for Suffolk in the Minor Counties competition. He was probably not destined for the first class umpires' list.*

We all treasure that which is elusive, which is maybe why Derek Randall did not plump for the obvious choice, the Centenary Test in Melbourne, where he produced an innings of sublime, yet typical flamboyance. Instead, he chose a Test in which he displayed distinctly unRandall-like qualities – endurance, dogged concentration and self-denial. It was the fourth Test at Sydney in January 1979.

Randall retired from first class cricket in 1993, at the age of 42, to much mourning. The unwitting clown prince of modern cricket was finally compelled to move to a smaller circus alongside Suffolk's minor county cricketers. With a warm chuckle we remember him as much for his somersaults as the concrete statistics of 28,000 runs and 47 Test appearances. This is not really fair, but hardly surprising.

For Randall's career did not always invite sober analysis. After all, this was the man, who on his debut for England overseas, stole a policeman's helmet in Poona and strutted around the boundary like a flannelled Charlie Chaplin. In Australia – where Rod Marsh had to remind him that 'this is not a garden party' as Randall instigated a conversation upon arrival at the crease – he responded to being hit on the head by Dennis Lillee by saying 'there's no point hitting me there, mate; there's nothing in it.' And only Randall could appear in an Adelaide bar late at night, wrapped in nothing but a towel, having locked himself out of his room with the bath running. He was a little more calculating at the crease, though still prone to moments of manic self-destruction, whether running between the wickets (he ran fast but sometimes in the wrong direction) or suddenly advancing down the pitch to the opposition's fastest bowler.

Randall announced himself as an international cricketer at the Centenary Test in 1977. This was his fifth appearance for England, but until then his top score was a paltry 37. Amid all the hullabaloo at Melbourne, Randall was more concerned about securing his Test place than joining in the revelry. He recalls: 'While the others were at cocktail parties, meeting the likes of Bradman and Larwood, I remember walking around Fitzroy Gardens (just outside the M.C.G.) for two hours and looking at those squirrel things (possums).'

His confrontation with Lillee in Melbourne was enthralling. He contrived numerous responses to the West Australian's numerous bouncers. He 'tennis-batted' one to the mid-wicket boundary; he ducked another and then rose to his full height, doffed his cap and bowed politely. No-one had ever done that to Lillee before. Another bouncer knocked Randall down, which prompted him to perform a spontaneous reverse roll. This was an innings which mesmerised two nations and ensured that the Centenary Test would be remembered for another 100 years. Yet this was not the game of his life. It must have been an interesting match at Sydney.

When Randall returned to Australia in 1978/9 with Brearley's team, he had the rare luxury of a guaranteed place in the side. Australia had been severely 'Packered' so there was no repeat of his duel with Lillee. Their team was desperately inexperienced and at time naïvely captained by Graham Yallop and with hindsight England's success looks too straight-forward to be memorable. England had won the first two Tests; at Brisbane – Randall was Man of the Match after hitting two 70s in a low scoring game – and at Perth. But Australia, inspired by the pace bowling of Rodney Hogg, had fought back to win in Melbourne. After two days of the Sydney Test, Australia had a first innings lead of 142 and looked certain to square the series.

In their first innings England had been bundled out for 152 with Hogg's partner, Alan Hurst, taking five wickets. Australia had responded with 294. With Willis, Gower and Botham suffering from a combination of a virus infection and heat exhaustion, the outlook was bleak. When Boycott was lbw to Hogg's first delivery in the second innings – 'he was none too happy with the decision,' recalls Randall – it was desperate.

Randall had been out for a duck in the first innings, caught by Wood at square leg, attempting to hook, the second time in the series that he had been dismissed in this way. At a Saturday team meeting Randall remembers receiving a 'mighty bollocking' from his captain for selling his wicket so cheaply. This time under the wary eye of Brearley at the other end, Randall avoided the bouncers, shunning the hook shot – 'I was determined not to do anything daft.'

Together they added 111. Randall liked batting with Brearley – 'he was a good runner and a steadying influence' – and as in the Centenary Test they retained their concentration by setting manageable targets, dividing each session into 15 minute segments. This ploy once led to the memor-able exhortation 'Stick at it, Brears, in 10 minutes, it will be 15 minutes to tea.' Typical Randall – undisputed logic expressed in scatter-brained form.

Randall remembers the Australians becoming increasingly impatient and frustrated. 'The match was played in searing heat; it was 20 degrees hotter than in the Centenary Test. At one point a television cameraman fell off his perch with sunstroke and the heat drained the Aussies in the middle as well. I remember not bothering with much practice on the fourth day so I could conserve my energy. The Aussies began to panic a bit; they knew they had to win this game and they over-attacked. The ball was beginning to turn sharply, but they only had one specialist spinner, Jim Higgs (the leg spinner, who bowled 59.6 eight ball overs). He grew impatient and started bowling around the wicket. I swept him a few times but mostly I just concentrated on keeping him out.'

In the end Randall batted 589 minutes for his 150, hitting just 13 boundaries and three of those were in the space of four deliveries from Rodney Hogg, armed with the second new ball. When Higgs finally wrapped up the English tail, Australia were left to score 205 in 265 minutes. A superlative opening spell from Mike Hendrick put them on the defensive, before the two spinners, Miller and Emburey, completed a remarkable victory, which ensured that the Ashes stayed with England. Randall, the barnacle, had saved them.

Result: England won by 93 runs

England

G. Boycott c Border b Hurst	8	lbw b Hogg	0
*J. M. Brearley b Hogg	17	b Border	53
D.W. Randall c Wood b Hurst	0	lbw b Hogg	150
G.A. Gooch c Toohey b Higgs	18	c Wood b Higgs	22
D.I. Gower c Maclean b Hurst	7	c Maclean b Hogg	34
I.T. Botham c Yallop b Hogg	59	c Wood b Higgs	6
G. Miller c Maclean b Hurst	4	lbw b Hogg	17
†R. W. Taylor c Border b Higgs	10	not out	21
J.E. Emburey c Wood b Higgs	0	c Darling b Higgs	14
R.G.D. Willis not out	7	c Toohey b Higgs	0
M. Hendrick b Hurst	10	c Toohey b Higgs	7
Extras (B 1, LB 1, W 2, NB 8)	12	(B 5, LB 3, NB 14)	22
1/18 2/18 3/35 4/51 5/66	152	1/0 2/111 3/169 4/237	346
6/70 7/94 8/98 9/141		5/267 6/292 7/307 8/334	
		9/346	

Bowling: *First Innings* – Hogg 11-3-36-2; Dymock 13-1-34-0; Hurst 10.6-2-28-5; Higgs 18-4-42-3. *Second Innings* – Hogg 28-10-67-4; Dymock 17-4-35-0; Hurst 19-3-43-0; Higgs 59.6-15-148-5; Border 23-11-31-1.

Australia

	First Innings		Second Innings	
G.M. Wood	b Willis	0	run out	27
W.M. Darling	c Botham b Miller	91	c Gooch b Hendrick	13
K.J. Hughes	c Emburey b Willis	48	c Emburey b Miller	15
*G.N. Yallop	c Botham b Hendrick	44	c&b Hendrick	1
P.M. Toohey	c Gooch b Botham	1	b Miller	5
A.R. Border	not out	60	not out	45
†J.A. Maclean	lbw b Emburey	12	c Botham b Miller	0
R.M. Hogg	run out	6	c Botham b Emburey	0
G. Dymock	b Botham	5	b Emburey	5
J.D. Higgs	c Botham b Hendrick	11	lbw b Emburey	3
A.G. Hurst	run out	0	b Emburey	0
	Extras (B 2, LB 3, NB 11)	16	(LB 1, NB 1)	2
	1/2 2/126 3/178 4/179 5/210	**294**	1/38 2/44 3/45 4/59	**111**
	6/235 7/245 8/276 9/290		5/74 6/76 7/85 8/85 9/105	

Bowling: *First Innings* – Willis 9-2-33-2; Botham 28-3-87-2; Hendrick 24-4-50-2; Miller 13-2-37-1; Emburey 29-10-57-1. *Second Innings* – Willis 2-0-8-0; Hendrick 10-3-17-2; Miller 20-7-38-3; Emburey 17.2-2-46-4.

Clive Rice

INDIA V SOUTH AFRICA

Calcutta, 11 November 1991

Born in Johannesburg on 23 July 1949, Clive Edward Butler Rice has a strong case for being the finest cricket never to play in a Test match. Of all the South Africans to suffer truncated careers because of the apartheid-induced sports boycott, Rice was the worst casualty. Not only was he one of the world's finest all-rounders of his day, when South Africa was welcomed back into the fold and the time came for him to sample the highest form of international competition, the cup was cruelly snatched from his lips. Captain against the rebel tourists of the 1980s and still at the helm for the historic visit to India in 1991, Rice was harshly sacked from the post before an official Test was played. So a lengthy spell leading Nottinghamshire to their most successful era since Larwood and Voce was Rice's main claim to fame. A top-order batsman, hostile fast bowler in his early days, fine slip and uncompromising captain, he took Notts to two County Championship pennants and the NatWest Trophy. With Richard Hadlee, he formed the most devastating double act in the English game. He was just as indispensable in his 20 years at Transvaal.

They moved with indecent haste but who could blame them? South African sports officials, locked in a time warp and with around two decades of international competition denied to them, picked up the phone as soon as F. W. de Klerk began to dismantle apartheid. And no-one was quicker on the draw than Dr Ali Bacher, who had captained South Africa's last and greatest Test side, who had organised rebel tours, who had taken cricket to the townships. Watching with scarcely disguised belief was Clive Rice, the de facto skipper who had spent long enough in England to qualify for the national side. Now 42 and with an interest in motor racing, he was still a formidably fit and determined captain of Transvaal. Finally, he thought, his time had come.

First came re-admission to the International Cricket Council in July, then a late inclusion in the World Cup the following year. But before that there would be an epoch-making tour to India, a country which South Africa had never played. 'To arrange an international tour in three days,' said Bacher, 'was quite an experience. But the importance of this was such that it could not be turned down. It goes way beyond cricket – there could not be a better venue for us to return.' Ironically, it was the cancellation of a similar short tour by Pakistan for fear of political reprisals that created the gap in India's calendar – and allowed South Africa to fill it. 'The game of your life,' says Rice, 'tends to be a match where you dominated the

147

proceedings and ended up with the Man of the Match award. But I have to differ as South Africa's re-entry into the international scene in Calcutta was a remarkable experience.

'After 21 years of isolation, this was not only an ambitious project but a dream come true for all the players and administrators in South Africa. Ali Bacher had come back from India for a meeting with the selectors, the team was assembled with a couple of days' notice and we departed in a week. A Boeing 707 loaded full of players, administrators and followers arrived at Calcutta airport to a welcome that even the President of the United States would have been proud of. The two-hour journey to the hotel saw the streets lined with millions of people. There were places where the motorcade had to stop and speeches were made. Eventually, we arrived at the team hotel, garlanded but shattered by the experience. From "polecats to heroes" in a week was something to comprehend.

'The world-wide interest in the match was incredible,' Rice continues. 'The media descended from everywhere to witness this memorable occasion and some 250 journalists were crammed into a hall for a press conference. All were desperately keen to get their piece of the action. The match at Calcutta, where 96,000 turned up, indicated the tremendous build-up and interest had continued after our arrival. The Guy Fawkes crackers that were exploding around the ground must have sounded like the battle of El Alamein, while the excitement and expectation created goose pimples as Cook and Hudson went out to bat. From the playing side, it was a wonderful occasion but we had to try to get on and win the match. There were tremendous distractions for everybody to overcome but we had to focus on scoring runs and bowling economically. Hudson was dismissed for nought, caught behind off Kapil Dev, but that shocked us back into reality and we started to rectify his early loss.' It was not easy. Rice admits: 'Losing the toss was pretty decisive.'

The South Africans had been hoping to field first as a way of settling their nerves but the crease offers no such hiding place. Even Bacher acknowledged: 'I would have been terrified to go out there.' But the visitors' apprehension had little to do with the bowling. No seat was left as the crowd filled the awesome concrete cavern that is Eden Gardens. They packed the gangways, the rafters, the aisles. They let off fire-crackers during the maiden overs, kept up a deafening racket between overs and when a wicket fell, erupted into what looked like a full-blown riot. The South Africans, blinking from their own black-hole of isolation, simply could not believe it. Says Rice: 'The explosions on the field would certainly not allow any player to 'fall asleep'. Indeed, the cacophony would have woken the dead but the problems were not confined to the batsmen. 'The real threat was players losing their concentration,' says Rice. 'In the field, when a ball was heading in a player's direction, fire-crackers were thrown and the guys were almost blown up! This was all part of fielding on the boundary in a foreign country and one of the many learning curves that our players had to adapt to.'

Back to the South African innings. At 28, Jimmy Cook was trapped lbw to Srinath and much now depended on Wessels, the only player to tour the sub-continent before, albeit with Australia. Fire-crackers were hopelessly inadequate weapons with which to prise out this doughty character and he provided the innings with much-needed ballast. After Kirsten had been bowled by Raju, Wessels and Kuiper put the 100 up but the sometime Aussie, full-time battler fell to Tendulkar and Kuiper also perished. It was never going to be enough and with Rice making only 14, the innings closed at 177 for eight.

If some of his colleagues seemed overawed by the occasion, Alan Donald was not. And by taking three for eight in his first four overs, he threatened to bowl South Africa to an 'impossible' victory. Shastri went without scoring, Sidhu for six and Manjrekar for one. At 20 for three, India were wobbling. But Donald lacked support and Tendulkar, who was fortunate to survive a run-out on three, took command. The teenager and Azharuddin took the score to 60 before the skipper was stumped, offering a wild slog. But in the debutant Amre, Tendulkar found the ideal partner and the pair's 56-run stand was ultimately decisive. Donald returned to remove both but he could not do it all and Kapil Dev and Prabhakar took the Indians to their target. Donald and Kapil Dev and Prabhakar took the Indians to their target.

Rice adds: 'As much as the game was played seriously and aggressively, the building of diplomatic relations off the field was more important and the players filled this role in a wonderful way. In fact, they went out of their way to build these relationships and I think it ultimately jeopardised their performances on the field. Also, we were including all the players on the tour in the first two games – I think after 20 years it would have been really disappointing for a player not to get an international cap because he was not the best for that position. The relief at scoring your first international run after all those years was amazing and a milestone in any player's career. When all of this is added up, it was a match of exceptional excitement and emotion, and the result did not matter. When people were wiping away the tears of joy, I would certainly rate it as the game of my life as it was much more than just a game of cricket.' On such an occasion, the cliché can be forgiven.

Result: India won by seven wickets

149

South Africa

S.J. Cook lbw Srinath 17
A.C. Hudson c More b Kapil Dev 0
K.C. Wessels b Tendulkar 50
P.N. Kirsten b Raju 7
A.P. Kuiper c Amre b Prabhakar 43
*C.E.B. Rice b Prabhakar 14
R.P. Snell c Amre b Kapil 16
B. McMillan run out 2
†D.J. Richardson not out 4
T.G. Shaw not out 0
    Extras (LB 13, W 11) 24
1/3 2/28 3/49 4/109   177
5/151 6/156 7/167 8/176
A.A. Donald did not bat

Bowling: Kapil Dev 9-2-23-2, Prabhakar 10-1-26-2, Srinath 10-0-39-1, Raju 10-0-32-1, Shastri 3-0-17-0, Tendulkar 5-0-27-1.

India

R.J. Shastri c Richardson b Donald 0
N.S. Sidhu c McMillan b Donald 6
S.V. Manjrekar b Donald 1
S.R. Tendulkar c Snell b Donald 62
*M. Azharuddin st Ric'son b Shaw 16
P.K. Amre lbw Donald 55
Kapil Dev b Kuiper 11
M. Prabhakar not out 12
K.S. More not out 0
    Extras (LB 2, W 11, NB 2) 15
1/1 2/3 3/20 4/60 5/116   178
6/148 7/177
S.L.V. Raju and J. Srintah did not bat

Bowling: Donald 8.4-0-29-5, Snell 6-0-35-0, McMillan 6-0-30-0, Shaw 10-0-46-1, Rice 5-0-14-0, Kuiper 5-0-22-1.

Barry Richards

Sheffield Shield, Perth, 20, 21, 22, 23 November 1970

Born in Durban, on 21 July 1945, Barry Anderson Richards was a schoolboy batting prodigy in his native Natal. Yet it was not until 1968 that world cricket awoke to the new giant in its midst: 2,395 runs in his first season for Hampshire signalling a swashbuckling entry in the county championship. For a decade he treated English and overseas bowlers with rampant disdain, smashing most of his 28,358 first-class runs for the county and, with West Indian Gordon Greenidge, revelling in one of cricket's more unlikely but brilliant opening partnerships. Sadly, his Test career consisted of a solitary series in 1969/70 when he helped South Africa thrash Bill Lawry's Australians 4-0. He continued his assault on the Aussies in 1970/71, his 1,538 runs (average 109.86) helping South Australia to regain the Sheffield Shield. Back in Natal in 1973/74, he hit a Currie Cup record 1,285 runs and did not let up when he joined Kerry Packer. Only boredom brought on premature retirement. A brilliant slip-fielder and occasional off-spinner, he once bagged 7-63 for Hampshire against The Rest of the World.

It is a measure of the princely genius of Barry Richards that even prime movers behind South Africa's sporting isolation privately regretted that his wondrous gifts were lost to the Test arena. Turning him into a mercenary was akin to condemning Napoleon to the Foreign Legion – and just about the only 'delivery' the dashing right-hander found unplayable. Indeed, you fancied that if anything could have prevented the sports boycott besides an end to apartheid, it would have been Richards's broad and flashing blade. But that is to trivialise a far greater deprivation even though one has to understand the frustration behind Richards's remark: 'When I first picked up a bat, politics and sport were simply two subjects at the opposite ends of a newspaper.' For a man whose timing was otherwise so exquisite, he was unfortunate to belong to a lost generation; blessed with one of the most sublime talents to grace the game, Richards was cruelly robbed of the chance to become an even greater legend and perhaps claim an opener's berth in cricket's all time XI.

Tall, powerfully built, curls of fair hair cascading over his collar, he flashed a smile like a square-cut, danced down the wicket like Nureyev, drove like a Maharajah. Unlike Gooch and Graeme Pollock, his bat was not a bludgeon; nor was it the rapier of a Compton or a Ranji; like his West Indian namesake, Richards combined power and artistry, accuracy and lofty disdain. Apathy was his greatest enemy but at the W.A.C.A. in 1970, he succeeded in dispatching even that searching opponent to the pickets for one rapturous day.

Richards had savoured his Test experiences. Against Lawry's men, his contribution had been 508 runs at an average of 72.57 and he even managed to complete a maiden Test 100 in the first over after lunch on his home ground. But it was but a tasty morsel when Richards hungered for a banquet. And once his country's departure from the Test arena was confirmed, he hardly needed the incentive of a dollar-a-run from Coca-Cola when Ian Chappell suggested a shot at the next best thing – a season in Sheffield Shield. The hard and true Australian tracks wore a come-hither look and Richards says: 'At 25, I was just about at my peak and welcomed a new challenge.' Settling in with South Australia, he soon found himself pitted against Shield winners, Western Australia, who boasted the experience of 'Garth' McKenzie and Tony Lock, and the youth of Dennis Lillee. To the best balanced and varied attack Down Under, Richards showed his respect with an uncharacteristically cautious start.

'I remember taking 15 minutes to get off the mark,' he says, 'and didn't have a very auspicious beginning. With eight-ball overs and a short session before lunch, there was just no sign of anything special.' But on a surface like matting and with a lightning outfield, the runs were not long in coming. Lillee made him hop a couple of times but Richards was the master long before leg-spinner Mann was introduced. The 100 came in 83 minutes and when Causby was out at 109, the mood of the home skipper was not improved when Ian Chappell bustled to the wicket. Richards recalls: 'The afternoon was when we really took charge but there was no particular pattern to it. I remember Lockie packing the cover field but as a bowler he avoided us. As for individual shots, I hit Lillee straight back over his head into the sightscreen for what should have been a six but for the most part the runs just flowed.'

He could have added 'in a mighty flood.' Discussing the innings over two decades later, you are aware just how easily runs came to him. No, your memory does not deceive – he really did step outside his leg-stump and late-cut an off-break, just as he thought nothing of pulling a quick ball well outside off-stump wide of mid-wicket's right hand. Most thrilling of all was when he deigned not to use his feet and simply flailed perfectly good-length deliveries to the fence, bowler bewildered, fielder not bothering to chase. As an improviser, he compared with Compton and Kanhai, but was somehow more regal, his cover driving worthy of Hammond. Yet he always gave the bowler a chance. Always? Perhaps it was Lock's reinforcements in the covers that maintained Richards's concentration for so long in Perth for it became a challenge for him to pierce this Maginot Line. But on that day he could have sent a cover drive through the eye of a needle and often did so, causing a despairing Lock to lose the last remnants of his hair.

Chappell gleefully joined the carnage but could not match Richards whose 100 came in just over two hours, his 150 in just under three. 'I gave a chance on 169,' he says, 'and Ian Brayshaw [who dropped a simple catch at mid-on] later told me: "I don't normally drop blokes on that score and then find they go and double it!" – I had not set out my stall to make a big one, but was very relaxed. I was enjoying it immensely and just carried on.' When Chappell was stumped for 129, the pair had put on 308 in 170 minutes. Pity poor Lockie – the score was 417 for two and the next man in was Ian's brother Greg . . .

Richards's 300 came with a rare, streaky shot over cover that almost went to hand. Fate decreed that it didn't and the South African became only the third player to reach the milestone in Sheffield Shield history – Charlie Gregory and Bill Ponsford being the others. But for once Greg failed and South Australia reached stumps at 513 for three, Richards 325 not out. 'No, I did not set out to score 300 in a day,' he maintains. 'I knew that very few people had done it but the enormity of it all only sank in later.' He said at the time: 'I am not a big scorer. It must have been the easy pace of the wicket.' The next morning he was sawn off at 356, given lbw to Mann after a 372-minute epic. Regrets? 'There were two,' he says. 'One was not hitting 50 boundaries and the other was not seeing it on television. Coming from South Africa, I was not used to television and by the time I thought about it – a month later – someone had wiped the tape!' But that was not all. 'I also recall celebrating with the Chappells and not going to bed at all. I was meeting a girlfriend who was flying in the next morning and went straight to the airport in a dishevelled state. When we got back to Adelaide, I discovered my unit had been broken into – with all the publicity surrounding the innings, the thieves knew I was away.'

For the record, South Australia declared at 575 for 9 and bowled the shell-shocked Shield-holders out twice to win by an innings and 111 runs. Richards, who could do no wrong, even got a wicket, having Rod Marsh caught by Ian Chappell in the second innings. 'That was the most enjoyable thing of all,' says Richards, who went on to score a mammoth 1,528 runs in the season. Only Sir Donald Bradman has hit more for the 'crow-eaters' in one summer.

South Australia

B.A. Richards lbw b Mann 356
J.J. Causby c Chadwick b Lock 38
*I.M. Chappell st Marsh b Lock 129
G.S. Chappell c Marsh b McKenzie 11
K.G. Cunningham c Inverarity b Lock . 13
K. Langley run out 7
E.W. Freeman c Irvine b Lock 6
†R. P. Blundell b Mann 0
A.A. Mallett not out 6
T.J. Jenner c McKenzie b Mann 5
J.R. Hammond
     Extras (NB 4) 4
1/109 2/417 3/447 4/551   575
5/553 6/563 7/564 8/575

Bowling: *First Innings* – McKenzie 19-2-101-1; Lillee 18-1-117-0; Brayshaw 12-1-69-0; Mann 20.6-1-120-3; Lock 16-1-108-4; Inverarity 8-0-56-0.

Western Australia

D. Chadwick c Blundell b Jenner	49	c and b Hammond	2
C. Scarff c Blundell b Hammond	11	b Cunningham	7
J.T. Irvine b Jenner	33	c and b G. S. Chappell	57
R.J. Inverarity c G. S. Chappell b Hammond	85	c and b G. S. Chappell	35
R.D. Meuleman retired hurt	28	absent hurt	–
I.J. Brayshaw lbw b Freeman	22	c Richards b Mallett	13
†R. W. Marsh c I. M. Chappell b Hammond	9	c I. M. Chappell b Richards	19
A.L. Mann c Blundell b Hammond	2	c I.M. Chappell b Hammond	1
D.K. Lillee c Cunningham b Hammond	12	b Hammond	6
G.D. McKenzie b Hammond	10	not out	18
*G.A.R. Lock not out	2	c Hammond b Mallett	8
Extras (LB 7, W 2, NB 17)	26	(B 1, NB 8)	9
1/33 2/88 3/110 4/239	289	1/3 2/15 3/102 4/137	175
5/256 6/261 7/270 8/285 9/289		5/141 6/142 7/161 8/175	

Bowling: *First Innings* – Freeman 15-1-53-1; Hammond 12.3-1-54-6; G.S. Chappell 8-1-23-0; Jenner 22-4-78-2; Mallett 18-5-37-0; Cunningham 9-2-18-0; Freeman 4-0-16-0; Hammond 9-2-25-3; G.S. Chappell 12-1-41-2; Jenner 8-0-25-0; Mallett 12.5-2-43-2; Cunningham 4-0-12-1; Richards 1-0-4-1.

Viv Richards

WEST INDIES V ENGLAND

Antigua, 11, 12, 13, 15, 16 April 1986

Viv Richards was born on 7 March 1952 in St John's, Antigua. For a decade he was the best batsman in the world with an uncanny ability to produce runs on the grand occasion. In 121 Tests he scored 8,540 runs, more than any other West Indian and he led his country on 50 occasions. He is also the first West Indian to hit 100 centuries. He retired from Test cricket in 1991. In county cricket he played for Somerset from 1974 until his controversial sacking in 1986 and for Glamorgan from 1990 to 1993.

English cricketers in recent years have often endured sleepless nights contemplating facing one of a posse of West Indian fast bowlers on the morrow, but Vivian Richards was the one *batsman* who could intimidate his opponents – even before he had received a ball. His journey to the crease, slow and measured, with a hint of a swagger, which became more marked as the years rolled by, was in itself a declaration of intent.

The cap confirmed this expression of superiority. In an age when a fast bowler's stock ball whizzed past the batsman's nostrils, Richards was one of the few to shun the helmet. His cap became his hallmark, a symbol that no bowler, however fast, could threaten his domination. For Richards was never satisfied with mere survival. Bowlers had to be subjugated, to recognise that he was the master. Sometimes this meant shunning the coaching book, relying instead on the keenest of eyes, phenomenal reflexes and the confidence to trust his instincts.

He reasoned that if he played an on-drive in classical style the ball would simply speed into the hands of the fielder at mid-on, so instead he flicked the wrists, playing the ball squarer – through the gaps. That whip through mid-wicket confounded the coaches. His front foot was planted down the wicket and his bat swung across his front pad. All wrong, yet Richards made it seem the safest shot in the world.

Richards, of course, was spoilt for choice in selecting his most memorable match. It might have been the Oval Tests of 1976 when he scored 291 or maybe a one-day international at Old Trafford in 1984 when he played an astonishing innings of 189 not out, which rescued the West Indies from a perilous position. However, he returned to his homeland, Antigua, for his chosen match, which took place on the England tour of 1985/6.

This was Richards' first series as captain against England and he had been anxious to maintain the awesome standards set by his predecessor, Clive Lloyd. By the time the two teams arrived in Antigua for the final Test, this had been achieved with ease. West Indies were 4-0 up and seeking to repeat the 'blackwash' of 1984. Such was England's disarray that Gower had to persuade Gooch, tired of anti-apartheid protests, to stay on for the match.

The Recreation Ground at St John's is inevitably a special place for Richards. He first played there in the early '70s when it was a ramshackle cricketing outpost. Now it is graced by two massive stands, one of which bears the name of Andy Roberts. In between them lies the Viv Richards pavilion. This pair put Antigua on the cricketing map; from 1981 St John's has become a regular Test venue for the West Indies and that is almost entirely due to these two sons of Antigua. The inaugural Test was played in March 1981 against England.

Richards recalls, 'This was a very important occasion for me. Not only was it in front of my home crowd but I had just got married and I wanted everything to be perfect. I did score 100 but, in truth, it had been a pretty edgy innings. I allowed the occasion to get to me.' In 1986 he was equally determined to add to the carnival atmosphere that is unique to Antigua with its ghetto-blasters pounding away in between overs and the impromptu metal bands, whose instruments comprise discarded hubcaps and lead piping. 'What could be more perfect than to achieve a second blackwash (the West Indies had defeated England 5-0 in 1984) in front of all my family and friends? Also, my father had just suffered a mild stroke. I was going to play well for my father – as simple as that. But when we batted my first innings proved to be a terrible disappointment (ct Gooch bowled Botham for 26).'

Nonetheless the West Indies amassed 474. In reply England just managed to avoid the follow on thanks to half centuries from Gooch and Wilf Slack and 90 from Gower. In their second innings the West Indies, with a lead of 164, needed quick runs to ensure the blackwash. Haynes and Richardson obliged with a brisk 100 partnership, but no-one was prepared for the mayhem that followed.

Richards continues: 'As I strode to the wicket the crowd gave me a truly thunderous ovation. It was true that my batting performances of the previous year had not been my best and there had been talk that "Richards is no longer hungry". But this crowd seemed to cast all that talk to the wind. I went to the wicket with about half an hour to go until tea and at the break I had 28. I felt particularly good. I remember hitting a couple of sixes off Ellison and Emburey, which seemed to set the ground alight. I was happy because my form was with me on my home ground, but I was not thinking of setting records, I just wanted to play well. After the break it just flowed. I started hitting fours and sixes and with every strike the crowd's noise seemed to intensify.'

Richards reached his 100 in 56 balls, the fastest ever in Test cricket in terms of balls received. Throughout Gower had stationed the majority of his fielders on the boundary, but the boundaries were not big enough.

The full record of the innings hints at the devastation:

0036126141 (24 off 10 balls)   0211041201 (36 off 20)
1120211100 (45 off 30)   0101624441 (68 off 40)
1200664612 (96 off 50)   00210461 (110 off 58)

Amid the assault two sixes off the unfortunate Emburey stood out. The first over long off landed outside the ground and later the carry was reckoned to be 125 yards; the second was a moral victory for Emburey. The off spinner tried a slower delivery, which beat him in the air. Richards was forced to stretch and play the shot with one hand on the bat. The ball still cleared long on by yards.

Richards remembers the jubilation when he reached his 100: 'I began to realise what it must be like to score for Liverpool at Anfield. Apparently the whole of the Caribbean had come to a standstill in celebration. There was a brief invasion of the pitch, which was marshalled by the local police force, but I got the impression that the police officers were far more concerned to shake my hand than send the spectators back to the stands. I was so happy that it had happened at the Recreation Ground. I knew then that, as long as I lived in St John's, I would always remember that day.'

A shell-shocked England side were bundled out for 170 in the final innings to complete the West Indian blackwash. Yet the match was more memorable for Richards' stunning innings. As *Wisden* faithfully records; 'If anyone forgets that extraordinary *tour de force*, it can truthfully be said that he did not deserve to see it in the first place.'
Result: West Indies won by 240 runs

West Indies

C.G. Greenidge b Botham 14
D.L. Haynes c Gatting b Ellison .... 131 (1) run out 70
R.B. Richardson c Slack b Emburey 24 (2) c Robinson b Emburey 31
H.A. Gomes b Emburey 24
*I.V.A. Richards c Gooch b Botham .. 26 (3) not out 110
†P.J.L. Dujon b Foster 21
M.D. Marshall c Gatting b Gooch 76
R.A. Harper c Lamb b Foster .... 60 (4) not out 19
M.A. Holding c Gower b Ellison 73
J. Garner run out 11
B.P. Patterson run out 0
    Extras (B 2, LB 11, W 1) 14   (B 4, LB 9, W 1, NB 2) 16
1/23 2/63 3/137 4/178   474   1/100 2/161   246
5/232 6/281 7/351 8/401 9/450

Bowling: *First Innings* – Marshall 24-5-64-3; Garner 21.4-2-67-4; Patterson 14-2-49-1; Holding 20-3-71-1; Harper 26-7-45-1; Richards 2-0-3-0. *Second Innings* – Marshall 16.1-6-25-2; Garner 17-5-38-2; Patterson 15-3-29-0; Holding 16-3-45-2; Harper 12-8-10-3; Richards 3-1-3-0.

England

G.A. Gooch lbw b Holding	51	lbw b Holding	52
W.N. Slack c Greenidge b Patterson	52	b Garner	8
R.T. Robinson b Marshall	12	run out	3
*D.I. Gower c Dujon b Marshall	90	c Dujon b Harper	21
A.J. Lamb c&b Harper	1	b Marshall	1
M.W. Gatting c Dujon b Garner	15	b Holding	1
I.T. Botham c Harper b Garner	10	b Harper	13
†P.R. Downton c Holding b Garner	5	lbw b Marshall	13
R.M. Ellison c Dujon b Marshall	6	lbw b Garner	16
J.E. Emburey not out	7	c Richardson b Harper	0
N.A. Foster c Holding b Garner	10	not out	0
Extras: (B 5, LB 6, NB 40)	51	(B 10, LB 10, W 2, NB 21)..	43

1/127 2/132 3/157 4/159   310   1/14 2/29 3/84 4/101   170
5/205 6/213 7/237 8/289 9/290   5/112 6/124 7/147 8/164
                                                9/168

Bowling: *First Innings* – Botham 40-6-147-2; Foster 28-5-86-2; Ellison 24-3-114-2; Emburey 37-11-93-2; Gooch 5-2-21-1. *Second Innings* – Botham 15-0-78-0; Foster 10-0-40-0; Ellison 4-0-32-0; Emburey 14-0-83-1.

Richie Richardson

Bridgetown, Barbados, 18, 19, 20, 22, 23 April 1992

Born on 12 January 1962 at Five Islands in Antigua, Richardson made his Test debut against India on the 1983/4 tour and was soon established in the West Indian team as an uninhibited strokeplayer and an enthusiastic 'lead guitarist'. He was appointed captain of the West Indies in the autumn of 1991 and since then has gained a reputation as a dignified leader – 'we play hard, but our opponents are not our enemies.' In 1993/4 Australia and the West Indies finally managed to complete a Test series without acrimony due largely to Richardson's attitude. In 1993 he was enlisted as Yorkshire's overseas player.

Richie Richardson's choice was a straightforward one – a historic match, which most observers of cricket or politics throughout the eighties would have deemed an impossibility. This was South Africa's first Test match since their exile from official international cricket in 1970 and, of course, it was the first time that South Africa had ever played a Test against the West Indies. Moreover, it was Richardson's first Test as captain of the West Indies. All these ingredients combined to form the prospect of a thrilling game to be contested in front of an eager Carribbean crowd at the Kensington Oval.

The game was indeed a classic, yet because of a bizarre boycott, ostensibly about the omission of the Barbadian pace bowler, Anderson Cummins, it was played in front of deserted stands. Richardson, the mildest of men, has never completely forgiven the Barbados public for their decision to stay away nor has anyone been able to explain convincingly the motives for the boycott. One hidden contributing factor may have been that the Barbados public were still uneasy about the rapidity with which South Africa had been welcomed back into the fold of international cricket. Cummins, after all, was a marginal choice to all but the most blinkered supporter.

Leaving aside the West Indies' obvious desire not to be defeated by a South African team after all those years when the black man was deemed inferior in southern Africa, this was a vital match for Richardson. After the retirement of Viv Richards in September 1991, Richardson had been preferred to Desmond Haynes as his successor. His first expedition – the Australasian World Cup – had been a failure. The West Indies, minus the experience of Richards, Greenidge and Dujon, had failed to qualify for the semi-finals. The Caribbean public were used to better things.

Moreover the records of Richardson's two predecessors in Test cricket made his task daunting, to say the least; in 74 Tests in charge Clive Lloyd had won 36 and lost 12; Viv Richards had won 27 of his 50 Tests and lost 8.

Richardson's burden was not helped by the reception he received in Jamaica for the first of the one-day internationals of this hastily arranged South African tour. Even though the West Indies won all three games comfortably, Richardson was constantly booed and heckled by the Sabina Park crowd, since he was held to be personally responsible for the omission of local favourite, Jeffrey Dujon, from the World Cup squad.

So to Barbados and a conspicuous absence of the drum beat and bugle blowing that is a hallmark of the Kensington Oval, where the West Indies had not lost a Test match since 1935. Kepler Wessels won the toss and adopted the usual policy in Bridgetown by choosing to field. Just before tea he may have been regretting his decision; for after a quickfire opening partnership of 99 between Haynes and Simmons, the West Indies had raced to 219-3 – Richardson's contribution a typically forthright 44. However, Richardson's dismissal, flailing outside the off stump against Richard Snell sparked a collapse as the West Indies' last seven wickets mustered a meagre 43 runs.

For the next three days South Africa were in charge of the match. Andrew Hudson was the cornerstone of the visitors' reply and became the first South African to score 100 on his Test debut. In all he batted for eight hours and 40 minutes until he was yorked for 163 by Kenneth Benjamin, the man preferred to Cummins. South Africa gained a first innings lead of 83 and on the eve of the rest day West Indies were 184-7. They were fortunate to have that many. Haynes had played the second ball of his innings from Donald onto his stumps but the bails refused to dislodge and Brian Lara, having completed his maiden Test 50 trod on his off stump when playing back to Bosch. Inevitably the television cameras spotted his transgression but the umpires did not.

Nonetheless that evening the South Africans were in buoyant mood as Richardson recalls 'both sides were invited onto the *Jolly Roger* boat for a party. The South Africans were celebrating since they thought they had the Test sown up. We had a good time too, but I knew we still had a chance in the game.' By the end of the fourth day this was still the minority view. The West Indies had rallied to 283 all out – a lead of 200 – thanks to a tenacious innings of 79 by Jimmy Adams on his Test debut and eccentric support from fellow Jamaicans, Walsh and Patterson. Curtly Ambrose then removed both openers cheaply, but the two most experienced members of the South African side, Wessels and Peter Kirsten took the score to 122-2 at the close.

So on the final morning South Africa needed another 79 runs for victory. Richardson stressed one crucial adjustment that his bowlers needed to make: 'We just had to bowl a little straighter rather than our normal off stump line since the bounce was becoming increasingly uneven.' But that technical adjustment was only half the story. The South Africans appeared paralysed by the prospect of a historic victory, while Walsh and Ambrose were inspired.

Here was the first indication that Richardson was capable of prompting his pacemen to awesome heights, forever fortifying their self-belief. Unlike his predecessor there were no histrionics on the pitch; underneath the maroon floppy hat he glided anonymously around the field exhorting his bowlers with a whisper rather than a whip. Walsh and Ambrose responded magnificently.

Walsh disposed of both overnight batsmen and the rest of the South Africans were impotent against him and Ambrose. Walsh's figures on that morning were 11-7-8-4, while Ambrose swiftly polished off a dispirited tail. When the last man, Donald, was bowled by Ambrose twenty minutes before lunch, South Africa were still 52 runs short of their target. At the conclusion of the match all 11 West Indian players linked hands on a lap of honour in front of 500 spectators. Richardson explained that 'we wanted to show the people of the Caribbean how united we are.'

This was to become a recurring theme of Richardson's captaincy: 'I believe we must stick together both socially and politically. We come from small communities and we have an insularity problem. The West Indian cricket team can give a great example of unity.'

The South African match also bolstered the confidence of Richardson as captain and the rest of his team. When confronted by similar situations against Australia in Adelaide in 1993 or England in Trinidad in 1994, the West Indians had the resolve and resilience to triumph against the odds and within the space of two years Richardson seemed as unchallenged as the West Indies captain as his two illustrious predecessors.

Result: West Indies won by 52 runs

West Indies

D.L. Haynes c Wessels b Snell	58	c Richardson b Snell	23
P.V. Simmons c Kirsten b Snell	35	c Kirsten b Bosch	3
B.C. Lara c Richardson b Bosch	17	c Richardson b Donald	64
*R.B. Richardson c Richardson b Snell	44	lbw b Snell	2
K.L.T. Arthurton c Kuiper b Pringle	59	b Donald	22
J.C. Adams b Donald	11	not out	79
†D. Williams c Hudson b Donald	1	lbw b Snell	5
C.E.L. Ambrose not out	6	c Richardson b Donald	6
K.C.G. Benjamin b Snell	1	lbw b Donald	7
C.A. Walsh b Pringle	6	c Richardson b Snell	13
B.P. Patterson run out	0	b Bosch	11
Extras: (LB 7, NB 17)	24	(B 17, LB 11, NB 20)	48
1/99 2/106 3/137 4/219 5/240 6/241 7/250 8/255 9/262	262	1/10 2/66 3/68 4/120 5/139 6/164 7/174 8/196 9/221	283

Bowling: *First Innings* – Donald 20-1-67-2; Bosch 15-2-43-1; Pringle 18.4-2-62-2; Snell 18-3-83-4. *Second Innings* – Donald 25-3-77-4; Bosch 24.3-7-61-2; Pringle 16-0-43-0; Snell 16-1-74-4.

South Africa

	First Innings		Second Innings	
M.W. Rushmere	c Lara b Ambrose	3	b Ambrose	3
A.C. Hudson	b Benjamin	163	c Lara b Ambrose	0
*K.C. Wessels	c Adams b Ambrose	59	c Lara b Walsh	74
P.N. Kirsten	c Lara b Benjamin	11	b Walsh	52
W.J. Cronje	c Lara b Adams	5	c Williams b Ambrose	2
A.P. Kuiper	c Williams b Patterson	34	c Williams b Walsh	0
†D.J. Richardson	c Ambrose b Adams	8	c Williams b Ambrose	2
R.P. Snell	run out	6	c Adams b Walsh	0
M.W. Pringle	c Walsh b Adams	15	b Ambrose	4
A.A. Donald	st Williams b Adams	0	b Ambrose	0
T. Bosch	not out	5	not out	0
Extras:	(B 4, LB 6, W 1, NB 25)	36	(B 4, LB 3, NB 4)	11
Total:		345		148

Bowling: *First Innings* – Ambrose 36-19-47-2; Patterson 23-4-79-1; Walsh 27-7-71-0; Benjamin 25-3-87-2; Arthurton 3-0-8-0; Adams 21.5-5-43-4. *Second Innings* – Ambrose 24.4-7-34-6; Patterson 7-1-26-0; Walsh 22-10-31-4; Benjamin 9-2-21-0; Adams 5-0-16-0.

Jack Russell

ENGLAND V AUSTRALIA

Lords, 22, 23, 24, 26, 27 June 1989

Jack Russell was born on 15 August 1963 at Stroud. He made his debut for Gloucestershire against the Sri Lankans in 1981 when he claimed eight victims in the match and was appointed the club's vice captain in 1993. His Test debut came in 1985. A perfectionist behind the stumps, a pragmatist with the bat in his hand, and self-taught artist, his work has become increasingly sought after; he has a shop in Chipping Sodbury and was commissioned by the Dean of Gloucester to draw Gloucester Cathedral to raise funds for its 900th Anniversary. He drinks a lot of tea and consumes lots of bananas.

Ever since Jack Russell made his debut for Gloucestershire back in 1981, no-one really doubted that he was a 'natural' of international potential. When taking catches behind the stumps the ball nestled in the palms of his gloves obediently rather than being grabbed against its will twixt thumb and forefinger. A Test career beckoned, provided that he could convince himself and the selectors – not renowned for the frequency of their visits to the West Country – that he was not a batting liability.

Ironically when that Test debut finally came – against Sri Lanka in 1988 – at the age of 25, Russell scored 94 as a nightwatchman, yet he kept like a novice. 'On average,' he says, 'I drop one catch a season standing back, but on that first day I missed two and got a finger to another.' These are not random recollections; Russell keeps a meticulous written record of his work, which, for example, reveals that up until September 1994 he had never missed a chance in Australia.

That Sri Lanka match was a relatively gentle introduction to international cricket. A sterner test came with the arrival of the Australians in 1989. In the first match at Headingley Russell kept immaculately, which meant, of course, that nobody noticed him behind the stumps as England crumbled to a humiliating 210 run defeat. However, attention was focussed on the supposed frailty of his batting, a problem that was to gnaw at his England career for years. The armchair critics, required to deliver an immediate verdict, even though their knowledge of Russell's batting was scant, decided that he could not play the short stuff.

Russell recognised that he had batted poorly at Leeds and that the Australians had unsettled him with their aggression with ball and tongue. Yes, he had batted without purpose, but the flak he received about being unable to cope with the bouncers he resented. However, the criticisms did crystallise his shortcomings at Headingley. 'I drove home from Leeds that night thinking about my batting and telling myself I was going to attack them and go for my shots whenever possible.'

So to Lord's and the second Test against Australia – Russell's choice. He didn't score a century nor did England pull off an astounding victory; in fact they were thrashed again and captain David Gower was pilloried on the Saturday evening for waltzing out of a press conference prematurely to jump into a taxi destined for the musical *Anything Goes*. But amid the carnage Jack Russell convinced himself that he could succeed at Test level with the bat.

On the eve of the match he had a long chat with his keeping mentor, Alan Knott, but the topic was batting, and the theme of Knott's message was simply 'bat as if your life is at stake.' Russell recalls 'in the nets I had bowlers hurling rubber balls at me from 16 yards and I just practised ducking and swaying out of the way. I was determined to be positive and not to be cowed by any verbal intimidation.'

Gower won the toss and England batted – wantonly – on a benign surface. England were soon 58-3 and despite a brisk partnership between Gooch and Gower, 185-6 when Russell came to the crease. The last four wickets managed to eke out another 101 runs, 64 from Russell, the highest score of the innings. Gone were the tentative jabs of Headingley. If the ball was in one of Russell's favourite arcs – wide of off stump – he cracked it to the boundary. In defence he played much straighter and more decisively, rather than offering the precarious angled bat of Leeds and he was in much more combative mood. 'I knew they would give me a lot of lip at Lord's because they sensed that I was vulnerable. Sure enough, Merv Hughes gave me an almighty earful; this time I shouted back whenever I hit him to the boundary (rough translation – "fetch that back, O obese Antipodean").'

Russell's innings did not alter the course of the match but he knew as he returned undefeated to the pavilion that he could cope with this Test match cricket; in fact he discovered that he enjoyed the supercharged atmosphere. England lost this Lord's Test by six wickets and would never recover any confidence in the summer of 1989; only the emergence of Robin Smith and Russell as genuine Test players could offer any consolation in that humiliating summer.

But after that Lord's innings the Australians never said a word to Russell at the crease and they had plenty of opportunities during his 351-minute century at Old Trafford in the fourth Test. The following winter a five-hour 55 in Barbados, which almost saved the match and the series was another milestone – 'it proved I wouldn't be crushed by the West Indian attack, as some players have been.'

Yet Russell's place has never been absolutely secure because of perceived batting frailties, which do not, however, tally with the statistics. Only three English keepers – Ames, Parks and Knott – have surpassed Russell's Test average of 27, from 31 Tests (Up to January 1994), though a Martian watching him bat for 10 minutes would find these figures bewildering. Russell's method, with the 'crab' stance has become ever more eccentric, perhaps another sign of confidence since it must require a lot of bottle to bat in public like that. When he unveiled his latest stance, the likes of Emburey and DeFreitas were stopped in their tracks with an amalgam of laughter or bewilderment as they ran up to bowl. However, such a method provokes the suspicion of selectors. But more detrimental to Russell's England career has been the inability to find an all-rounder to replace Ian Botham. Instead the selectors, following Keith Fletcher's pet theory have compensated by asking Alec Stewart to keep wicket in a prolonged experiment, which never really worked. Hence the relief of the purists – and of Russell himself – when he was recalled to the England squad for the Caribbean tour of 1994.

Result: Australia won by six wickets

England

G.A. Gooch c Healy b Waugh	60	lbw b Alderman	0
B.C. Broad lbw b Alderman	18	b Lawson	20
K.J. Barnett c Boon b Hughes	14	c Jones b Alderman	3
M.W. Gatting c Boon b Hughes	0	lbw b Alderman	22
*D.I. Gower b Lawson	57	c Border b Hughes	106
R.A. Smith c Hohns b Lawson	32	b Alderman	96
J.E. Emburey b Alderman	0	not out	36
†R.C. Russell not out	64	c Boon b Lawson	29
N.A. Foster c Jones b Hughes	16	lbw b Alderman	4
P.W. Jarvis c Marsh b Hughes	6	lbw b Alderman	5
G.R. Dilley c Border b Alderman	7	c Boon b Hughes	24
Extras (LB 9, NB 3)	12	(B 6, LB 6, NB 2)	14

1/31 2/52 3/58 4/131 5/180   286   1/0 2/18 3/28 4/84   359
6/185 7/191 8/237 9/253   5/223 6/274 7/300 8/304
                                             9/314

Bowling: *First Innings* – Alderman 20.5-4-60-3; Lawson 27-8-88-2; Hughes 23-6-71-4; Waugh 9-3-49-1; Hohns 7-3-9-0. *Second Innings* – Alderman 38-6-128-6; Lawson 39-10-99-2; Hughes 24-8-44-2; Waugh 7-2-20-0; Hohns 13-6-33-0; Border 9-3-23-0.

Australia

G.R. Marsh c Russell b Dilley	3	b Dilley	1
M.A. Taylor lbw b Foster	62	c Gooch b Foster	27
D.C. Boon c Gooch b Dilley	94	not out	58
*A.R. Border c Smith b Emburey	35	c sub b Foster	1
D.M. Jones lbw b Foster	27	c Russell b Foster	0
S.R. Waugh not out	152	not out	21
†I.A. Healy c Russell b Jarvis	3		
M.G. Hughes c Gooch b Foster	30		
T.V. Hohns b Emburey	21		
G.F. Lawson c Broad b Emburey	74		
T.M. Alderman lbw b Emburey	8		
Extras (LB 11, NB 8)	19	(B 3, LB 4, NB 4)	11
1/6 2/151 3/192 4/221	528	1/9 2/51 3/61 (4 wkts)	119
5/235 6/265 7/331 8/381 9/511		4/67	

Bowling: *First Innings* – Dilley 34-3-141-2; Foster 45-7-129-3; Jarvis 31-3-150-1; Emburey 42-12-88-4; Gooch 6-2-9-0. *Second Innings* – Dilley 10-2-27-1; Foster 18-3-39-3; Jarvis 9.2-0-38-0; Emburey 3-0-8-0.

Bob Simpson

Adelaide, 28, 29, 31 January & 1 February 1966

AUSTRALIA V INDIA

Perth, 16, 17, 18, 20 & 21 December 1977

Robert Baddeley Simpson was born in Marrickville, Sydney, on 3 February 1936, nine years after his parents emigrated from Scotland. His father had played left-half for Stenhousemuir and Falkirk, but young Bob's early sporting passion was for golf. After switching to the willow, he made his first-class debut for New South Wales at 16, but had to work for his success, moving to Perth in 1956 and spending a summer with Accrington in the Lancashire League. Becoming an opening bat was, however, the best move he made. In 1959/60, he averaged 300.66 in the Sheffield Shield and totalled 445 in the Tests against the West Indies. He returned to N.S.W. to amass 359 in one dig against Queensland. Arguably the finest 'slipper' of all time and a more than useful leggie, he took over from Richie Benaud as Australia's captain in 1964, yet that first Test 100 still eluded him. In his 46th innings, he made it worth the wait with an epic 311 at Old Trafford to ensure the Ashes stayed with Australia. In 1968, after 29 Tests in charge, he retired still at his peak at 32. Nine years later, he answered the call of a desperate Australian Cricket Board whose team had been decimated by Kerry Packer. Making possibly the greatest comeback in Australian Test history, Simpson scored 176 against India. He retired for good after touring the West Indies in 1978. Nine years later, with his country once again in need after a hammering by Mike Gatting's England, he became Australia's coach. A World Cup triumph and three Ashes victories followed.

It is not because of his monumental contribution to Australian cricket that Bob Simpson has two games in his name, even though it spans four decades. Nor is it his celebrated 'cometh the hour' rescues: it's simply the way he defied one of the oldest and truest adages in sport. At the age of 42, Simpson came back after almost 10 years of retirement to produce an innings as valuable as any in his previous career. And of all his great digs, it is the 176 that he ground out against India on his favourite Perth track that is remembered most fondly by Australians. For all that, he admits: 'I forget I had a second career.' It is from his first that he plucked his original offering – a double century against England at Adelaide. But once his memory is jogged, he admits that 'the comeback against India probably has equal standing' in his personal archives. 'It's either one or the other,' he said and even when his triple centuries were tossed in as possible tie-breakers, he stuck with the above two. They may not have been instant box-office but both could have been directed by Cecil B. DeMille. And you do not need *Wisden* to tell you that Australia won both games. Which was, of course, an unspoken pre-requisite.

When Mike Smith, who led the first England tourists to fly to Australia, vowed to play 'brighter cricket' , the sceptics were wondering if he'd had time to get to know his players. No-one doubted the skipper's sincerity but the likes of Boycott, Barrington and Edrich had not been chosen with the barrackers in mind. And with Australia opening with Simpson and Lawry, it was never going to be hit and giggle. Simpson had taken residency in Manchester to snuff out England in the previous series so he was unlikely to submit to calls from the bar. No matter, after three Tests England were one up, thanks to Bob Barber's blistering 185 in Sydney. Simpson? He'd missed the drawn first Test with a broken wrist, returned for another draw in the second and then went down with chicken-pox before the third. 'Having lost that by an innings,' he says, 'we really had to do something special in Adelaide to hold on to the Ashes. Yet I hadn't really played any cricket.' Australia need not have worried.

Four changes were made from the side humiliated in Sydney but it was the reprieved McKenzie (left out until replacement Peter Allan went down with sore shins) who bowled England out for a dismal 241 to set up the victory charge. 'It was a wonderful display of controlled swing bowling,' said Simpson, who chipped in himself with two smart slip catches. 'The fielding was the best I've seen from our fellows since the Trinidad Test. We were determined to get them out for less than 300 but we needed to score at a run a minute to win the match.'

Simpson and Lawry were among the first pair of openers that a cricket fan would choose to save his life; their immortal partnership of 382 against the West Indies being the pinnacle of their legendary defiance. But to force a victory? There is nothing like being one down in an Ashes series to focus even the most circumspect mind and, while remaining massively reassuring in defence, the pair kept the board clicking. If not quite racing, their opening stand of 244 was among the most positive of their five century partnerships against England. And according to Bill O'Reilly, 'Simpson had never played better. He square-cut confidently and his footwork countering the spinners was classical,' wrote the old master in the *Sydney Morning Herald*. It was Simpson's first century in Adelaide, his second against England and his fifth in all Tests. His 100 came in 207 minutes and he gave one chance – to Boycott at 84.

Having lost a stone in weight before the match, the last thing Simpson (not out 159) needed was an overnight stomach bug and he looked wan the next day as he laboured a further 200 minutes taking his score to 225 (the highest by an Australian against England at Adelaide). After losing a few more pounds in a nine-hour stay, he blamed himself 'for not scoring fast enough' in a total of 516. But he still led his men with great purpose in the field as Neil Hawke (five for 54) ran through the England second innings. Despite a typically gritty 102 from Barrington, Smith's men failed to make Australia bat again, the series was all-square and the Ashes were to remain Down Under.

1977 . . . For a player who, as a youth, was waved airily to slip by Keith Miller and persuaded to open the batting by Neil Harvey, Simpson is very much his own man. Although it was not known at the time, he resisted the blandishments of Kerry Packer before responding to an S.O.S. from Australia's beleaguered establishment, reeling from the mass exodus of stars to World Series Cricket. A seasoned campaigner was sorely needed and Simpson had kept his eye in playing grade cricket for Western Suburbs in Sydney. But was it enough to counter the wiles of Chandra, Bedi and Prasanna?

With six untried youngsters and Jeff Thomson, Simpson juggled his resources so effectively that Australia won an exciting first Test at the Gabba by 16 runs, 89 in the second innings from Simpson and seven wickets in the match from Thommo going a long way towards victory. With Packer's World Series running simultaneously, there were two fascinating contests – and it was largely down to Simpson that Australia v India was as riveting as the A.C.B. v Packer. After India had been restricted to 402 by a valiant effort from Thomson in heatwave conditions, Australia's youngsters were in dire trouble at 65 for three when, as Simpson puts it, 'a supposedly old man of 41 walked to the wicket. I had a bit to prove – that age is no barrier if the mental strength is still there – and I remember it was about 40 degrees – pretty hot for batting one and a quarter days.' But first with John Dyson and later with Steve Rixon, Simpson hauled Australia from the brink of disaster to almost parity – and enthralled the viewing public. All the old shots were there and after making 176, he said simply: 'I enjoyed that.'

To bat that long and make that many after a decade's absence from the Test arena would be a mighty, heroic effort by any standards, but to do so in this heat and in this sweltering political climate, it was a genuine epic. 'I was soon at home,' says Simpson, 'Perth is my favourite wicket and there was no reason why, with application and a little luck, a batsman could not score runs.' It was shorter than certain other celebrated leaseholds but was the pivotal knock of a series he rates as 'every bit as good as the one against the West Indies in 1959/60.' And writing in his autobiography *Simmo,* he stresses: 'This innings backed my conviction that players can continue long past 30 without being unduly worried about the physical aspects.'

With a lead of just eight runs, India made 330 in their second knock, leaving the Australians the tall order of 339 in the fourth innings to go two up. Thanks to a century from nightwatchman Mann and 83 from Toohey, they got there by two wickets, Thomson smashing Bedi over cover for the winning hit. The A.C.B. were beside themselves and appointed Simpson as skipper for the 1978 tour to the Caribbean. But this series was far from finished. India coming back to win the next two Tests before Australia triumphed in the decider by 47 runs, Simpson having made another 100. For a man whose reputation is cast in granite, it was straight out of *Boys' Own.* Or was it *the Golden Oldies*?

Australia v England 1965-66 (Fourth Test)
Result: Australia won by an innings and nine runs

England

G. Boycott c Chappell b Hawke	22	lbw b McKenzie	12	
R.W. Barber b McKenzie	0	c Grout b Hawke	19	
J.H Edrich c Simpson b McKenzie	5	c Simpson b Hawke	1	
K.F. Barrington lbw b Walters	60	c Chappell b Hawke	102	
M.C. Cowdrey run out	38	c Grout b Stackpole	35	
*M.J.K. Smith b Veivers	29	c McKenzie b Stackpole	5	
†J.M. Parks c Stackpole b McKenzie	49	run out	16	
F.J. Titmus lbw b McKenzie	33	c Grout b Hawke	53	
D.A. Allen c Simpson b McKenzie	2	not out	5	
D.J. Brown c Thomas b McKenzie	1	c and b Hawke	0	
I.J. Jones not out	0	c Lawry b Veivers	8	
Extras (LB 2)	2	(LB 2, NB 8)	10	

1/7 2/25 3/33 4/105 5/150 6/178   241   1/23 2/31 3/32 4/114   266
7/210 8/212 9/222   5/123 6/163 7/244 8/253
9/257

Bowling: *First Innings* – McKenzie 21.7-4-48-6; Hawke 23-2-69-1; Walters 14-0-50-1; Stackpole 5-0-30-0; Chappell 4-1-18-0; Veivers 13-3-24-1. *Second Innings* – McKenzie 18-4-53-1; Hawke 21-6-54-5; Walters 9-0-47-0; Chappell 22-4-53-0; Stackpole 14-3-33-2; Veivers 3.7-0-16-1.

Australia

*R.B. Simpson c Titmus b Jones 225
W.M. Lawry b Titmus 119
G. Thomas b Jones 52
T.R. Veivers c Parks b Jones 1
P.J.P. Burge c Parks b Jones 27
K.D. Walters c Parks b Brown 0
I.M. Chappell c Edrich b Jones 17
K.R. Stackpole c Parks b Jones 43
N.J.N. Hawke not out 20
†A.T.W. Grout b Titmus 4
G.D. McKenzie lbw b Titmus 1
    Extras (B 4, LB 3) 7
1/244 2/331 3/333 4/379 5/383   516
6/415 7/480 8/501 9/506

Bowling: Jones 29-3-118-6; Brown 28-4-109-1; Boycott 7-3-33-0; Titmus 37-6-116-3; Allen 21-1-103-0; Barber 4-0-30-0.

Umpires: C.J. Egar and L.P. Rowan

Australia v India 1977-78 (Second Test)
Result: Australia won by two wickets

India

S.M. Gavaskar c Rixon b Clark	4	b Clark	127
C.P.S. Chauhan c Gannon b Simpson	88	c Ogilvie b Thomson	32
M. Amarnath c Gannon b Thomson	90	c Rixon b Simpson	100
G.R. Viswanath b Thomson	38	c Rixon b Clark	1
D.B. Vengsarkar c Rixon b Clark	49	c Hughes b Gannon	9
B.P. Patel c Rixon b Thomson	3	b Gannon	27
S.M.H. Kirmani† c Rixon b Thomson	38	lbw b Gannon	2
S. Venkataraghavan c Simpson b Gannon	37	c Hughes b Gannon	14
S. Madan Lal b Gannon	43	b Thomson	3
B.S. Bedi b Gannon	3	not out	0
B.S. Chandrasekhar not out	0	not out	0
Extras (B 1, NB 8)	9	(B 1, LB 4, NB 10)	15

1/14 2/163 3/224 4/229 5/235   402   1/47 2/240   (9 wkts dec.) 330
6/311 7/319 8/383 9/391   3/244 4/283 5/287 6/289
                                        7/327 8/328 9/330

Bowling: *First Innings* – Thomson 24-1-101-4; Clark 17-0-95-2; Gannon 16.6-1-84-3; Mann 11-0-63-0; Simpson 11-0-50-1. *Second Innings* – Thomson 21.5-3-65-2; Gannon 18-2-77-4; Clark 18-1-83-2; Mann 8-0-49-0; Simpson 8-2-41-1.

Australia

J. Dyson c Patel b Bedi	53	c Vengsarkar b Bedi	4
C.S. Serjeant c Kirmani b Madan Lal	13	c Kirmani b Madan Lal	12
A.D. Ogilvie b Bedi	27	(4) b Bedi	47
P.M. Toohey st Kirmani b Bedi	0	(5) c Amarnath b Bedi	83
R.B. Simpson* c Vengsarkar b Venkataraghavan	176	(6) run out	39
S.J. Rixon† c Kirmani b Amarnath	50	(8) lbw b Bedi	23
K.J. Hughes c Patel b Bedi	28	lbw b Madan Lal	0
A.L. Mann c Vengsarkar b Bedi	7	(3) c Kirmani b Bedi	105
W.M. Clark c Patel b Chandrasekhar	15	not out	5
J.R. Thomson c Amarnath b Venkataraghavan	0	not out	6
J.B. Gannon not out	0		
Extras (LB 25)	25	(B 8, LB 10)	18

1/19 2/61 3/65 4/149 5/250   394   1/13 2/33 3/172   (8 wkts) 342
6/321 7/341 8/388 9/388   4/195 5/295 6/296 7/330
                                          8/330

Bowling: *First Innings* – Madan Lal 15-1-54-1; Amarnath 16-2-57-1; Chandrasekhar 33.6-6-114-1; Bedi 31-6-89-5; Venkataraghavan 23-4-55-2. *Second Innings* – Madan Lal 11-0-44-2; Amarnath 3-0-22-0; Bedi 30.2-6-105-5; Chandrasekhar 15-0-67-0; Venkataraghavan 28-9-86-0.

Umpires: R.A. Bailhache and R.A. French

Robin Smith

HAMPSHIRE V SURREY

NatWest final, Lord's, 7 September 1991

Born in Durban, South Africa on 13 September 1963, Robin Smith followed his elder brother, Chris, into the Hampshire and England sides of the '80s after completing the four year qualification period. He was a prolific schoolboy sportsman in Natal, setting national junior records in the 100 metre hurdles and the shot putt as well as breaking scoring records at cricket and rugby (as a full back). He made his debut for Hampshire in 1982 and for England in 1988. Since then his Test match average has hovered around the 50 mark, the sure sign of quality. He is renowned as a selfless, wholehearted cricketer – he often fields under the helmet for England – and he hits the ball as hard as any modern batsman.

Cricketers usually betray something of themselves in the middle. Contrast innings by Boycott and Botham and it is not too tricky to tell which of them has been invited to appear in pantomime. When Gooch and Gower were in partnership, the Bollinger drinker was, I think, discernible. However, Robin Smith can confuse us.

Watch him crack those square cuts with the ferocity of a cuckolded lumberjack and the assumption is that here is a forthright, self-assured character, who knows he's very good. Meet him off the field and he is always cheerful and unfailingly polite, yet remarkably self-deprecating about his cricket, diffident even. Why this should be the case after 45 Tests for England and a batting average of 46 is a puzzle.

As a batsman he is all too aware of his Achilles heel and it is a rare one among modern cricketers. He does not enjoy batting against spin bowlers – especially unorthodox ones like Anil Kumble or Shane Warne. Both have jeopardised his Test place and however much Smith has theorised and sought advice, the solution has remained elusive. But against pace bowlers and in particular the awesome West Indians, Smith is the first player the selectors write down on the teamsheet. He is one of very few professional cricketers who is genuinely exhilarated by the ball whistling past his nostrils.

His method against the quicks is neither classical nor particularly elegant. Indeed on his first England tour to the Caribbean in 1990 he was often ridiculed by the locals. Before each innings he got a colleague to throw cricket balls at his head from a distance of five yards and he ducked and weaved appropriately. This was regarded as 'defeatist' though it was far more realistic practice than the usual diet of gentle half volleys that

172

batsmen indulge in before the game. West Indian onlookers soon changed their mind. His method of counteracting short, straight bowling may have been occasionally humiliating – 'basically I tried to hit the deck as fast as I could,' but it worked. Smith raised by a cricket-mad father in Durban had learnt early in his life the virtue of realistic practice.

David Gower, a colleague at Hampshire for four years confirms this. He remembers Smith taking to the nets at Southampton with a bowling machine when he heard that he had been picked for the first Test against the West Indies in 1991. Gower in a nearby net (yes, I promise) heard proceedings even if he didn't see them – 'there was the whistle of the ball flying out of the machine at high speed and frequently the thud of the ball hitting Robin's body, followed by a strangled "aaargh".' Gower, incidentally, chose to remain where he was against mortal opposition.

Predictably Smith's choice centres on a confrontation with a fast bowler and also highlights his loyalty to his county side, Hampshire. The innings he most savours was a typically combative Test century against the West Indies at Lord's in 1991, his most flamboyant one-day innings was that astonishing *tour de force* at Edgbaston against the Australians in 1993 when he smashed 167 not out and still ended up on the losing side, but for the match of his life he chose a game in which his contribution led to victory – Hampshire's NatWest final against Surrey in 1991. The fast bowler in question was Pakistan's Waqar Younis.

Hampshire had arrived at Lord's in some disarray. By chance they had been scheduled to play at the Oval against Surrey in the match preceding the final and Waqar Younis had caused havoc. His match figures were 12-92 as Hampshire slumped to a 171 run defeat. In addition he had broken the little finger of the Hampshire captain, Mark Nicholas, as he tried to fend off a vicious lifter so that he was immediately ruled out of the final. Advantage Surrey before a ball was bowled.

Gower, despite a dearth of initials (three is usually the minimum requirement), was entrusted with the Hampshire captaincy for the day, won the toss and chose to field. Surrey began slowly; their inexperienced opener, Robinson, was forced to retire hurt having been struck on the head by Aqib Javed, who bowled with surprising haste as if fed up with hearing and reading about the exploits of his more exalted Pakistani colleague. But Alec Stewart, Graham Thorpe and David Ward restored the innings so that after 60 overs Surrey had set Hampshire the demanding target of 241 for victory.

Hampshire's response was sedate but solid. Waqar's brief first spell, which is usually his least threatening, was overcome by Paul Terry and Tony Middleton. They had added 90 in 27 overs when Middleton called Terry for another quick single only to see him run out by a direct hit from Thorpe at mid-wicket. As Smith entered the stage Waqar was instructed to loosen up by his captain, Ian Greig. The promised confrontation was about to take place.

Smith recalls, 'Waqar bowled at searing pace. I defended and ducked, intent on survival.' Waqar's four over spell was wicketless, a rare occurence in 1991, when he scavenged 113 first class wickets and before it finished, Smith had produced one rasping cover drive. Greig was forced to rest Waqar and save him for the final fling. Smith and Middleton took the score to 160 but with victory on the horizon for Hampshire wickets started to tumble. Middleton, Gower (lbw to Waqar), and James all departed in swift succession. By now Waqar was steaming in from the Pavilion End and it was getting dark.

Smith was fearful for his new partners: 'Sighting the ball from the Pavilion End at Lord's is hard enough in clear daylight, but with dusk approaching it was almost impossible for batsmen who had just arrived at the wicket. It was easier for me since I had time to acclimatise.' While the others groped myopically against Waqar, Smith's eye and concentration remained sure. 24 were needed off three overs when Jon Ayling hit two timely boundaries. That 58th over produced 14 runs but also the freakish dismissal of Smith, run out when Murphy gathered a rebound from the stumps and threw down the wicket. Hampshire were then 10 runs short of a victory, fashioned by Smith's 78 from only 94 balls.

With two balls remaining Ayling struck the winning runs. Soon Gower found himself hoisting the trophy into the night sky and that drubbing at the Oval was now a dim, inconsequential memory as Smith modestly accepted the Man of the Match award from Colin Cowdrey.

Result: Hampshire won by four wickets

Surrey

D.J. Bicknell b Ayling	....	13
J. D. Robinson not out	....	3
†A. J. Stewart b Ayling	....	61
G.P. Thorpe c James b Connor	....	93
D.M. Ward c Maru b Connor	....	43
M.A. Lynch c Ayling b Connor	....	10
*I.A. Greig not out	....	7
Extras (B 2, LB 4, W 3, NB 1)	....	10
1/25 2/139 3/203 4/222 5/233		240

M.P. Bicknell, J. Boiling, Waqar Younis, A.J. Murphy did not bat.

Bowling: *First Innings* – Aqib Javed 12-2-54-0; Connor 12-4-39-3; Ayling 12-0-39-3; James 9-3-33-0; Maru 6-0-23-0; Udal 9-0-46-0.

Hampshire

V.P. Terry run out	....	32
T.C. Middleton b Murphy	....	78
R.A. Smith run out	....	78
*D.I. Gower lbw b Waqar Younis	....	9
K.D. James c Stewart b Bicknell M	....	0
J.R. Ayling not out	....	18
†A.J. Aymes run out	....	2
R.J. Maru not out	....	1
Extras (LB 17, W 5, NB 3)	....	25
1/90 2/160 3/192 4/193		243
5/231 6/238		

S.D. Udal, C.A. Connor, Aqib Javed did not bat.

Bowling: *First Innings* – Waqar Younis 12-0-43-1; M. Bicknell 11.4-1-32-1; Murphy 12-0-56-1; Robinson 12-0-43-0; Boiling 12-1-52-0.

John Snow

Sydney Tests, 9-14 January & 12-17 February 1971

Born 13 November 1941, John Snow played for Sussex from 1961 to 1977, when he joined the 'Packer Circus'. In 1980 he came out of retirement to help Warwickshire win the Sunday League. At best his fluid action made him the most potent English fast bowler since Fred Trueman, though he was sometimes criticised at Hove for preserving his energies for the big occasion. He was also a capable lower order batsman, who in 1966 added a crucial 128 runs with Ken Higgs in a famous last wicket stand against the West Indies. In 49 Tests for England he claimed 202 wickets. Apart from his triumphs in Australia in 1970/71, he took a record 27 wickets in four Tests in the Caribbean on the 1967/8 tour, the last time England were victorious in the West Indies. Unlike Trueman he published two volumes of poetry in between tormenting opening batsmen.

It is curious how the most talented English fast bowler since Freddie Trueman undertook just one tour of Australia. In 1965/6 David Larter, the gangling Northamptonshire paceman, whose rise and fall in professional cricket was as meteoric as that of the Bay City Rollers in the hit parade, was preferred to John Snow. Fair enough; Larter had captured 87 cheap wickets the season before and there may have been enticing parallels to be drawn among the selection committee of that other Northamptonshire meteor, who really did terrorise Australians, Frank Tyson. In fact Larter never added to his 10 Test caps in 1965/6 as he broke down, thereby gaining the unique, though hardly coveted distinction of touring Australia twice without playing a Test match.

In 1974/5 John Snow knew that he would not be picked, even though the bulk of the English public as well as the cricket professionals thought he would – and should – be the mainstay of the fast bowling attack. The only son of a Worcestershire country rector, educated in a southern public school and given to penning poetry, was reckoned to be a bit of a troublemaker. He had bundled over Sunil Gavaskar in a Test match and was punished by being dropped; he had occasionally been accused of not trying for his county, Sussex, but what really undermined his prospects of touring was the fact that he had the temerity to question how the game was being run. 'My pet grouse was the insecurity of cricketers as they prepared for the winter. You had to wait until the middle of September to know if you were touring, which made it impossible to make any concrete plans; they must have known who would comprise the bulk of their

175

touring party by mid-August.' He declined one England tour for this reason and it was hardly surprising that when Kerry Packer came along offering much higher financial rewards and a more professional, sympathetic treatment of players that Snow, in the autumn of his career, was one of his early signatories. By the '90s winter contracts were indeed issued to senior players confirming the sense of Snow's argument and after a decade out of the game he was invited to join England's band of specialist coaches.

The one Ashes tour that he did complete in 1970/1 under the captaincy of Ray Illingworth was the pinnacle of his career. 'That tour represented what I always wanted to do: to participate in an Ashes victory in Australia.' Snow found it hard to select one match on the tour preferring to view the entire series as one marathon contest. In the end we permitted him to choose the two decisive Tests in Sydney. In the first Snow was supreme, taking 7-40 to enable England a 299 run victory. In the second his contribution was not so tangible, but for tension, drama and elation the game demanded inclusion.

The 1970/1 tour was a triumph for Illingworth, preferred as England captain – after much debate – to the perennial bridesmaid Down Under, Colin Cowdrey, but no-one could call it a harmonious expedition. England's management team were as compatible as a gaggle of former Tory Prime Ministers. Captain and vice-captain, Cowdrey, were not natural bedfellows, while Illingworth and his players were incensed when manager, David Clark, mused to the Australian press that he would rather lose the series 3-1 than endure a succession of draws. This reflected a set of priorities unknown in Pudsey. Another bone of contention was the addition of a seventh Test match after the Melbourne Test had been washed out; the players were anxious to be rewarded for their 'overtime' and the visit of the President of the M.C.C., Sir Cyril Hawker, which was expected to be a gentle goodwill exercise, was soon transformed into a troubleshooting mission. Snow was the centre of a minor storm early in the tour when he was admonished by Illingworth for 'buggering about in the field and upsetting other bowlers' in an early match in Adelaide. But there was plenty of mutual respect between them. Illingworth recognised that Snow was the most potent bowler on either side and that his energies should be saved for the Tests, Snow that he should not undermine the efforts of his colleagues to win a Test place.

After two draws and a washout, England arrived in Sydney, knowing that this was Australia's 'result' pitch, which was expected to turn. England dominated with Boycott excelling with the bat in both innings and Underwood taking four wickets in Australia's first innings so that Illingworth was able to declare, leaving Australia the improbable target of 416 for victory; more realistically they had to bat for nine and a half hours; they lasted half that time. Snow recalls; The pitch was slow in pace, but there was a worn patch just short of a length, which allowed the leg cutter to go. Ian Chappell, the emergency opener to protect Stackpole, was dismissed first ball by a lifter and one really reared at "Garth" McKenzie and he had to retire hurt. Otherwise I remember there was just enough movement and some brilliant catches in the slip area, one by Peter Lever to get rid of Stackpole and another by Willis in the gully from

Rod Marsh.' The fast bowlers' union were sticking together.

Snow is not the sort to wax lyrically about the quality of his own bowling on that day, so we must leave that to others. E. W. Swanton wrote, 'I had not seen an Englishman bowl either faster or better than Snow at Sydney since Tyson.' Illingworth was prepared to compare him to Trueman – 'Fred could swing the ball more, but with Snow's height, he had the ability to bounce the ball into the batsman from just short of a length.' So England took the lead in the marathon.

A draw at Melbourne was followed by another in Adelaide, where Illingworth stunned critics by declining to enforce the follow-on. Snow explains: 'The pitch in Adelaide was flat; I had a bad back and we were all conscious that the final Test was at Sydney, where there definitely would be a result.' Illingworth, compelled to play four Tests in six weeks, was conscious of conserving the energy of his key players.

So to the explosive finale at Sydney with England already deprived of their key batsman, Boycott. The pitch was damp at the start and bowler-friendly as England were bundled out for 184. Ian Redpath and Greg Chappell ensured an Australian lead and in the closing stages of their innings Terry Jenner was hit on the head, ducking into a bouncer from Snow. Umpire Rowan warned Snow and captain Illingworth was fuming – with Rowan rather than Snow – one of the few occasions when he lost his temper on a cricket field. When Snow withdrew to long leg at the end of the over, one spectator grabbed Snow's shirt and empty beer cans were thrown in his direction. Illingworth promptly led his players from the field, returning after seven minutes during which England were warned that the match might be forfeited unless he returned. Illingworth's action was vilified by most observers though the brief delay did bring an end to the crowd's unruly behaviour.

After England had scored 302 in their second innings, Australia were set 223 to win. Snow bowled Eastwood with his sixth ball but in the fifth over he dislocated his finger, which was entangled with the boundary railings as he attempted to catch a hook from Stackpole. Thereafter the match was a blur for Snow – England, superbly marshalled by Illingworth, won by 62 runs. He recalls, 'At the hospital I was pumped full of pethidine; I told them I didn't want any sleeping tablets, but they ignored me, so the following day at the ground I was semi-conscious. I did my best to celebrate with the team afterwards but by 10 o'clock I had collapsed in a heap. That injury prevented me going on to New Zealand, so I travelled in the Far East, which was what I'd wanted to do after the Ashes series anyway.' He's still travelling now. As a successful travel agent, he ships cricket lovers and writers around the world with a laid-back efficiency and equanimity, totally at odds with his reputation as the firebrand fast bowler of the '60s and '70s.

9, 10, 12, 13, 14 January
Result: England won by 299 runs

England

G. Boycott c Gleeson b Connolly 77   not out 142
B.W. Luckhurst lbw b Gleeson 38   c I Chappell b McKenzie ... 5
J.H. Edrich c Gleeson b G Chappell 55   run out 12
K.W.R. Fletcher c Walters b Mallett 23   c Stackpole b Mallett 8
B.L. D'Oliveira c Connolly b Mallett 0   c I Chappell b G Chappell . 56
*R. Illingworth b Gleeson 25   st Marsh b Mallett 53
†A.P.E. Knott st Marsh b Mallett 6   not out 21
J.A. Snow c Lawry b Gleeson 37
P. Lever c Connolly b Mallett 36
D.L. Underwood c G Chappell 0
    b Gleeson
R.G.D. Willis not out 15
     Extras (B 5, LB 2, W 1, NB 12) 20   (B 9, LB 4, NB 9) 22
1/116 2/130 3/201 4/205   332   1/7 2/35 3/48 4/181   319
5/208 6/219 7/262 8/291 9/291   5/276

Bowling: *First Innings* – McKenzie 15-3-74-0; Connolly 13-2-43-1; Gleeson 29-7-83-4; G. Chappell 11-4-30-1; Mallett 16.7-5-40-4; Walters 3-1-11-0; Stackpole 7-2-31-0. *Second Innings* – McKenzie 15-0-65-1; Connolly 14-1-38-0; Gleeson 23-4-54-0; G. Chappell 15-5-24-1; Mallett 19-1-85-2; Walters 2-0-14-0; Stackpole 6-1-17-0.

Australia

*W.M. Lawry c Edrich b Lever 9   not out 60
I.M. Chappell c Underwood b Snow . 123   c D'Oliveira b Snow 0
I.R. Redpath c Fletcher b D'Oliveira 64   c Edrich b Snow 6
K.D. Walters c Luckhurst b Illingworth . 55   c Knott b Lever 3
G.S. Chappell c&b Underwood 15   b Snow 2
K.R. Stackpole c Boycott b Underwood . 33   c Lever b Snow 30
†R.W. Marsh c D'Oliveira b Underwood 8   c Willis b Snow 0
A.A. Mallett b Underwood 4   c Knott b Willis 6
G.D. McKenzie not out 11   retired hurt 6
J.W. Gleeson c Fletcher b Underwood ... 0   b Snow 0
A.N. Connolly b Lever 14   c Knott b Snow 0
     Extras (NB 11) 11   (B 2, NB 1) 3
1/14 2/38 3/137 4/160 5/189   236   1/1 2/11 3/14 4/21   116
6/199 7/208 8/208 9/219   5/66 6/66 7/86 8/116 9/116

Bowling: *First Innings* – Snow 14-6-23-1; Willis 9-2-26-0; Lever 8.6-1-31-2; Underwood 14-3-66-4; Illingworth 14-3-59-1; D'Oliveira 9-2-20-2. *Second Innings* – Snow 17.5-5-40-7; Willis 3-2-1-1; Lever 11-1-24-1; Underwood 8-2-17-0; Illingworth 9-5-9-0; D'Oliveira 7-3-16-0; Fletcher 1-0-6-0.

12, 13, 14, 16, 17 February
Result: England won by 62 runs

England

J.H. Edrich c G Chappell b Dell	30	c I Chappell b O'Keeffe	57
B.W. Luckhurst c Redpath b Walters	0	c Lillee b O'Keeffe	59
K.W.R. Fletcher c Stackpole b O'Keeffe	33	c Stackpole b Eastwood	20
J.H. Hampshire c Marsh b Lillee	10	c I Chappell b O'Keeffe	24
B.L. d'Oliveira b Dell	1	c I Chappell b Lillee	47
*R. Illingworth b Jenner	42	lbw b Lillee	29
†A.J.E. Knott c Stackpole b O'Keeffe	27	b Dell	15
J.A. Snow b Jenner	7	c Stackpole b Dell	20
P. Lever c Jenner b O'Keeffe	4	c Redpath b Jenner	17
D.I. Underwood not out	8	c Marsh b Dell	0
R.G.D. Willis b Jenner	11	not out	2
Extras (B 4, LB 4, W 1, NB 2)	11	(B 3, LB 3, NB 6)	12
1/5 2/60 3/68 4/69 5/98	184	1/94 2/130 3/158 4/165	302
6/145 7/156 8/165 9/165		5/234 6/251 7/276 8/298 9/299	

Bowling: *First Innings* – Lillee 13-5-32-1; Dell 16-8-32-2; Walters 4-0-10-1; G. Chappell 3-0-9-0; Jenner 16-3-42-3; O'Keeffe 24-8-48-3. *Second Innings* – Lillee 14-0-43-2; Dell 26.7-3-65-3; Walters 5-0-18-0; Jenner 21-5-39-1; O'Keeffe 26-8-96-3; Eastwood 5-0-21-1; Stackpole 3-1-8-0.

Australia

R.H. Eastwood c Knott b Lever	5	b Snow	0
K.R. Stackpole b Snow	6	b Illingworth	67
†R.W. Marsh c Willis b Lever	4	b Underwood	16
*I.M. Chappell b Willis	25	c Knott b Lever	6
I.R. Redpath c&b Underwood	59	c Hampshire b Illingworth	14
K.D. Walters st Knott b Underwood	42	c D'Oliveira b Willis	1
G.S. Chappell b Willis	65	st Knott b Illingworth	30
K.J. O'Keeffe c Knott b Illingworth	3	c sub b D'Oliveira	12
D.K. Lillee c Knott b Willis	6	c Hampshire b D'Oliveira	0
T.J. Jenner b Lever	30	c Fletcher b Underwood	4
A.R. Dell not out	3	not out	7
Extras (LB 5, W 1, NB 10)	16	(B 2, NB 5)	7
1/11 2/13 3/32 4/66 5/147	264	1/0 2/22 3/71 4/82	160
6/162 7/178 8/235 9/239		5/96 6/131 7/142 8/154 9/154	

Bowling: *First Innings* – Snow 18-2-68-1; Lever 14.6-3-43-3; D'Oliveira 12-2-24-0; Willis 12-1-58-3; Underwood 16-3-39-2; Illingworth 11-3-16-1; Fletcher 1-0-9-0. *Second Innings* – Snow 2-1-7-1; Lever 12-2-23-1; D'Oliveira 5-1-15-2; Willis 9-1-32-1; Underwood 13.6-5-28-2; Illingworth 20-7-39-3.

Alec Stewart

Bridgetown, 8, 9, 10, 12, 13 April 1994

Alec Stewart was born on 8 April and followed his father, Mickey, into both the Surrey and England dressing rooms. Indeed Stewart senior was his son's cricket manager when he began both his county and international careers. But any charges of nepotism were soon dismissed. In public Mickey referred to his son as 'England's number 3' rather than Alec; moreover Alec's performances soon demonstrated his right to play international cricket, whoever the manager. Meticulously polite off the field, combative on it, Stewart is currently captain of Surrey and vice-captain of England.

For Alec Stewart there were two matches in contention. Both took place in the Caribbean, rarely the venue for memorable English performances. The first was his Test debut in Kingston, Jamaica in 1990. Whatever happens in your first Test is chiselled in the memory for the rest of your life.

In this match, Stewart's contribution was modest; he scored 13 in the first innings and was not out 0 when Wayne Larkins hit the winning runs in the second, However, England's victory by nine wickets was their first against the West Indies for 16 years and 30 Test matches. It was the most unexpected Test victory imaginable, defying all cricketing logic. No-one outside the England team, which was led by Graham Gooch and managed by Alec's father, Mickey, had been able to envisage England competing with the West Indies, let alone beating them.

Four years later when England returned to the Caribbean, Gooch had resigned the captaincy and Stewart senior had given way to Keith Fletcher. Alec was now England's vice captain with 32 Test caps to his name. In the interim the selectors had flirted with making him keep wicket for England, even though he was reluctant to take on that role on a regular basis for Surrey.

Fortunately, when Mike Atherton took over the captaincy it was decided that Stewart should play as a specialist opening batsman. On the 1994 West Indies tour, the wisdom of this decision was confirmed beyond any doubt in the fourth Test match of the series in Bridgetown, Barbados – Stewart's choice. 'There I batted better than at any time in my life – and, even more important, we won.'

This victory was as unexpected as the one in Jamaica. The West Indies had only lost one match in Bridgetown in their history – a bizarre rain-affected game in 1935 against Bob Wyatt's tourists, notable for two cavalier declarations. The portents for the England side were dreadful in 1994. They had lost the first three games of the series and in the previous Test in Trinidad they had been routed for 46 by Curtly Ambrose when needing 194 for victory. Such a devastating experience could easily lead to the complete disintegration of the tourists' resolve, which had been the case on the 1985/6 tour.

Hordes of English tourists had arrived in Barbados for the game wondering whether all their savings had been wasted. They outnumbered the home supporters in the compact stands of the Kensington Oval and were increasingly vociferous as the game progressed. Stewart acknowledges that they gave the English team 'an enormous fillip'.

Richie Richardson won the toss and opted to field, so England had an immediate opportunity to exorcise the memory of the 46 all out debacle against Ambrose and Walsh. So much depended on the openers, Atherton and Stewart, the only two batsmen in the English side who had shown any conviction against the West Indian pace bowlers in the first three Tests. Both withstood the opening barrage with aplomb and, aided by a lightning fast outfield, runs came swiftly. When, after an hour's play this pair had added 47 together, there was raucous cheering from the English supporters, relief tinged with irony that this nightmarish landmark had been passed.

Together they added 171 when Atherton edged to Lara at first slip for 85. Stewart pressed on to his first Test century against the West Indies and a feature of his innings was the certainty with which he pulled the West Indian fast bowlers whenever they pitched short. From the start, a man had been stationed at deep square leg for Stewart but he was seeing the ball so early that he was able to crack anything short through mid-wicket. For a while the West Indies bowlers were non-plussed. They were not used to visiting batsmen taking on the short-pitched ball with such relish.

Stewart's technique gives him more time than most to pull the ball. He is a back-foot player, having learnt his cricket on the bouncy pitches at the Oval and in West Australia, where he played grade cricket for eight years. Nonetheless, the explanation of his fondness for the pull shot is surprising: 'I like to pull if the bounce is uneven, which I know is contrary to the coaching manuals. By attempting to hit short balls on unreliable surfaces it makes sure that I keep my eye on the ball. If the bounce is true it is much easier to duck with impunity. In the Caribbean it rarely was so I was reluctant to duck.' Instead he kept pummelling the ball to the legside boundary.

He also recognised that he had tightened up as any opening batsmen. 'In the Barbados Test of 1990 I played two cameos (45 and 37); in both innings I was caught in the slips flashing outside the off stump. By 1994 I had learnt my lesson and I knew where my off stump was.' Indeed in the innings he disdained anything outside off stump unless it was eminently hittable. As the bowlers grew frustrated, they started to direct the ball at Stewart's pads. This is where his strength lies and time and time again he clipped the ball through mid-wicket with exquisite timing.

After Stewart's dismissal – played on to Winston Benjamin for 118 – the

English innings subsided to 355 all out. However, a sterling performance by Angus Fraser enabled England to gain a first innings lead of 51 – and it would have been much more but for the patience of the 19-year-old Chanderpaul and the belligerence of the West Indian tail. Fraser's 8-75 were the best figures achieved by an Englishman against the West Indies and just reward for the stalwart Middlesex workhorse.

Goaded by the prospect of an unthinkable defeat in Barbados, the West Indian pacemen stormed in at the start of England's second innings, but again Stewart stood firm. He hit another century – no Englishman had ever hit two in the same match against the West Indies – and if anything, this innings was more impressive than the first for several reasons. Stewart had good cause to feel jaded after his first innings efforts; England at 79-3 looked as if they might surrender the initiative as they had done so melodramatically at Trinidad so the pressure was on. Moreover, the West Indies bowled more intelligently against him – there was nothing short to hit. Indeed on the fourth morning, Stewart, who began the day on 62, could muster only 13 runs in two hours. Yet in the afternoon, supported by his county colleague, Graham Thorpe, Stewart was able to up the tempo at the appropriate moment. He finished with 143 out of a total of 394-7 so that Atherton was able to set the West Indies an unlikely target of 446 for victory.

By teatime on the last day the West Indies were all out for 237, with Caddick and Tufnell sharing eight wickets between them. Stewart was Malcolm Marshall's obvious choice as Man of the Match, his performance having catapulted him into the highest echelon of world batsmen; at last, England had a candidate to play against that hypothetical Martian XI. Moreover, Alec Stewart could no longer be regarded as 'Mickey's boy'; rather Stewart senior had now been demoted to 'Alec's Dad'.

Result: England won by 208 runs

England

*M.A. Atherton c Lara b K. Benjamin	85	c Lara b Walsh	15
A.J. Stewart b W. Benjamin	118	b Walsh	143
M.R. Ramprakash c Murray b W. Benjamin	20	c Chanderpaul b Walsh	3
R.A. Smith c Murray b W. Benjamin	10	lbw b K. Benjamin	13
G.A. Hick c Murray b Ambrose	34	c Lara b Walsh	59
G.P. Thorpe c sub b K. Benjamin	7	c Arthurton b Walsh	84
†R.C. Russell c Chanderpaul b Ambrose	38	not out	17
C.C. Lewis c Murray b Ambrose	0	c Walsh b Adams	10
A.R. Caddick b Ambrose	8		
A.R.C. Fraser c Chanderpaul b Walsh	3		
P.C.R. Tufnell not out	0		
Extras (LB 7, NB 23)	30		
1/171 2/223 3/242 4/265 5/290	355	1/33 2/43 3/79 4/197	394
6/307 7/307 8/327 9/351		5/344 6/382 7/394	

Bowling: *First Innings* – Ambrose 24.2-5-86-4; Walsh 24-3-88-1; W. Benjamin 22-4-76-3; K. Benjamin 20-5-74-2; Chanderpaul 10-4-23-0. *Second Innings* – Ambrose 22-4-75-0; Walsh 28-5-94-5; W. Benjamin 22-3-58-0; K. Benjamin 20-1-92-1; Chanderpaul 10-3-30-0; Adams 6.5-0-31-1.

West Indies

D.L. Haynes c Atherton b Fraser	35	c Thorpe b Tufnell	15
*R.B. Richardson c Atherton b Fraser	20	c Ramprakash b Caddick	33
B.C. Lara c sub b Lewis	26	c Tufnell b Caddick	64
K.L.T. Arthurton c Russell b Fraser	0	b Tufnell	52
J.C. Adams c Thorpe b Fraser	26	c Russell b Caddick	12
S. Chanderpaul c Ramprakash b Tufnell	77	c sub b Hick	5
†J. R. Murray c Thorpe b Fraser	0	c Thorpe b Caddick	5
W.K.M. Benjamin c Hick b Fraser	8	c Stewart b Tufnell	3
C.E.L. Ambrose c Hick b Fraser	44	b Lewis	12
K.C.G. Benjamin not out	43	c Hick b Caddick	0
C.A. Walsh c Tufnell b Fraser	13	not out	18
Extras:	12		18
Total:	304		237

Bowling: *First Innings* – Fraser 28.4-7-75-8; Caddick 24-2-92-0; Lewis 17-2-60-1; Tufnell 32-12-76-1. *Second Innings* – Fraser 17-7-40-0; Caddick 17-3-63-5; Lewis 8.2-1-23-1; Tufnell 36-12-100-3; Hick 4-2-3-1.

Chris Tavare

Old Trafford, 13-18 August 1981

Chris Tavare was born on 27 October 1954. A zoologist at Oxford University, where he gained three blues, Tavare made his debut for Kent in 1974 and captained the county in 1983/4 before being replaced by Chris Cowdrey. In 1989 he joined Somerset and he led them from 1990 until his retirement in 1993. A right-hand batsman and superb slip fielder, he played 31 Tests for England and spent most of that time blocking for his country, but in county cricket he was capable of destroying attacks in unorthodox style. Inevitably the golfer he most admires is Paul Azinger 'because he's also got a funny grip.' One other oddity – he was seldom heard to swear on a cricket field.

Once Ian Botham declined to choose this match, it was snapped up by Chris Tavare. Yes, he was the man at the other end when Botham smashed a century in 86 balls, the perfect anonymous foil. 'I have never experienced an atmosphere like the Saturday of the Old Trafford Test, 1981 before or since,' explains Tavare. 'There was a packed crowd and the Ashes were in the balance. When Botham entered, whirling his bat over his shoulders, the whole ground was transformed and the air of expectation among the spectators was enormous; they were not to be disappointed.'

To set the scene, albeit briefly, since the 1981 Tests against Australia are now firmly embedded in cricket's folklore: Botham began the series as captain, but resigned after registering a pair in the second Test at Lord's, just in time to avoid the ignominy of being sacked. Mike Brearley was installed as captain. At Headingley Botham batted miraculously; at Edgbaston he bowled miraculously. Surely cricketing mortality was due to return?

Tavare had not played in any of these matches. After two Tests against the West Indies in 1980 he had been dropped; now he was recalled in an attempt to resolve England's problem number 3 slot. His reputation as an obdurate blocker – deserved in Test cricket, but not on the county circuit – was already established. This was a vital game for his own international future though amid all the excitement of an incredible series, his recall warranted little attention.

At Old Trafford Brearley won the toss and England batted in difficult conditions. 'The ball seamed around and kept low,' recalls Tavare. 'We lost wickets early (Boycott and Gooch) to Lillee and Alderman; in a curious way this helped me as it meant that I was justified in adopting my defensive method; there was no pressure to score quickly, just to stay there.' (Tavare, you may recall, lost his Test place in 1984 following a dour 14 in two hours against Sri Lanka at Lord's; a brisk eight and he would have survived.)

Botham went for a duck to Lillee and England were grateful for a ninth wicket partnership of 40 between Tavare and Paul Allott on his Test debut – 'I remember Paul being greatly offended when I tried to shield him from the bowling; after a couple overs I didn't bother.' Allott made 52 not out and with Tavare top scoring (69) England finished with a modest total of 231.

In their first innings Australia batted like a shell-shocked team. To a man they went for their shots, but it didn't work. Within 31 overs they were bowled out for 130, Botham taking 3-28 as well as snapping up three slip catches off the bowling of Bob Willis. So England were batting again by Friday evening, losing Gooch cheaply – bowled by Alderman. Boycott and Tavare took the score to 70-1 at the close and England were in charge.

Saturday morning's play must have been a grave disappointment for a capacity crowd. Lillee and Alderman both probed away menacingly and both Boycott and Tavare were operating in their most defensive modes, a combination more powerful than Mogadon. 29 runs were added for loss of three wickets and England were losing the initiative; Boycott and Gatting were lbw to Alderman while Gower succumbed to Lillee. In two hours Tavare had contributed nine runs. Brearley was batting at six and this was Tavare's first match under his leadership; already Tavare had been impressed by his incisive observations during team talks. He remembers walking out to bat with Brearley after lunch with nerves jangling. 'You would have expected our conversation to revolve around how we were going to cope with Lillee and co., but it didn't. Brearley knew that I'd studied zoology at Oxford and as we headed towards the middle he instigated a conversation about behavioural patterns. I'm sure this helped to relax me.' However, it didn't do Brearley much good. He was soon caught down the leg side off Alderman to make the score 104-5, giving England a precarious lead of 205 on a pitch gradually easing. The crowd erupted at Botham's trademark bat-twirling entry.

Tavare recalls, '"Beefy" started very slowly, which I always regarded as a good sign. His first 30 balls produced three singles and I remember saying to him between overs, "Are you trying to do me out of a job in this team?"' Then Botham started to attack Bright; a cut for four was followed by a lofted cover drive. This prompted Kim Hughes to take a second new ball, whereupon Botham exploded. Now he had one escape; a sliced drive against Alderman was dropped by Whitney running backwards at mid-off; undeterred he set about Lillee.

'Lillee put two men back on the legside boundary and bounced him. Botham hooked and each time I thought "That's out" as the ball skimmed towards the fielder, but it just kept going into the stands.' Lillee's first over with the new ball yielded 22 runs, 19 from Botham's bat, the most in the history of England/Australia Tests. Thereafter Tavare describes Botham's batting as 'savage': 'I just sat back and watched, determined not to get out.' Occasionally he had to run like a hare rather than a tortoise to survive as Botham's calling was not at its most reliable. Afterwards Botham declared 'I like batting with "Tav". He seems to understand my calls even when I mean the opposite.'

Botham drove Lillee straight at head height – fortunately the Australian was still bent double in his follow through as the ball whistled past – and then pulled Alderman for another massive six. He reached his century in the first over after tea in the grand manner, a six off Bright. It had taken 86 balls, the quickest in England since 1902. When he was caught behind off Whitney for 118 his partnership with Tavare had been worth 148 in 123 minutes, the worth to the paying spectator was incalculable.

Tavare added another 40 with Alan Knott before his 423-minute marathon was ended by Alderman. In all, he had batted 12 hours in the match for 148 runs and Botham was quick to recognise his contribution: 'I got a lot of plaudits for my hundred but "Tav" never got due praise for his unselfish, determined batting in both innings.' England needed those runs, for in Australia's second innings Graham Yallop and Allan Border, despite a broken finger, scored fine centuries. But Australia's total of 402 was still 103 runs short of their target and the Ashes were won.

Chris Tavare now began a run of 25 consecutive Tests for England; there was the odd skittish innings – at Melbourne and the Oval in 1983 against New Zealand – but suspicious of his own talent and ever conscious of the team's need, he blocked most of the time. His method often earned him harsh criticism, though rarely from his teammates. Bob Willis, who recognised the need for rest and recuperation for a fast bowler, delighted in his forward defensive just as front row forwards appreciate a safe touch kick from their fly-half rather than any fancy stuff. He may have been in a minority but he once declared with feeling. 'I just love watching "Tav" bat.'

Result: England won by 103 runs

England

G. Boycott c Marsh b Alderman	10	lbw b Alderman	37
G.A. Gooch lbw b Lillee	10	b Alderman	5
C.J. Tavare c Alderman b Whitney	69	c Kent b Alderman	78
D.I. Gower c Yallop b Whitney	23	c Bright b Lillee	1
J.M Brearley lbw b Alderman	2	c Marsh b Alderman	3
M.W. Gatting c Border b Lillee	32	lbw b Alderman	11
I.T. Botham c Bright b Lillee	0	c Marsh b Whitney	118
A.P.E. Knott c Border b Alderman	13	c Dyson b Lillee	59
J.E. Emburey c Border b Alderman	1	c Kent b Whitney	57
P.J.W. Allott not out	52	c Hughes b Bright	14
R.G.D. Willis c Hughes b Lillee	11	not out	5
Extras (LB 6, W 2)	8	(B 1, LB 12, NB 3)	16

1/19 2/25 3/57 4/62 5/109   231   1/7 2/79 3/80 4/98 5/104   404
6/109 7/131 8/132 9/175   6/253 7/282 8/356 9/396

Bowling: *First Innings* – Lillee 24.1-8-55-4; Alderman 29-5-88-5; Whitney 17-3-50-2; Bright 16-6-30-0. *Second Innings* – Lillee 46-13-137-2; Alderman 52-19-102-5; Whitney 27-6-74-2; Bright 26.4-11-68-1. *Second Innings* – Lillee 46-13-137-2; Alderman 52-19-102-5; Whitney 27-6-74-2; Bright 26.4-11-68-1.

Australia

G.M. Wood lbw b Allot	19	c Knott b Allott	6
J. Dyson c Botham b Willis	0	run out	5
K.J. Hughes lbw b Willis	4	lbw b Botham	43
G.N. Yallop c Botham b Willis	0	b Emburey	114
M.F. Kent c Knott b Emburey	52	c Brearley b Emburey	2
A.R. Border c Gower b Botham	11	not out	123
R.W. Marsh c Botham b Willis	1	c Knott b Willis	47
R.J. Bright c Knott b Botham	22	c Knott b Willis	5
D.K. Lillee c Gooch b Botham	13	c Botham b Allott	28
M.J. Whitney b Allott	0	c Gatting b Willis	0
T.M. Alderman not out	2	lbw b Botham	0
Extras (NB 6)	6	(LB 9, W 2, NB 18)	29
1/20 2/24 3/24 4/24 5/58	130	1/7 2/24 3/119 4/198	402
6/59 7/104 8/125 9/126		5/206 6/296 7/322 8/373	
		9/378	

Bowling: *First Innings* – Willis 14-0-63-4; Allott 6-1-17-2; Botham 6.2-1-28-3; Emburey 4-0-16-1. *Second Innings* – Willis 30.5-2-96-3; Allott 17-3-71-2; Botham 36-16-86-2; Emburey 49-9-107-2; Gatting 3-1-13-0.

Jeff Thomson

AUSTRALIA V WEST INDIES

Sydney, 3, 4, 5, 7 January 1976

Born in Bankstown, Sydney on 16 August 1950, Jeffrey Robert Thomson hit Test cricket like a meteorite. Ox-like strength and all-round athleticism helped him make an early name throwing javelins, eggs, cricket balls and one well-documented tantrum. He broke records, was banned for life at soccer for clocking a referee, yet did not complain when his parents couldn't afford to send him to the West Indies with the Australian Schoolboy cricketers. An amiable, fun-loving surfie, he might have become an Olympic decathlete had his fearsome fast bowling not been ripping through the New South Wales grades. Even so, his career had a false start or two, with a disastrous Test debut (0 for 110 v Pakistan) on a broken foot and a move to Queensland before he terrorised the English tourists in 1974/75. In lethal tandem with Dennis Lillee, 'Thommo' took 33 wickets in five Tests and wreaked similar havoc on the 1975/76 West Indians. But his devastating sling-shot action was not destined to last and injuries limited him to exactly 200 Test wickets. A worthy total but one that does not convey the fear he induced in the finest batsmen. It is doubtful if anyone has ever bowled faster.

'A wild and woolly colonial', 'a one-day wonder', 'undisciplined hurler', were some of the epithets a grudging English press used to greet Thomson's arrival on the international scene in 1974. As a renowned 'Pom-hater', Thommo just loved it when those same critics choked on their ill-chosen phrases as he smashed England to submission – a devastating side-effect of his wicked 'throat ball'. Humble pie was the dish of the tour, boxes were reinforced and full-stops became glottal stops as typewriters trembled. In his biography, *Thommo Declares,* he claimed: 'I could never cop Poms ... generally speaking, that is. As soon as they lobbed her in '74, I couldn't wait to have a crack at 'em. I thought "Stuff that stiff upper lip. Let's see how stiff it is when it's split."'

Well, split lips were minor worries during that humiliating tour when the Ashes were lost, the dressing room resembled Emergency Ward 10 and an ageing Colin Cowdrey was called out of retirement. Distraught, Mike Denness even dropped himself but if, two decades later, the skipper, Fletcher, Amiss & Co. thought they were safe from their tearaway tormentor, they should think again. For Thommo, until recently Queensland's coach, chooses a game against the West Indies as his greatest. Why? 'Because,' he says, 'there were no bunnies in their batting line-up.'

Thommo is, of course, much more affable than he sounds just as his 'hatred' of batsmen was hyped by blood-stained ball pens, he is not still trying to put the Englishmen down. Why, he even played for Middlesex and under Brearley at that! He is merely being his own harshest critic and no-one can blame him for rating Richards, Lloyd (Clive), Rowe, Fredericks, Greenidge and Kallicharran more adept at dealing with the short ball than Fletcher, Denness, Amiss, Lloyd (David) and Luckhurst. However, when he had done with the West Indies, there was not a deal to choose between them and their predecessors. Clive Lloyd took the lesson to heart and determined that no West Indies side would ever be so humiliated again. Indeed, Thomson's performance was to have historic repercussions on the game as it was here that the West Indies decided there was no answer to fearsome fast bowling. As Brearley once put it: 'Broken marriages, conflicts of loyalty, the problems of every-day life fall away as one faces up to Thomson.'

His approach was deceptively short and devoid of menace. Then came a skip like a javelin thrower's, a pivot of the shoulders and, with that mane of blond hair flowing, the ball would be hurled with primordial intent. There were wides, there were no-balls; there were full tosses and runs sometimes to be had but, as *Wisden* stated, 'his very inaccuracy had merit in that the batsmen never knew what to expect.' The measured run-up made the action all the more explosive and Greg Chappell said of him: 'His throat ball would come straight up like a snake out of the grass at your feet.' Keith Miller claimed: 'Thommo frightened me when I was sitting 200 yards away,' while Bill O'Reilly wrote: 'I unhesitatingly class him as the most lethal fast bowler in Australian cricket.' Words like 'typhoon', 'terror' and 'tornado' became middle names and someone once had the temerity to label him 'a million dollar airport with a two-bob control tower.' That critic was not a batsman. It falls to former England seamer and respected scribe Mike Selvey to provide the most graphic description of the first ball he saw Thommo bowl: 'It was very fast and pitched just short of a length before taking off like a missile, searing past Tony Greig's nose and Rod Marsh's despairing leap before splintering the sight screen. My flesh went cold.'

But that may have been just a loosener – Thomson thinks he was even faster the following season. 'I reckon,' claims the man himself, 'I was at my fastest against the Windies. In the Sydney Test, I was really flying. Really getting amongst 'em. I had not had a great season but was fired up and wanted to knock 'em over. They had some big names but that meant nothin' to me once I had that ball in my hand. And with Dennis Lillee out with pleurisy, it really was up to me.' Australia were already two-one up in the series with the West Indies' batting having revealed an unsuspected fragility. Thomson and Lillee had both been amongst them but still no-one was prepared for the devastation Thomson alone would wreak at the S.C.G.

Instead of seizing upon the absence of Lillee to level the series, Lloyd's men folded to Thomson in the second innings. But the warning signs were there even during an apparently respectable first dig of 355. Although Thomson went for 117 in his 25 overs, he made a telling impact. Besides taking one of the most memorable catches of all time, he captured three wickets and caused as many casualties: in a fearsome blitz, he struck Lloyd on the jaw, Julien on the hand and Holding in the face with the last ball of the first day. But worse was to come.

Justice, however, must first be done to Thommo's snaring of Murray, whom he caught off Walker out near the fence. O'Reilly wrote in the *Sydney Morning Herald*: 'It is useless to try to describe the distance he ran, the headlong dive at the ball and the desperate job he made of it as he rolled over on the ground. It was the greatest outfield catch I have ever seen — none of the others come within a street of it.' At the end of the second day, with Greg Chappell having trouble with Andy Roberts and Australia (164 for four) still almost 200 adrift, West Indies looked to be in the box seats. But they had reckoned without Chappell's master class on the third day and Thommo's mayhem on the fourth.

Dropped by Boyce off Roberts at 11, Chappell went on to a magnificent 182 not out to shepherd Australia to 405 and a priceless lead of 50. It was enough for Thomson to unleash his thunderbolts and West Indies, still reeling from his first innings assault, collapsed. Bowling as fast as even he has ever done, he was the 'terror', 'typhoon' and 'tornado' all in one. After blasting an initial breach the previous evening, he had Rowe held brilliantly by a diving Marsh to reduce the visitors to 52 for five. Then he sent Holding's leg stump cartwheeling, but Lloyd and Murray resisted until lunch. After the break, Thomson came out determined to finish the job. 'It had looked good for them at one stage,' he said, 'If they'd won, the series would have been level but now we had the chance to clinch it. I just tore into them.'

In two overs, he had Lloyd held by Marsh and Boyce by Redpath at slip. With Walker chipping in to remove Julien and Roberts, it did not take long — Thomson eventually flattening Murray's off-stump. Australia made the 82 they required for the loss of three wickets. The slogan coined had been: 'Ashes to ashes, dust to dust, if Lillee don't get you, Thommo must.' He had got the Windies. And Test cricket would not be the same again.

Result: Australia won by seven wickets

West Indies

R.C. Fredericks c I.M. Chappell ..... 48 b Thomson		c Turner b Gilmour 24	
B.D. Julien not out 46	(9)	lbw b Walker 8	
A.I. Kallicharran c Redpath .... 9 b Thomson	(2)	c Walker b Thomson 7	
L.G. Rowe b Walker 67		c Marsh b Thomson 7	
I.V.A. Richards c I.M. Chappell ...... 44 b G.S. Chappell	(3)	c Thomson b Gilmour 2	
*C.H. Lloyd c Turner b Walker 51		c Marsh b Thomson 19	
†D.L. Murray c Thomson b Walker 32		b Thomson 50	
K.D. Boyce c and b Mallett 16		c Redpath b Thomson 0	
M.A. Holding hit wkt b Thomson 2	(5)	b Thomson 9	
A.M.E. Roberts c Marsh b Walker 4		b Walker 2	
L.R. Gibbs c Marsh b G. S. Chappell . 5		not out 0	
Extras (B 5, LB 14, NB 3, W 9) . 31			
1/44 2/87 3/160 4/213 5/233 355		1/23 2/32 3/33 4/47 5/52 128	
6/259 7/321 8/321 9/346		6/95 7/75 8/120 9/126	

Bowling: *First Innings* – Thomson 25-5-117-3; Gilmour 13-2-54-0; Walker 21-8-70-4; Cosier 3-1-13-0; Mallett 13-4-50-1; G.S. Chappell 4.2-0-10-2; I.M. Chappell 1-0-10-0. *Second Innings* – Thomson 15-4-50-6; Gilmour 12-4-40-2; Walker 9.3-3-31-2; G.S. Chappell 2-0-5-0; Mallett 1-0-2-0.

Australia

I.R. Redpath c Murray b Holding ... 25	b Boyce 28
A. Turner c Lloyd b Boyce 53	c Murray b Holding 15
G.N. Yallop c Murray b Julien 16	not out 16
I.M. Chappell c Murray b Holding ... 4	c sub (C.G. Greenidge) ...... 9 b Kallicharran
*G.S. Chappell not out 182	not out 6
G.J. Cosier b Holding 28	
†R.W. Marsh c Gibbs b Julien 38	
G.J. Gilmour run out 20	
M.H.N. Walker c Lloyd b Roberts 8	
J.R. Thomson c Richards b Roberts .. 0	
A.A. Mallett lbw b Roberts 13	
Extras (B 3, LB 8, NB 5, W 2) .. 18	(LB 4, W 4) 8
1/70 2/93 3/103 4/103 5/202 405	1/45 2/51 3/67 (3 wkts) 82
6/319 7/348 8/377 9/377	

Bowling: *First Innings* – 20.6-3-94-3; Holding 21-2-79-3; Boyce Gibbs 18-3-52-0; Julien 15-2-87-2. *Second Innings* – Roberts 4-1-12-0; Holding 7-0-33-1; Boyce 4-0-14-1; Kallicharran 2-1-7-1; Gibbs 1-0-4-0; Richards 0.1-0-4-0.

Umpires: T.F. Brooks and R.R. Ledwidge

Frank Tyson

AUSTRALIA V ENGLAND

Sydney, 17, 18, 20, 21, 22 December 1954

Born in Bolton on 6 June 1930, Frank Holmes Tyson was rejected by his native Lancashire but joined Northants after reading English Literature, French and History at Durham University. Erudite and physically powerful, he could recite a sonnet and then release a missile. With his terrifying pace, he blazed through Australia in 1954/55 to enable England, under Len Hutton, to retain the Ashes. Team-mate Trevor Bailey, writing in From Larwood to Lillee *stated: 'Whenever there is talk of fast bowling, I always say without fear of contradiction that the quickest bowler I have ever seen, or played against, was Frank Tyson.' At the height of his powers, he was awesome, and fully justified the sobriquet 'Typhoon'. But injuries took their toll, restricting him to just 76 wickets in 17 Tests at 18.56. Like Larwood before him, he did not enjoy a long career and settled in Australia, teaching, coaching, commentating on and writing lucidly about the game.*

'To bowl quick,' Frank Tyson wrote in his autobiography, *A Typhoon Called Tyson,* 'is to revel in the glad animal action; to thrill in physical prowess and to enjoy a certain sneaking feeling of superiority over the other mortals who play the game. No batsman likes quick bowling, and this knowledge gives one a sense of omnipotence.' Tyson had always wanted to bowl quick – as evidenced by his 30-yard run-up – and the sight of him pounding in from the sightscreen with the 'keeper halfway back to the boundary drew intakes of breath on every ground in England in the early 1950s. But the gasps were drowned by the euphoria of regaining the Ashes after 18 years. The Aussies had a glimpse of Tyson but Freddie Brown, still in charge at Northants, shrewdly whisked him off soon after he'd taken two wickets in a withering first over. But when the team's boat sailed for Australia in the autumn, Tyson was on it.

When it docked at Fremantle, there could have been no more welcoming gangplank than Perth's lightning pitch but the 24-year-old bowled anywhere but at the stumps. Still, he was in the side for the first Test at Brisbane when Hutton won the toss and asked Australia to bat on a rain-affected wicket. Tyson took one for 160 off 29 wayward overs and England lost by an innings and plenty. Chastened by the experience, the tourists left out Bedser (whose one for 131 had not been helped by shingles and seven dropped catches) for the second Test, the pace burden falling squarely on Tyson and his reliable accomplice Statham, with Bailey in support. Between Brisbane and Sydney, Tyson had cut his run but with

192

four changes in the England team and a new Australian captain, Arthur Morris taking over when both Ian Johnson and Keith Miller were unfit, little notice was taken.

It did not rate a mention when England, put in by Morris, were bundled out on a green top the first day. However, English spirits had lifted in the late afternoon. 'It was only some courageous hitting by Johnny Wardle and Brian Statham, who put on 44 for the last wicket,' recalls Tyson, 'which enabled us to reach 154.' Wardle's efforts were described by one Australian writer as 'hilarious carpet-beater's wallops,' but the Yorkshireman's 35 was England's top score. And when Morris fell (caught by Hutton at leg-slip) off the last ball of the day, Australia were 18 for one and England, for the first time in the series, saw a glimmer.

When Australia reached lunch on the second day at 86 for two, not many pundits were backing the visitors but, with the 44,879 crowd entranced, Tyson rose to the occasion. In a 70-minute spell, bowling unchanged with Bailey, he took two for 23 in six overs. Not spectacular figures but the Hill hummed as this balding, wild bull finally harnessed his speed to peg Australia back, turn the game and, ultimately, the series. 'We were back in the game when Trevor Bailey and I each took four wickets and limited the Australian first innings lead to 74,' says Tyson. 'The scribes had written us off for this Test, Brisbane having been a game of black misfortune.'

To Bailey's fast-medium off-stump sniping, Tyson was the artillery barrage, a deathly hush descending over the great ground as he turned at the end of his shortened run. For a lover of the classics, it was, unlike Larwood and Lindwall, sheer brute strength and anything but poetry in motion. He started like a man who, in a tearing hurry to get indoors, remembered only at the last second to wipe his boots on the mat. After these irritated stutters, he broke into a shuffle and then, finally, long, raking strides of deadly intent. The very earth seemed to shake at the pounding and the crowd fell silent, the slips crouched and the terrified batsman stood as if before a firing squad. As Tyson neared the delivery stride, he twice pushed the right hand down toward the waist, as if measuring his aim, and then, in an apocalyptic climax, he would arch his broad back, catapult his upper body in a sling action and let go at a speed that has rarely been surpassed. It was quite simply awesome and, when he found his line and length, it was unplayable.

Australia hopped and jumped to 228 all out – a useful lead but there had been a marked psychological shift. England's secret weapon had found his range, finishing with four for 45 and a lot of bruised Australians. However, when Hutton and Graveney went in the same over from Johnston to leave England at 55 for three just before lunch on the third day, it looked as if the paceman's efforts were about to be wasted. But in strode Colin Cowdrey, who, like Tyson, was on his first tour, to join Peter May. In the first of many great partnerships they enjoyed, the young university graduates completely mastered the bowling to put on 106 before Cowdrey went for 54. Edrich came in and England had a lead of 130 at the end of the day. 'Peter May scored a brilliant hundred,' says Tyson, 'and we reached 296 to set Australia 223.' 'Easy,' said most Australians.

England had collapsed from 222 for four to 250 for nine but Statham and Appleyard added 46 for the last wicket. Tyson remembers 'being hit on the head by a Lindwall bouncer,' but the ageing Australian, returning the compliment after being dismissed by a similar ball from Tyson, did not generate anything like the same pace. Still, Tyson tottered and fell, and was helped off with a bump the size of an egg on the back of his head. An X-ray revealed no serious damage and he returned to a warm reception. 'But I was angry,' he recalls. And when Australia began the quest for 223, it certainly looked it. Glad animal? You bet. E. W. Swanton described Tyson and Statham as 'tigerish,' while *The Times* preferred 'lions' . Openers Morris and Favell somehow avoided their claws to get to 27 before Statham trapped Morris lbw off the last ball before tea. Favell soon followed (caught Edrich bowled Tyson) but Harvey and Burke survived until the close. The odds were still on a home victory.

After an over apiece from Tyson and Statham on the fifth morning, those odds shortened, the pitch appearing dead, the weather sunny with a cooling breeze blowing off Botany Bay. England's hopes of assistance from either a crumbling wicket or cloud cover were dashed but, roaring in from the Randwick End, Tyson had that wind behind him. It was all he needed. With searing yorkers he removed Burke and Hole in his second over. Harvey and Benaud steadied the ship but it was Tyson who split them – as a fielder. 'I took a steepling catch at square-leg, much against my expectations, to dismiss Benaud off Appleyard,' he says. At lunch, the match was on a knife-edge but few favoured England – until Tyson yorked Archer in the second over of the afternoon. Australia needed 101 with four wickets left. When Davidson was brilliantly caught by a diving Evans off Statham, a tense situation was given added piquancy with the appearance of Lindwall. He became the fourth victim to be yorked by Tyson but Harvey was still there. It was not over yet.

Harvey punished both England pacemen and was capable of winning the match on his own. But when Langley was bowled by Statham, 74 were still wanted and only Bill Johnston was left. For 40 minutes, the masterly Harvey protected his partner so well, Johnston only faced nine balls in seven eight-ball overs. Thirty-nine were added as Harvey edged into the nineties and an improbable victory beckoned. Statham, who had been bowling into the wind since lunch, had to be taken off and when Bailey was dispatched for two fours, England's frustration mounted. But, finally, Tyson, who was also ready for a rest, had the last word. 'Boy, was I glad when Evans caught Johnston down the leg-side of a back-pocket flick.' England won by just 38, Tyson finishing with six for 85, 10 for 130 in the match. 'For me,' he adds, 'it represented the turning of the tide. It would be easy to simply choose the Melbourne Test [when he took 7-27] but it was not as good a game of cricket. And Neil Harvey was magnificent.' But it was Tyson's match as *Wisden* confirmed: 'Not for a long time has a star burst upon the cricket firmament with such startling suddenness . . .' Frank was 'a glad animal' for the rest of the tour.
Result: England won by 38 runs

England

*L. Hutton c Davidson b Johnston	30	c Benaud b Johnston	28
T.E. Bailey b Lindwall	0	c Langley b Archer	6
P.B.H. May c Johnston b Archer	5	b Lindwall	104
T.W. Graveney c Favell b Johnston	21	c Langley b Johnston	0
M.C. Cowdrey c Langley b Davidson	23	c Archer b Benaud	54
W.J. Edrich c Benaud b Archer	10	b Archer	29
F.H. Tyson b Lindwall	0	b Lindwall	9
†T.G. Evans C Langley b Archer	3	c Lindwall b Archer	4
J.H. Wardle c Burke b Johnston	35	lbw b Lindwall	8
R. Appleyard c Hole b Davidson	8	not out	19
J.B. Statham not out	14	c Langley b Johnston	25
Extras (LB 5)	5	(LB 6, NB 4)	10

1/14 2/19 3/58 4/63 5/84   154   1/18 2/55 3/55 4/171   296
6/85 7/88 8/99 9/111   5/222 6/232 7/239 8/249
    9/250

Bowling: *First Innings* – Lindwall 17-3-47-2; Archer 12-7-12-3; Davidson 12-3-34-2; Johnston 13.3-1-56-3. *Second Innings* – Lindwall 31-10-69-3; Archer 22-9-53-3; Davidson 13-2-52-0; Johnston 19.3-2-70-3; Benaud 19-3-42-1.

Australia

L.E. Favell c Graveney b Bailey	26	c Edrich b Tyson	16
*A.R. Morris c Hutton b Bailey	12	lbw b Statham	10
J.W. Burke c Graveney b Bailey	44	b Tyson	14
R.N. Harvey c Cowdrey b Tyson	12	not out	92
G.B. Hole b Tyson	12	b Tyson	0
R. Benaud lbw b Statham	20	c Tyson b Appleyard	12
R.G. Archer c Hutton b Tyson	49	b Tyson	6
A.K. Davidson b Statham	20	c Evans b Statham	5
R.R. Lindwall c Evans b Tyson	19	b Tyson	8
†G.R.A. Langley b Bailey	5	b Statham	0
W.A. Johnston not out	0	c Evans b Tyson	11
Extras (B 5, LB 2, NB 2)	9	(LB 7, NB 3)	10

1/18 2/65 3/100 4/104 5/122   228   1/27 2/34 3/77 4/77   184
6/141 7/193 8/213 9/224   5/102 6/122 7/127 8/136
    9/145

Bowling: *First Innings* – Statham 18-1-83-2; Bailey 17.4-3-59-4; Tyson 13-2-45-4; Appleyard 7-1-32-0. *Second Innings* – Statham 19-6-45-3; Bailey 6-0-21-0; Tyson 18.4-1-85-6; Appleyard 6-1-12-1; Wardle 4-2-11-0.

Umpires: M.J. McInnes and R. Wright

Polly Umrigar

Trinidad, 4, 5, 6, 7, 9 April 1962

Born in Sholapur, Maharashtra, on 28 March 1926, Pahlan Ratanji Umrigar was described by L. N. Mathur in his Portrait of Indian Test Cricketers *as a 'vibrant, vivacious and vigorous' all-rounder. As a student, Umrigar hit 115 not out off the 1948/ 49 West Indies and after a 15-year, 59-Test career was India's heaviest run-getting (3,631, average 42.22) when he retired. His 130 not out – after being dropped and then recalled – made him a national hero as it steered India to a historic first Test victory over England in Madras in 1952. A tall, imperious stroke-maker and fine fielder, his off-cutters and out-swingers made him a useful change bowler. 'Polly', as he was universally known, could also be an astute captain, leading Bombay to five successive wins in the Ranji Trophy. On each of his two tours to England, he made three double centuries and, at his best, batted with a rare majesty. At his worst, he was 'sorted out' by Fred Trueman, seven Test innings in England yielding just 43 runs in 1952. But he eventually came to terms with fast bowling and totalled 16,023 first-class runs for an average of 52.53. Since his retirement, he has been a prominent figure in Indian cricket administration.*

It looked like the best batting side ever to leave India. Led by the doughty Nari Contractor, there was the elegance of Manjrekar and Borde, the adventure of the Nawab of Pataudi, the panache of the debonair Durani, the grandeur of Umrigar. And they had just defeated Ted Dexter's England at home. As for the West Indies, while the islands' population were rejecting the Federation, Frank Worrell had welded a side that displayed a rare unity and confidence. And they were fresh from an epic tussle in Australia. All the makings of a fine series then – as long as India's batsmen didn't display what *Wisden* called, 'that hysterical uneasiness against pace.'

But after the players had been given shamefully little time to prepare for the Caribbean, the first two Tests were quickly lost. Worse, much worse, however, was to come. In a now-infamous incident in a match with Barbados, Contractor was hit on the head by a Charlie Griffith bouncer. The crack was heard in the Indian dressing room and was to reverberate through the game. Contractor was operated on in hospital and his life was saved, but he never played Test cricket again. This near-tragedy was hardly likely to boost India's confidence against fast bowling and although Manjrekar made a heroic 100 in the same match, the team never fully recovered. They did, however, restore some pride in the fourth Test which, although they lost it by seven wickets, proved a turning point in the evolution of Indian cricket.

'When any cricketer scores a 100 in a Test match,' says Polly Umrigar, 'it is to my mind a memorable Test match. And for me there are three in particular which stand out. There was my first hundred in a Test, when I was called up as a replacement and helped put India on the way to our first victory. There was also my first double 100, the first by an Indian batsman, against New Zealand in 1955/56. But my greatest game has to be the fourth Test against the West Indies in Trinidad when we toured in 1961/62.'

With the series already lost, it looked like the slaughter would continue when Kanhai carved up the Indian bowlers on the first day for a scintillating 139. But when Umrigar, who had earlier bowled Hunte, trapped the great improviser lbw, the carnage was contained. Troubled by fibrositis in his back, Umrigar's effectiveness had been intermittent until now. As *Wisden* put it, 'but for Umrigar's sustained accuracy during many long spells, India would have been subjected to a far greater gruelling.' The man, himself, recalls: 'I bowled 56 overs and captured five wickets for 107 runs.' But he could not prevent Worrell and Hall putting on an undefeated 98 for the last wicket to undermine Indian confidence even further.

By the end of the second day, the visitors had lost five wickets to Wes Hall for just 61, still nearly 400 behind. In trying to repair the damage on the third day, Umrigar made 56, acting skipper Pataudi 47 and Borde 42, but they still had to follow on 247 behind. When Sardesai completed a pair, morale in the Indian dressing room plummeted yet again but, in a bold gamble, Pataudi promoted the dashing Durani from number 9 to number 3. With marvellous driving and courageous, flamboyant hooking, the all-rounder changed the mood in the Indian camp. Suddenly, batting looked a little less suicidal and Umrigar, who had had his problems against Hall as he had against Trueman, carried on where Durani left off. His confidence bolstered by his first-innings half-century, only his second of the series, he set about the West Indian bowling with something akin to vibrancy, vivacity and vigour.

'In this innings,' he says, 'which was my 12th hundred in Tests, I was able to attack all the bowlers and knocked Worrell, Sobers, Gibbs and Rodriguez out of the firing line. When Worrell brought back Hall and Stayers with the new ball, I really attacked them to take the second innings total beyond 400. I found useful partners in Bapu Nadkarni, with whom I carried the score to 371 after a stand of 90 runs, and Budhi Kunderan. The total went to 422 with my score being 172 not out.' Umrigar hit 22 fours and made his runs out of 230 in just 248 minutes. The bald stats are staggering enough but the effect that Durani and Umrigar's innings had on Indian cricket went well beyond a previously demoralised dressing room.

With just 176 runs to get to take a 4-0 lead, the West Indies reached the target for the loss of three wickets, Nurse and Sobers being together when the winning runs were hit. In the fifth Test, the margin was 123 runs, Worrell's men confirming they were a major competitive force with one of the finest sides in West Indies' history. In Kanhai, there was one of the masterly innovators, in Hall one of the genuine express bowlers, in Gibbs a marvellous off-spinner and in Sobers, probably the greatest all-rounder of all. With hindsight, India had been ill-equipped to take them on in the Caribbean without a pace bowler and a top-class spinner. But even in defeat, India's emergence as a cricket nation had taken a major step.

Writing in his *History of Indian Cricket*, Mihir Bose asked: 'Was it 1959 [when a negative India had returned from England demoralised] all over again? Not quite,' he answers. 'In contrast, the younger players now returned from the West Indies suggesting that in the ruins there was the real prospect of a brighter future.' The 1962 side were infinitely more colourful and entertaining: they had seen their captain hit on the head and almost killed, and they had fought back. For Umrigar, who had been there throughout the highs and lows of the 1950s, it was his last overseas tour and he comfortably topped the Test batting averages with 49.44. He had bowled well when fitness allowed but, above all, it was his valedictory tour. 'In the pavilion after my 172 not out,' he says, 'I received compliments from the greatest fast bowler I have faced – Wes Hall. "This time," he said, "somebody has really stood up and attacked my bowling." To my mind,' says Umrigar, 'this is a great compliment to receive from a player of his standing.' Indeed, he had proved the critics wrong in a glorious knock that helped usher in the new generation of brave, young Indian batsmen. And all cricket-lovers will thank him for that.

Result: West Indies won by seven wickets

West Indies

C.C. Hunte b Umrigar	28	c Kunderan b Durani	30
E. McMorris c Sardesai b Nadkarni	50	b Durani	56
R.B. Kanhai lbw b Umrigar	139	c Nadkarni b Durani	20
S.M. Nurse c b Durani	1	not out	46
G.StA. Sobers lbw b Jaisimha	19	not out	16
W.V. Rodriguez b Umrigar	50		
†I.L. Mendonça b Umrigar	3		
L.R. Gibbs lbw b Nadkarni	15		
*F.M.M. Worrell not out	73		
S.C. Stayers c Surti b Umrigar	12		
W.W. Hall not out	50		
Extras (LB 4)	4	(B 3, LB 1, NB 4)	8

1/50 2/169 3/174 (9 wkts dec.) 444 1/93 2/100 3/132 (3 wkts) 176
4/212 5/258 6/265 7/292 8/316 9/346

Bowling: *First Innings* – Surti 26-4-81-0; Jaisimha 18-4-61-1; Umrigar 56-24-107-5; Durani 18-4-54-1; Borde 23-4-68-0; Nadkarni 35-14-69-2. *Second Innings* – Surti 21-7-48-0; Jaisimha 4-1-5-0; Umrigar 16-8-17-0; Durani 31-13-64-3; Borde 1-1-0-0; Nadkarni 28-13-34-0.

India

First Innings		Second Innings	
D.N. Sardesai b Hall	0	(9) c Worrell b Gibbs	0
V.L. Mehra b Hall	14	b Hall	62
R.F. Surti c Nurse b Hall	0	(7) c Mendonça b Gibbs	2
V.L. Manjrekar c Mendonça b Hall	4	c Nurse b Sobers	13
M.L. Jaisimha c Mendonça b Hall	10	(1) c Mendonça b Stayers	15
P.R. Umrigar st Mendonça b Sobers	56	not out	172
*Nawab of Pataudi jr c Sobers b Rodriquez	47	(5) c Kanhai b Sobers	1
C.G. Borde c Nurse b Rodriguez	42	c Sobers b Gibbs	13
S.A. Durani c Worrell b Rodriguez	12	(3) c Rodriguez b Sobers	104
R.G. Nadkarni c Rodriguez b Sobers	1	run out	23
†B.K. Kunderan not out	4	c Rodriguez b Gibbs	4
Extras (B 1, LB 4, NB 2)	7	(B 9, LB 3, NB 1)	13

1/0 2/0 3/9 4/25 5/30   197   1/19 2/163 3/190 4/192   422
6/124 7/144 8/169 9/175   5/221 6/236 7/278 8/278
                                                 9/371

Bowling: *First Innings* Hall 9-3-20-5; Stayers 8-1-23-0; Gibbs 19-5-48-0; Sobers 25-6-48-2; Rodriguez 19-3-51-3. *Second Innings* Hall 18-3-74-1; Stayers 10-2-50-1; Gibbs 56.1-18-112-4; Sobers 47-14-116-3; Rodriguez 9-1-47-0; Worrell 3-0-10-0.

Umpires: B Jacelon and H.B. de C. Jordan

Doug Walters

Perth, 13, 14, 15, 17 December 1974

Born on 21 December, 1945, in Dungog, an up-country town in New South Wales, Kevin Douglas Walters learned his cricket on an ant-bed pitch at his parents' dairy-farm. A batting prodigy, he played for his state just a few days after his 17th birthday and, at 19, became only the fifth Australian to make a 100(155) in his first Test. He got another in his second. National service interrupted his brilliant career for two years but normal service resumed in 1967. A slim, wiry figure beneath that baggy green cap, Walters hit with tremendous power and could carve any attack to ribbons in a session. He could also make big scores, notching 253 in the Sheffield Shield and, against the West Indies at Sydney, became one of only four players in history to score a double century and a century in the same Test. A useful medium-pacer (strike rate 67.24), he was a wonderful field either at slip or in the covers, where his pick up and throw would deter most greyhounds. Although he never did himself justice in England, his career stats confirm him as a great – 5,357 Test runs at 48.26. They do not, however, come near to conveying his icon status Down Under – especially in his beloved Sydney.

Say what you like about robotic efficiency, but sports fans like their heroes to be human. A penchant for a tinnie, a fag and a practical joke can go a long way to overcoming any statistical deficiency in the eyes of true believers; just as a wry sense of humour, an unobtrusive manner and a liking for cards can bring forgiveness for off-stump fallibility. All these and bush origins earmarked Doug Walters as a dinkum Aussie – after all, if you come from a place called Dungog, you can hardly be up yerself, can you?

Of course, wielding a cricket bat as if it were a scalpel helped – not to mention a happy knack of breaking partnerships with the ball. Safe hands and a habit of throwing down the stumps with only one of them to aim at didn't do any harm, either. Western Australian batsman Ian Brayshaw once said: 'He is so fast the only thing he can't do is keep wicket to his bowling.' Even so, the affection that Australian crowds had for Walters was extraordinary – and difficult to understand in England. Billed as yet another in the never-ending line of 'new Bradmans', Walters had everyone's sympathy – even though an early batting average of 94 suggested he might be closer to emulating the Don than any other would-be impersonator. In the army, he asked for no special favours and by the time English conditions – aka John Snow – had exploited his cross-bat, he had secured a place in the hearts of his countrymen. One session of vintage 'Freddie' was worth a series of failures and, as E. W. Swanton put it, 'Who better than Doug Walters when the mood is on him?'

If Walters did not quite manage to milk the cows and Pommie bowling on the same morning – 'I was never very keen on milking' – one of his greatest assets was his poker-face imperturbability. Henry Blofeld hints at this with his story about a Walters innings – or should it be hand? – when, padded-up and next man in, he was in the pavilion playing cards. At the fall of the wicket, Walters placed his cards face-down on the table, his cigarette in an ash-tray and walked to the middle to be out first ball. He was soon back in the dressing room, cards in hand, fag in mouth, as if nothing had happened. His explanation? 'I had a good hand at the time . . .' Or so it was claimed.

His dry humour made him a popular figure and if his bat was crooked, he knew how to play straight off the field. When asked if he'd made any adjustments late in his career, he replied: 'I'm just plain Doug Walters and my technique is bad. I'm not going to change it at 35.' It was his refusal to change at 25 that confounded the hapless England tourists of 1974/75. Just as they thought Lillee's back trouble would diminish his threat, they were convinced that Walters was a soft touch. He had cut a forlorn figure in the previous Ashes series and had been dropped after scoring just 71 runs in four Tests. But no sooner had a rejuvenated Lillee and a rediscovered Thomson been unleashed on Mike Denness' men, than Walters took centre on his favourite track. After being softened up by the pacemen, England were about to be put to the sword.

Thomson had blitzed the tourists so badly at Brisbane that they sent an S.O.S. for 41-year-old Colin Cowdrey, who four days after blinking into the Australian sun, found himself staring down the barrel at Thomson and Lillee. Courageously though he batted, it was finger-in-the-dyke stuff and England were dismissed for 208. Walters, who had taken two for 13, had to wait until just before tea (192-4) on the second day before getting a dig – which was not as ideal as the departing Greg Chappell (62) had suggested: 'There you are Doug – I've set it up for you,' said Chappell as the two men crossed. 'Now you can get a 100 in the last session!' Walters had done similar between lunch and tea in the West Indies but was just relieved to have his cuppa at three not out.

Resuming at 201 for four, Australia were in charge but England's cause was far from hopeless – another wicket would bring in the tail and the prospect of restricting the Australian lead. The trouble for England was that Willis, who fancied a go at Walters, had been bowling for an hour and the new ball was due an hour after tea. Denness opted to rest him and it was left to 6'7" Tony Greig to exploit Walters' perceived weakness to the rearing delivery on the off-stump. After warming up with seven of the eight runs taken off Greig's first over after lunch, Walters went on the rampage. The 50 partnership with Edwards came in 38 minutes, Walters whipping anything short, however wide of off-stump, through mid-wicket with tremendous power. Phil Wilkins wrote in the *Sydney Morning Herald;* 'Walters' right foot went back and his bat came through like the ivory tusk of a bull elephant.'

As the afternoon wore on and the bowling and fielding wilted, he unveiled his complete repertoire including his famous, feet-together pull that Trevor Bailey called his 'come-to-attention' shot, a legacy perhaps of his army days. But he was also a devastating cutter and driver, and not even the normally parsimonious Titmus could put the brakes on. Only Chris Old escaped a goring. Walters raced to 50 in 48 minutes off 50 balls and Chappell was suddenly not feeling so guilty. Perhaps the session century was on? 'When I was 67 at drinks,' says Walters, 'I thought I'd make Greg's prediction come true rather easily. I felt that if I was still there at the close, I'd have 120 or 130 – and it was just one of those magic days. We all have them at some stage and this was one of mine. But I lost the strike for a few overs and, with it, lost momentum.' Suddenly Arnold and Willis were steaming in with the new ball and a defensive field; there were just two overs remaining and 14 were still wanted. 'I thought it had gone out of the gate,' admits Walters. But three twos and a single off the seventh ball of Arnold's last over kept it alive – until Edwards took one off the eighth ball to a huge groan from the terraces.

And so to the final over of the day, bowled by Willis. Loss of strike was not Walters' only problem now – cramp in one hand made it difficult for him to grip the bat. But he had not given up – not even when Edwards hit two off the first ball. Three off the third gave Walters the strike and the crowd buzzed once more as Willis pounded in. Seven wanted off six balls. 'The first ball I received was short and I went to hook,' he recalls. 'I got a top edge and it was four over Alan Knott's head.' The crowd went wild but still six were needed. And Willis was at full pelt. 'I was used to getting three or four short balls an over,' says Walters, 'but he kept the next few well up.' With two gullies for an edge and two men on the long-leg boundary for the hook, it was riveting stuff. But four balls in the block hole were almost more than the crowd could bear. Walters, 97 not out, did well to dig them out. One ball left, three for the ton, six for the session century. Willis hurtled in. 'I just wanted to get on the back foot,' says Walters. He got his wish – it was the bouncer. 'As soon as I connected, I knew it was six,' he says. As the ball sailed over the mid-wicket fence, the crowd swarmed on to the field to mob their hero: 'It was the most satisfying innings I've played,' he adds, 'and made better by us winning the Test.'

It remains to add two footnotes to Walters character: first, modesty made him reluctant to choose such a personal triumph until he obligingly left the queue for the Centenary Test; second, when he returned to the dressing room, he found it empty, apart from his skipper Ian Chappell who admonished him for 'irresponsible batting'. At that his team-mates, avenging previous pranks, could not contain themselves any longer and emerged from hiding to proffer their congratulations. Then he lit a fag.
Result: Australia won by nine wickets

England

D. Lloyd c G.S. Chappell .... 49 b Thomson	c G.S. Chappell b Walker . 35	
B.W. Luckhurst c Mallett b Walker 27	(7) c Mallett b Lillee 23	
M.C. Cowdrey b Thomson 22	(2) lbw b Thomson 41	
A.W. Greig c Mallett b Walker 23	c G.S. Chappell .... 32 b Thomson	
K.W.R. Fletcher c Redpath b Lillee ... 4	c Marsh b Thomson 0	
*M.H. Denness c G.S. Chappell .... 2 b Lillee	(3) c Redpath b Thomson 20	
†A.P.E. Knott c Redpath b Walters .. 51	(6) c G.S. Chappell b Lillee ... 18	
F.J. Titmus c Redpath b Walters 10	c G.S. Chappell b Mallett . 61	
C.M. Old c G.S. Chappell .... 7 b I.M. Chappell	c Thomson b Mallett 43	
G.G. Arnold run out 1	c Mallett b Thomson 4	
R.G.D. Willis not out 4	not out 0	
Extras (NB 5, W 3) 8	(LB 4, NB 11, W 1) 16	
1/44 2/99 3/119 4/128 5/132 208 6/132 7/194 8/201 9/202	1/62 2/106 3/124 4/124 293 5/154 6/156 7/219 8/285 9/293	

Bowling: *First Innings* – Lillee 16-4-48-2; Thomson 15-6-45-2; Walker 20-5-49-2; Mallett 10-3-35-0; Walters 2.3-0-13-2; I. M. Chappell 2-0-10-1. *Second Innings* – Lillee 22-5-59-2; Thomson 25-4-93-5; Walker 24-7-76-1; Walters; Mallett 11.1-4-32-2.

Australia

I.R. Redpath st Knott b Titmus 41	not out 12	
W.J. Edwards c Lloyd b Greig 30	lbw b Arnold 0	
*I.M. Chappell c Knott b Arnold 25	not out 11	
G.S. Chappell c Greig b Willis 62		
R. Edwards b Arnold 115		
K.D. Walters c Fletcher b Willis 103		
†R.W. Marsh c Lloyd b Titmus 41		
M.H.N. Walker c Knott b Old 19		
D.K. Lillee b Old 11		
J.R. Thomson c Knott b Old 0		
A.A. Mallett not out 11		
Extras (B 7, LB 14, NB 2) 23		
1/64 2/101 3/113 4/192 5/362 481 6/416 7/449 8/462 9/462	1/4 (1 wkt) 23	

Bowling: *First Innings* – Willis 22-0-91-2; Arnold 27-1-129-2; Old 22.6-3-85-3; Greig 9-0-69-1; Titmus 28-3-84-2. *Second Innings* – Willis 2-0-8-0; Arnold 1.7-0-15-1.

Umpires: R.C. Bailhache and T.F. Brooks

Bob Willis

ENGLAND V AUSTRALIA

Headingley, 16, 17, 18, 20, 21 July 1981

Born in Sunderland on 30 May, 1949, Bob Willis played county cricket for Surrey and Warwickshire. He was capped by England – before he had won his county cap – when he was flown out as a replacement for Alan Ward on the 1970/1 Ashes tour. He went on to play 90 Tests, in which he took 325 Test wickets, despite a body and bowling action that defied the conventional models for a successful pace bowler. He overcame these handicaps via rigid self-discipline and determination. He captained England in 18 Tests, winning seven and losing five despite the fact that his mammoth run up temporarily exiled him from the rest of his team.

Mike Brearley or Ian Botham might have chosen this match but didn't, Graham Dilley would have done if we had let him. Kim Hughes or Allan Border probably would have considered it, but in the end it was appropriate that Bob Willis, the central figure on the last day, should be left with arguably the most stunning Test match this century. It was only the second time in Test history that a side had won after following on. And Bob Willis nearly missed it.

In the previous Test at Lord's, which had ended in a sombre defeat and the resignation/sacking of Ian Botham, Willis had developed flu symptoms. Willis recalls: 'I missed Warwickshire's next game at the Oval. On the Saturday Alec Bedser (the Chairman of Selectors) rang to say that I was not picked for Headingley since Mike Brearley was unhappy about selecting players not fit enough to play in the current round of Championship matches. I explained to Alec that I was not playing at the Oval specifically to ensure that I would be fit for the Test match. I agreed to play in a second XI match for Warwickshire on the Monday "to prove my fitness" and the selectors agreed to change their minds. Alec Bedser arranged for the secretary of Derbyshire to intercept Mike Hendrick's invitation to play in the Test before it reached him.'

After three days of the Test Willis must have wondered whether his intervention had been worthwhile. In Australia's first innings he had bowled 'reasonably well' but without taking any wickets. The pitch was obviously unreliable yet the Australians had compiled 401-9 declared throughout two rain-interrupted days, with John Dyson, the craggy New South Wales opener scoring a century. On the third England were bundled out for 174 by Lillee, Alderman and Lawson. Botham, after his pair at Lord's had scored 50 to add to his six wickets. But his rejuvenation, now that he had been unshackled from the captaincy, was a minor consolation for England, especially when, following on, they lost Gooch for a duck that evening.

Throughout the first three days all had been gloom from every vantage point, except the Antipodean. Headingley had been cold and uninviting, the cricket pedestrian, even mediocre at times, and there was an air of resignation that England's dire sequence of results would inevitably continue. This was the mood at the Botham residence on the eve of the rest day. Traditionally Botham held a party every year at this time and Willis remembers that 'several of us there thought we might be playing our last Test matches. Certainly I did. I had been dropped for the last two Tests of 1980 when I was having severe no-ball problems and had great difficulty bowling a legitimate delivery. In the West Indies in 1980/1 I had to return home early because of a knee injury. Another humiliating English defeat and that might be it.'

Like everyone else Willis checked out of the team's Leeds hotel on the Monday morning. Boycott was passively defiant for a while but England slumped to 105-5 when Botham entered and then to 135-7 at the arrival of Dilley, still needing 92 to make the Australians bat again. Odds of 500-1 on an English victory may have tempted Lillee and Marsh but not many others at Headingley.

Who does not know what happened next? Botham and Dilley 'just decided to have a go.' A few statistical reminders: this pair added 117 in 80 minutes, Dilley cracking nine fours in his 56, mostly through regal cover drives. Botham's first 50 took him 112 minutes, but he went from 39 to 103 in only 17 strokes – a six, 14 fours and two singles. His partnership of 67 with Chris Old took 53 minutes. Bob Willis contributed two in a last wicket partnership of 37, which in retrospect was crucial to the outcome of the match. When Botham left the field that Monday evening, 145 not out after 210 minutes at the wicket, the crowd massed in front of the pavilion singing 'For he's a jolly good fellow' and waving Union Jacks. At least he had cheered everyone up.

On the Tuesday Australia needed 130 to win. Brearley decided to open the bowling with Botham down the hill and Dilley, partly on the basis that these two players had to be on a high after their batting performances. Botham's first two balls were struck for four by Graeme Wood but he soon had the left-hander caught behind driving. For the sixth over Brearley called on Willis to bowl up the hill. Willis recalls: 'Legend has it that Brearley denied me the new ball and made me bowl up the hill to get my goat up and there's some truth in that. After bowling five overs I asked to have a go at the other end.' Both Bob Taylor behind the stumps and Botham thought Willis deserved choice of ends and Brearley agreed.

Brearley told Willis not to worry about no-balls. Willis undertook to bowl fast and just short of a length – maybe in the first innings he had been too preoccupied with accuracy on a pitch renowned to help pace bowlers. 'I found my rhythm immediately. When I bowled at my best I was in a cocoon, distracted by nothing except the next delivery. The pitch was now misbehaving. If you hit the cracks the ball either squatted or went vertical.' Even so just before lunch Australia were 56-1. Then a perfect bouncer was fended away by Trevor Chappell to give Bob Taylor a simple catch. However, the next two wickets, which fell in the last over before lunch, were the result of brilliant fielding. Hughes was caught at third slip by the diving Botham and three balls later Yallop was held by Gatting at short leg. At lunch Australia were 58-4 and for the first time in the match Willis, never a natural optimist, felt that England could win. During lunch Brearley mulled over the remaining Australian batsman, speculating how they might play. Willis, he decided – unsurprisingly – would probably bowl down the hill until the death and began with Old up the hill because the Yorkshiremen favoured bowling at left-handers. Sure enough Border was soon bowled through the gate by Old to make the score 65-5. Willis then removed Dyson, Marsh and Lawson in quick succession. In six overs he had taken six wickets, after bowling 37 overs in the match without taking a wicket and Australia were 75-8.

Now Lillee and Bright offered some resistance adding 35 together. 'Lillee was stepping away to the leg side and gliding the ball over the slips so I had to change my length and bowl fuller,' recalls Willis. Immediately Lillee scooped a catch to mid-on and when Bright was comprehensively yorked England had won by 19 runs. Still in a trance-like state Willis rushed to the pavilion and took to the bath, only to be hauled out to talk to Peter West of the BBC. He gave what he admits was 'probably an ill-judged' interview – deadpan and distinctly unecstatic. He was feeling drained and all the criticisms of the England side in the previous months had hurt. 'By the time I had finished with the interviews, half the side had vacated the dressing room; they were going off to prepare for Gillette Cup games with their counties. I had a few beers with Beefy in the dressing room. When I was driving home the Test victory was the lead item on the BBC's PM programme. It was only then that the significance of what I had achieved began to hit home.'
Result: England won by 19 runs

Australia

J. Dyson b Dilley	102	c Taylor b Willis	34
G.M. Wood lbw b Botham	34	c Taylor b Botham	10
T.M. Chappell c Taylor b Willey	27	c Taylor b Willis	8
*K.J. Hughes c&b Botham	89	c Botham b Willis	0
R.J. Bright b Dilley	7	(8) b Willis	19
G.N. Yallop c Taylor b Botham	58	c Gatting b Willis	0
A.R. Border lbw b Botham	8	b Old	0
†R.W. Marsh b Botham	28	c Dilley b Willis	4
G.F. Lawson c Taylor b Botham	13	c Taylor b Willis	1
D.K. Lillee not out	3	c Gatting b Willis	17
T.M. Alderman did not bat		not out	0
Extras: (B 4, LB 13, W 3, NB 12)	32	(LB 3, W 1, NB 14)	18
1/55 2/149 3/196 4/220 5/332	401	1/13 2/56 3/58 4/65	111
6/354 7/357 8/396 9/401		5/68 6/74 7/75 8/110	

Bowling: *First Innings* – Willis 30-1-72-0; Old 43-14-91-0; Dilley 27-4-73-2; Botham 33.2-11-95-6; Willey 13-2-31-1; Boycott 3-2-2-0. *Second Innings* – Willis 15.1-3-43-8; Old 9-1-21-1; Dilley 2-0-11-0; Botham 7-3-14-1; Willey 3-1-4-0.

England

G.A. Gooch lbw b Alderman	2	c Alderman b Lillee 0
G. Boycott b Lawson	12	lbw b Alderman 46
*J.M. Brearley c Marsh b Alderman	10	c Alderman b Lillee 14
D.I. Gower c Marsh b Lawson	24	c Border b Alderman 9
M.W. Gatting lbw b Lillee	15	lbw b Alderman 1
P. Willey b Lawson	8	c Dyson b Lillee 33
I.T. Botham c Marsh b Lillee	50	not out 149
†R.W. Taylor c Marsh b Lillee	5	c Bright b Alderman 1
G.R. Dilley c&b Dilley	13	b Alderman 56
C.M. Old c Border b Alderman	0	b Lawson 29
R.G.D. Willis not out	1	c Border b Alderman 2
Extras: (B 6, LB 11, W 6, NB 11)	34	(B 5, LB 3, W 3, NB 5) 16

1/12 2/40 3/42 4/84 5/87   174
6/112 7/148 8/166 9/167

1/0 2/18 3/37 4/41   356
5/105 6/133 7/135 8/252
9/319

Bowling: *First Innings* – Lillee 18.5-7-49-4; Alderman 19-4-59-3; Lawson 13-3-32-3. *Second Innings* – Lillee 25-6-94-3; Alderman 35.3-6-135-6; Lawson 23-4-96-1; Bright 4-0-15-0.